HOUSE
HISTORIES

HOUSE HISTORIES

A GUIDE TO TRACING THE GENEALOGY OF YOUR HOME

Sally Light

Including Chapters on How to Operate a
Homebased "House Histories" Business

Ninth Printing, August, 2005

Library of Congress Catalogue Card Number: 88- 83479
    ISBN: 0-9614876-1-5

Published in the United States by
    Golden Hill Press, Inc., Spencertown, New York 12165
Text Illustrations by Margaret Eberle.
This book was set in Times Roman and Souvenir Demi by
    Ari Iacovini of Just Your Type, Great Barrington, Massachusetts

Printed on acid-free paper.

To Mary,
who has persevered . . . .

Table of Contents

SECTION VI: Appendices

Acknowledgements

There are always so many people to thank who have helped along the way in the production of a book. The many individuals around the country who provided valuable technical information have been acknowledged in the Bibliography. There are still several other who have been available to advise, edit and proofread on numerous occasions. These are the ones who deserve special recognition here.

Mary L. Zander has spent countless hours advising, pushing and editing even during a difficult time in her life. Lorraine Zagorola has spent countless hours editing. Dr. Otto Sonntag gave of his time as a consulting editor. Paula J. Treder, A.I.A. read the text and added her valuable comments, particularly in the architecture sections. James Henson, Esq. gave suggestions for the legal chapters. David F. Stoddard, C.G.R.S. graciously reviewed the genealogical and handwriting sections. Glen D. Kistler, C.E., U.S. Army Ret'd., contributed his perspective for the surveying chapters as a resident of a state surveyed under the Township and Range system. Martin D. Ritz, Lic. Sur., read and corrected the survey chapters from his perspective living in a state laden with the indiscriminate survey system. Katherine Thompson, Town Historian and author of books on regional history, read the text and enhanced certain sections. Dr. Peggy Haskell edited the text from her perspective as a linguist, even while on vacation. Nancy J. Kern helped complete certain research on various technical aspects of the text. Christopher M. Bailey, C.P.A., gave suggestions for the business chapters. In addition to these, Tom and Chris Sauter, Roberta B. Keller, Edie Mesick, Dolores Winkler and Lisa-Marie Light all helped proofread the text.

Sue Dunham and Suzanne E. Winkler typed various sections under unrealistic deadlines. Suzanne also managed to pinch hit for me in various professional aspects when I needed her most.

Over the years there have been several individuals who have always responded generously to my queries. This also happened while preparing the text. I would like to recognize them for their many contributions: Terry Hallock, A.I.A; Marion L. Kern, Town Historian; Elliot M. Sayward, Editor Emeritus, The Chronicle of EAIA; William E. Gustafson; Dr. Roderic H. Blackburn; Neil Larson and Dorothy J. Bailey.

To each of these individuals I would like to extend my most heartfelt gratitude for all that they have done. Without their help this book would not have been completed.

Introduction

Anyone can do a house history or become a house historian. Whether you are doing this for your own house or as a business, it does not require special credentials. Rather, the main ingredients are interest and a willingness to perform the variety of tasks necessary to complete the research. There are five general steps that you will take: on site inspection, oral inquiries, document search, analysis of information found and writing up of results.

Site inspection provides you with a general idea of what architectural eras the house exhibits. You will check out the site, the outbuildings and the house itself, inside and out, to get a visual idea of size and general layout of house and grounds. (A flashlight, pen and notebook, 25' measuring tape and a camera are all the equipment you will need.) Some of a house's unique characteristics can be easy to spot; others are more subtle. This book will help you develop the observant eye needed to detect variations in timbers, floor boards, wall thicknesses and coverings, woodwork and doors and their fastenings, room sizes and ceiling heights.

Oral inquiries to past owners, town historians, and others may help steer you in the right direction and add to your data. Next, you will start the "paper chase" with a visit to the local courthouse, where deeds, mortgages, surveys, maps and wills are found. There you will apply the only new skills that you may need—how to read early handwriting and to draw rough outline maps of the early written survey descriptions. These skills are easily learned from this book. Explanations and examples then are given to guide you in organizing a completed house history.

Certain personal traits are helpful in doing a house history. In addition to being observant and outgoing, it helps to have a curiosity which drives you to find out about local history or architecture, and enough imagination to suggest other avenues when you hit a snag. Also, a persistence which, if you find you do not know an answer, will drive you to hunt until you find it. Or, at least, until you find out that no one else seems to know the answer either.

Once you have done the inspection and research suggested in this book, your completed house history will reflect the different technologies, people and zeitgeist—the spirit of the times—that have shaped the house. The book is designed to unravel the mysteries associated with all three.

Technology

In a house history, technology refers to the effect of scientific developments on building materials and on the ways they are utilized in house construction. Glass, paint, nails and wood veneers are common examples of materials which have changed in themselves, and in their applications over the years, because of new technology. They leave clues for the house historian.

Because they are the most visible and easily traced, the technologies associated with a house usually are the first thing you will document. Again, technology refers to materials and methods used in the building trades. Many advancements occurred in these in the 19th century, which in turn affected house building and alteration. For instance, better quality steel produced new types of saws, and the steam engine a new type of power to drive these saws and other machinery. Quality steel and power tools also produced wire nails in abundance, and a different frame style of house construction evolved. As plate glass technology improved, window panes became larger until a single pane for each half of a double hung window became common in the 20th century. As the chemistry of paints developed, new colors were introduced.

Such technologies identify a house as being in or out of a specific time period. Size(s) of window panes, the color of the original paint or the type of saw tooth marks, will help date a house, as will other facets of its construction. A house may have a metal roof, the invention of which marks the roof historically. The fabric—brick, wood or stone—used to clothe the house can help place the house in a specific time period. The style of a house can date it. The invention in the mid-19th century of the mowing machine, and the introduction of the lawn mower on the mass market in the 1870's, affected landscaping around the house, encouraging the placement of homes in the midst of vast lawns. All these are examples of technologies which affected the construction, look, and style of a house and of its later alterations.

Because this book emphasizes pre-20th century houses, modern plumbing, heating and lighting systems have not been directly addressed in the text. Most of these houses existed before such technology came into being or was widely used. When older houses were adapted for inside running water since no space had been allowed for a bathroom, the new toilets often were placed on the porch, or over a port-cochere, if no other interior space were available. Central heating, gas and electricity used channels in the walls or made holes in the floor for piping, but had little or no effect on interior space. Also, the advent of balloon framing allowed more use of inside wall space for hot air and electric conduits. By the 20th century, these technologies affected home-building, in that interior spaces had to be designed to accommodate the systems.

Spirit and Fashion of An Era / Zeitgeist

Houses also are influenced by fashion—the outward manifestation of the era during which they were built or altered. It is easy to see why houses changed. When the right combination of technology and fashion coincide, a new era evolves. Yesterday, as today, people are "trendy," and want whatever is "up-to-date." If they can afford it, they make changes.

A classic example of a trendsetter in house building and house setting is the work of landscape architect Andrew Jackson Downing. He advanced the philosophical ideals of the mid-19th century by writing what became a popular book on architectural drawings and landscape gardening, *Cottage Residences*, in which he utilized the architectural drawings of Alexander Jackson Davis and others. Downing believed in integrating the out of doors with the inside of the house by means of large windows, from which the view of a beautiful lawn and extensive gardens could be enjoyed. He promoted the porch, verandah or piazza as a place of retreat during inclement weather when garden walks could not be taken for exercise. Downing also believed that the color of the house should integrate it with its surroundings. Thus he preferred the neutral shades of grey or fawn. The influence of Downing's book can be seen in the Italianate, Gothic and Second Empire houses of the mid-to-late 19th century.

Although all houses perform the basic, life-maintaining function of a shelter, there are certain other functions, not essential, that vary with social custom and fill other needs that people have. These needs include privacy, personal expression, cleanliness and financial independence. Such non-basic needs also help produce houses with differing architectural styles, room arrangements and settings. For example, in the early 19th century, before cloth was manufactured in the mills, it was woven at home. Since a loom takes up a lot of space, part of a larger room, or a separate room, was needed to perform this ordinary household task. In contrast, in the 20th century, our emphasis on cleanliness and on firm bodies, to enhance sexual beauty and physical health, can call for bathrooms large enough to include jacuzzis and saunas, or even exercise areas. A weaving room was desirable in the 19th century; a large bathroom might be today. Both room arrangements express the spirit of the times. They are the practical expressions of their eras.

3

People

Until the mid-20th century, interest in older houses was focussed more on the mansions of the wealthy. There was less interest in how ordinary people lived and coped. The United States and its constitution are now over 200 years old and various bicentennials—and some tricentennials—of counties, towns and buildings are being celebrated annually. These have acted as a catalyst to help interest us in discovering more about these ordinary people who comprised, and still form, the backbone of our society. Such people built houses, owned them, lived in them, put up the additions and changed the windows. When doing a house history, if you do not learn about the people who lived in the house, you are missing its heart.

While researching old houses, you begin to realize, from deeds, mortgages and other documents, how many men had two or three wives, due to the high death rate from childbirth and related causes. Men also died young, not only from disease, but from accidents. Thus prior to the 20th century, families often were composed of children who had to adapt to more than one "mother" or "father," and stepsister and stepbrother relationships much like today's "his, hers and ours" families.

How does this tidbit of social history relate to the house history? A house may be made larger when two families, rather than two individuals, "marry." At the same time it may be changed in style, or an outbuilding may be added, because a person with a new occupation has joined the family.

Inheritances also initiate changes. While researching a house, you may discover that a newly married granddaughter and her husband moved in with a widowed grandmother, yet this date does not coincide with the time changes were made to the house. They occur later, for no easily discernable reason. Then, when you read the grandmother's will, you discover that granddaughter inherited the property and money roughly around the date that corresponds to the changes in the house.

The houses you research reveal people expressing their personalities, planting the lilacs and apple trees in the dooryard, building a swinging cat door in the wall next to the front door, burying their young son near the barn after he died from a fall from a tree. A house historian is of necessity a special kind of social historian, whose discoveries about the lives of our forefathers include the significant and poignant, as well as the trivial or amusing explanations behind the changes in houses.

Interacting with prevailing technologies and current social fashion, the house builder, the individual home owner and family, and, later, new owners each adapted the house to suit their own specific needs over the years. The answers to when and why, for your house, may lie in whether, for example, the house was designed for a single family or for a family and their servants or slaves. You may need to find out the occupations of those who lived in the house. Was the family of modest means or well off? What could they afford in a house, and how have they left their mark on the house and its setting? All of these things—the original and changing technologies connected with the house, the social eras in which it has existed, the people who occupied it—will leave the clues to help you understand it from its beginnings to the present.

Section I

Inspecting the House and Site

Your first step in researching a house is to inspect it, since it is much easier to research if you have seen its style and have a general idea of its age. Even if it is your own house, do not neglect this careful inspection. A home owner has lived with and adapted to a house's oddities and may no longer recognize some characteristics as having significance. Whether you are seeing the house for the first time or not, looking at its separate parts—roof, chimneys, doors, windows, outbuildings, foundations, boundary walls—will give you clues to help you puzzle out its whole story. This Section will suggest the things to look for during this inspection, and the conclusions that may be drawn from them about dates, origins and reasons for alterations.

During your inspection, keep in mind that a house is an organic structure which typically has undergone one or more changes over the years. These alterations or additions usually result from the need for *repairs*, the needs of various owners to have the house *function* differently and fluctuations in *fashion*. Accustom yourself, as you walk around and through the house, to comparing what appears to be *original* construction with what may be *changes* from original construction. This will give you some initial hints for your house history, although you may not at first understand why or when the changes were made.

There are obvious reasons why the most common exterior and interior repairs are made to a house. For example, sun and wind slowly tend to weather window sills and siding on southern or western exposures. (By the time these are replaced, styles have changed, so the replacements may vary in style from the original. Fashion has had its influence.) Or, water tends to damage foundations on the north or east. Indeed, foundation sills often rotted because 20th-century shrubbery and plantings were placed too close to the 18th- or 19th-century foundation, retaining moisture and blocking sunlight.

Often a needed repair was modified or influenced by *technological advances*. When cast iron, coal-burning stoves promised warmer rooms and no more wood-cutting, fireplaces were plastered up and round holes cut into their flues for stovepipes. So, when a fireplace chimney needed repair to make it less of a fire hazard, the home owner may have decided that this was the time to change to a coal stove. Or, when wide-board oak or pine flooring became so worn or termite-infested that it was unsafe, the new, narrow-width hardwood flooring may have been used to replace it. Such changes were an outgrowth of the technological advances made in housing materials and methods. *Fashion* may speed up or delay the widespread use of a new technology. There are many instances in which a technological advance was not widely utilized until years after its invention because it was not perceived as fashionable or "trendy."

Changes also were made to conform to contemporary social practice or to enhance the house's *functioning*. For example, in early houses a creamery often was added in the summer kitchen wing to house the large table and churn needed when butter-making became a cottage industry. Or, perhaps household and farm help needed bedrooms, so a new ell was added. If the addition was exclusively for farm hands, there probably was no access between their second floor bedrooms and those of the family. The hands used separate stairs or a trap door and ladder to the kitchen area on the first floor. Because farm hands often were young, unmarried men from poor families, or had been "liberated" from the poorhouse to work for low wages, the farmer worried about their socializing with his daughters. The separate entrances kept them physically isolated from the main part of the house.

In the next seven chapters, guidelines are given for the kinds of things you should particularly note, record or sketch as you do your inspection of the house and site. This overview is very comprehensive but not all inclusive — you may run into some unique detail not covered here. Illustrations of the most common architectural forms you will encounter are included. If some aspect of your research requires very specialized information, check the Resource Section for further help.

To prepare for your site visit, bring the camera, snap rule, flashlight, pen and pad on clipboard noted previously. Wear comfortable pants and practical shoes, because you may be crawling around in an attic or cellar, barn or other outbuilding, conducive to dustballs, spider webs and worse. Take complete exterior pictures of the house and grounds. Also take interior shots of unique details that raise questions. Later you can use these photos as a means to help research and identify these details.

1

The Setting:
Site, Grounds and Outbuildings

To get a comprehensive picture of the total site, look at the house in relation to its outbuildings and to the lay of the land. Walk around, trying to see not only what is there now, but what may have been there before. Is there, for example, an empty foundation hole? This could indicate that an original building burned down. Or, do these foundation dimensions correspond to those of an ell or wing on the existing house, indicating that the ell was moved to its present site?

Are there other landscape features which may tell you something? Perhaps an old lane passing along the depth of the property, front to rear, is an abandoned road. This would explain the present house location, facing this lane, which once was a main road. Or, is the empty foundation hole located near what is now the main road, but once was an old trail used for cattle and sheep drives? Perhaps when it became too busy a thoroughfare, the previous owner moved the house away from the traffic.

Examine any ridges or hollows that appear to be man-made, that is, not corresponding to the natural terrain. These could have been dug for a specific purpose, such as loading wagons, digging gravel or stone, or sawing wood in a pit. Perhaps this is where the house building materials came from or were prepared? (Use methods suggested in Section II to provide other kinds of evidence to help confirm or reject such speculations.)

If your house is in a village, how close are the neighbors? Are most of the lots a standard size—1/8 to 1/4 acre—or are they different sizes and irregular shapes? The differences may arise from the way they were sectioned off from a larger property, something your research can establish. Note the styles and apparent ages of houses and buildings adjacent to yours. Are there similar details, pointing to a common carpenter, mason or builder? Close neighbors and their houses—the social and physical environment—may supply evidence that is as significant as the target house itself in explaining some of its origins, and add a dimension to its history. The story of a house is not told in total isolation.

Water Sources

What is the source of water? The very earliest houses almost always will be found next to a running brook or stream. Near the house may be the remains of an old spring house, built over a dug-out hillside spring or next to a stream. There may be evidence of a stone dam, which could indicate an old mill site. The house timbers might have been cut there.

If there is a shallow, open cistern in the cellar, look for its source. If there is a hill behind your house, it might contain a gravity-fed spring, with old—late-19th- to early-20th-century—lead pipes still buried in it, carrying the water to your cellar cistern. Before lead pipes came into use in the latter part of the 19th century, hollowed-out logs served as conduits for water. Check the shape of the well if you can. In the early 19th century, wells usually were bottle-shaped, while cisterns were rounded, relatively shallow receptacles, which collected water from roof gutters and other sources of run-off.

If you cannot see an original water source, it probably is buried. Previously existing old cisterns or wells may be found under an ell added later, or under porches or very close to what was the kitchen. Even though the water source may have been filled in, you will recognize it by the well-laid rock or brick dry wall. If you can, try to date the foundation or ell above it; you then can assume that the cistern was earlier.

Archaeology and Trash Sites

In the bottoms of wells or in any body of water near a house, it is not uncommon to find old tools or old bottles, especially whiskey bottles. These can be dated by experts and they may tell something about the medicines used by early occupants, or about family members. (While dismantling a rotted front porch, some new home owners discovered over 150 whiskey bottles dating from the 1880's. After a record search, it was established that a man had lived in the house with his elderly parents, and continued to live there, a happy recluse, after their deaths.)

All farm houses had a designated dump site, originally located at the back of the house near the food preparation room. Later, in the 19th century, when beautiful lawns were more in vogue, dump sites were located behind outbuildings, away from the road. If it has not already been raided, a dump site can be a "gold mine" of treasures, full of shards, metal gizmos and household or farm items which may add data and dates to your house history.

Most people do not actually excavate their land to find archaeological artifacts. They may, however, when rebuilding a road or driveway, or adding a building to the property, locate a foundation or dump site. Occasionally a family burial plot is discovered. In more than one such instance, bodies have been dug up, sometimes preserved by the peculiarities of the soil and climate. If, when digging in your garden or elsewhere, you uncover something that looks unusual, or an artifact, call an expert and describe your find. Your town historian, or the state historic preservation officer can help you contact an archaeologist, who will advise you what to do.

Outbuildings

Outbuildings housed functions that were undesirable to have inside the house itself. An outbuilding could be, for example, a dairy barn, pig sty, outhouse or smithy. Establishing the functions of the outbuildings may give you clues to the occupations of some of the previous owners. Usually the various outbuildings were built over a period of time, and their functions also changed over the years. Since they were not necessarily built at the same time as the house, these buildings usually do not give clues to the date of the house construction. At times a shared construction method may give a general clue to dating. The existence or function of outbuildings also can offer corroboration of facts you have obtained through other methods of researching the house.

Stone Walls

Although other types of fencing were used — notably wooden, zigzag rail fencing — all of these were less permanent than stone walls. Stony property usually was avoided for use until the better soils were depleted or the population became so dense that these lands had to be utilized in the 18th and 19th centuries. When stony land had to be used for grazing, the stones were cleared. The fieldstone walls made from these often delineate property boundaries, and dooryards, paddocks and fields.

Stone walls often outlined even very large property holdings. For example, in 1935, the Rombout Patent of 1722 in what is now Dutchess County, New York, was verified through aerial photographs showing the stone walls around the perimeter of these holdings. These photographs were compared to the surveys made in 1722, which had utilized wide stone walls to mark the boundaries of the property. Although the Patent had long since been broken into smaller parcels and parts of the wall removed, the perimeter in 1935 still maintained its original integrity, as shown by the remaining walls and the variations in vegetation where the wall had been removed.

Plantings

What plants are located in the dooryard? Depending on the species, plantings also can be roughly dated. When barberries are found near the house, with apple trees located nearby, these usually are 18tn- or early-19th-century plantings. Day lilies, cinnamon rose and lilacs were 19th-century plantings. Many of these have survived for over 100 years. Although barberry bushes were intentionally destroyed in wheat-producing regions because they were intermediate hosts in the life cycle of the stem rust which is harmful to wheat, oats, rye, barley and other small grains and grasses, they still exist in other regions. There are other early, long-lived plantings characteristic of specific regions, which your local cooperative extension agent can identify.

Besides helping to date the house, such plantings can add information to your story. The plants may have been prized for their sweet perfume or for their medicinal value. "Remedy" books were published in the 19th century with recipes for multiple uses of plantings. Even the humble dandelion was imported for its various uses, as were mustard and many other 20th-century "weeds."

2

Exterior Elements
of the House

After you have inspected the house site and landscaping and have collected data on them, walk around the house itself. Measure the widths and depths of each facade—all the lengths and sides of the house. Make a diagram of these, being sure to include and label all wings, ells and shed additions. As you learn more about the house, these measurements, by their symmetry or variation may help confirm your speculations about how the house was built or what changes were made to it and how or when. This chapter explains what to look for.

Asymmetry: Variations in Dimensions

Professionals working with early houses are familiar with the fact that houses can be categorized roughly by their dimensions as being within a given period or belonging to a particular style. As a simple, proportional example of this, remember that Dutch houses and barns tended to be square while English houses and barns such as Georgian and Federal (1735-1820) were more rectangular. Houses of a specific era or style often were built according to the general dimensions commonly used for that style. There was, so to speak, an "ideal" house with "ideal" dimensions. In reality, houses did not always conform exactly to these. They varied according to the ethnicity of the builders, the availability of proper tools, and because of the general lack of standardization of measurements.

It was not until 1889 that the United States adopted a standard length for our "foot." Before that, there were variations of this measurement, making it difficult for a builder to establish an exact linear distance as a unit of measurement. Compounding this, when someone who was not a carpenter by trade, or who did not have a measuring tool was building a house, he may have created his own "foot" by cutting a board at an arbitrary length. He then simply used multiples or divisions of this board to measure the dimensions of the house.

Another explanation for variations in some center-entrance house dimensions is that in the late 18th to early 19th century it was not unusual for these houses to be built in sections. Although such a house may appear symmetrical, it is not exactly so, because it was built room by room, and the front door moved as the house expanded. To establish whether this is the case with your target house, measure the bays on each side of the front entrance, or measure the distance from the exterior door frame to the edge of the wall. The entrance actually may be one to three feet off center, as are the windows. Or, the windows on one side of the door may not be exactly the same distance from the edge of the house or door as are the windows on the other side. If the floor also appears to have been built in sections which agree with these divisions, then the house probably was built in sections. This was characteristic of houses until the 1820's.

When asymmetrical houses were in fashion later in the 19th century—for example, the Queen Anne (1880-1900) style's off center entrance, corner tower and multiplaned roof line—it was not unusual to "modernize" an older, symmetrical house by bricking up or removing windows to make it asymmetrical. Porches often were added to help accomplish this. Even if such a house is re-sided, you may be able to see where such changes were made in the original fabric. Look for waves in the wood, vinyl or metal siding, or for obvious breaks in brick or stone siding.

Foundations

Examine the exterior foundation. Does it appear to have been constructed all at one time or in stages? That is, are there breaks in the foundation material or style, indicating that it was added on to? A very clear example of this would be an uncoursed, rubble foundation which abruptly becomes a coursed, cut-fieldstone foundation. (Illustration 1.)

You can assume that a dry-wall, rubble foundation—that is, one made of uncoursed, unmortared stone—generally is older than one with mortared brick laid on top of the fieldstone. The older foundations were small and rectangular in form, while irregular "z"-shaped foundations show the influence of the designs of Alexander Jackson Davis and others after 1842.

When wings or ells were attached to the original house, a full cellar often was not dug under them. Rather, the footings for the walls were placed beneath the frost line and a two-foot, dead-air space left under the addition. In such cases, when adding heat or electricity in the 20th century, builders have had to dismantle part of the foundation from the cellar of the main section in order to draw the pipes or lines through to the ell.

STONE BONDS

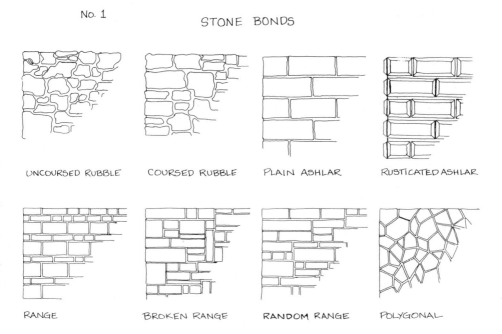

UNCOURSED RUBBLE   COURSED RUBBLE   PLAIN ASHLAR   RUSTICATED ASHLAR

RANGE   BROKEN RANGE   RANDOM RANGE   POLYGONAL

In some cases, not even footings were dug. Instead, about two feet of rubble was stacked under the sills to provide a foundation for the additions. These additions often were the first to be torn down because of settling, racking or rot. In order for a wing to last more than 100 years, its walls must be placed on secure footings. There also must be air circulation, so that excessive moisture does not accumulate and cause wood to rot.

Chimneys

Chimneys in permanent houses were made of stone or brick, or a combination using stone for the foundation and the firebox and brick as the flue. Chimneys in temporary houses often were made of a log and clay combination. The logs were corner-notched and laid up like a small log house. Although clay chinked the logs and lined the flue, fire was a constant worry. You are particularly likely to find the remains of a log chimney in 18th- and 19th-century log houses. These may no longer be recognizable as log houses for they later were covered with clapboarding or other materials.

How many chimneys are there in the house you are researching? One or two were common in a small house, four in a larger house. Are they interior or exterior chimneys? If there is one center chimney measure or eye-ball it to confirm if it truly is in the center of the house, or to one side of the center. (Illustration 2.)

NO. 2   CHIMNEY LOCATIONS

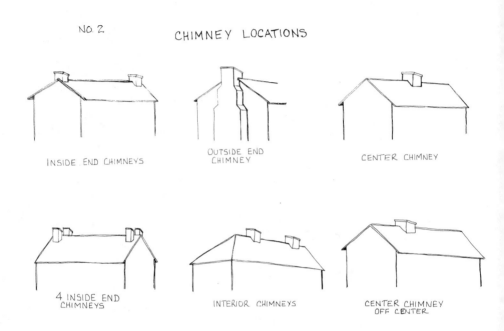

INSIDE END CHIMNEYS   OUTSIDE END   CENTER CHIMNEY
                             CHIMNEY

4 INSIDE END   INTERIOR CHIMNEYS   CENTER CHIMNEY
CHIMNEYS   OFF CENTER

If an interior chimney is off center, it may indicate that the house was a 17th- to 18th-century, two-room German house, in which the kitchen (küche) was wider than the parlor (stube). Or, an off-center chimney may mean that the house was extended on what now appears to be the "long" axis or "long" side of the house. This was possible if no ridgepole was used in constructing the original roof. Pairs of rafters could be added to lengthen the house, but the center chimney was too massive to be moved.

Center chimneys were characteristic of smaller, 17th- to 19th-century northern homes. They often were located immediately behind the center entrance and massively constructed, designed to serve as the carrier of perhaps three flues in a one-and-a-half story house. A flue came from each fireplace located in the two small rooms on either side of the center entrance, and the third flue from the kitchen or back room, which had a cooking fireplace with adjacent oven. These flues merged into one main flue in the chimney. (Illustration 3.)

CENTER CHIMNEY WITH THREE FIREPLACES
AND AN OVEN

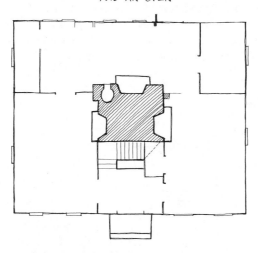

Two interior, end chimneys often identify a larger, northern, 18th- to 19th-century center-entrance home with a room on each side of the entrance. In 18th-century, wooden Dutch homes, most brick fireboxes of end· chimneys were exposed for four or five feet from the ground, through the clapboarding, to minimize the fire hazard. (Illustration 4.)

NO. 4

FIREBOX EXPOSED ON A CLAPBOARD HOUSE

19

If the house has multiple chimneys in a variety of planes and locations, it may indicate that one or more additions were made at different times. Typically, a large ell was added perpendicular to a smaller, center-chimney house. This ell had end chimneys, one being placed adjacent to the side wall of the original center-chimney house. Then, a smaller wing was added on to the ell, in telescope fashion, with an end chimney on its exterior wall.

NO. 5

EXTERIOR BEEHIVE OVEN

In the South, during the 17th, 18th and 19th centuries, end chimneys sometimes were placed on the exteriors of brick or stone houses to keep them cooler. Brick or stone exterior end chimneys on any *frame house,* however, also may be a 20th-century addition. The style of brick, their bonding, and the shape of the chimney will help date it.

Sometimes, especially in the mid-Atlantic states during the late 18th to early 19th centuries, a beehive oven might be placed on the exterior, with access to it from inside the house. This exterior oven placement helped keep the house cooler. (Illustration 5.) In still other instances, especially in the South, the oven was located outside in the yard.

Roofs

Look at the roof of the house. Is it a gable, hip, gambrel, mansard, shed or a multiple of styles? (Illustration 6.) You probably can identify the original section of the house by spotting the roof additions. For instance, shed roofs usually were added onto a gable — the gable being the most common roof style.

Gambrel roofs had more second floor head room, inviting the addition of shed-roofed dormers. A gambrel sometimes was added on to an original gable roof. Mansard roofs were late 19th-century additions, a means of converting a third floor attic into full-ceilinged bedrooms for household help or for tenants.

NO. 6

ROOFS

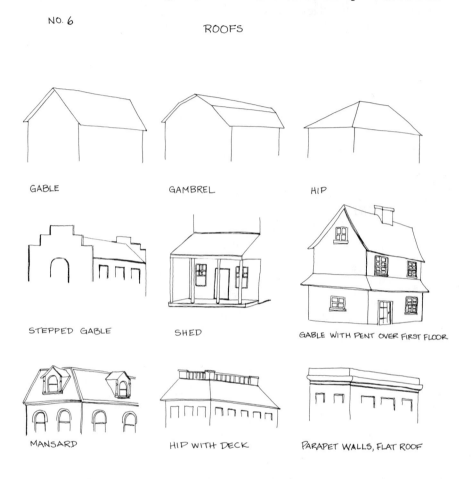

GABLE

GAMBREL

HIP

STEPPED GABLE

SHED

GABLE WITH PENT OVER FIRST FLOOR

MANSARD

HIP WITH DECK

PARAPET WALLS, FLAT ROOF

The roofing material may or may not be useful for dating a house, because roofs have to be replaced more often than other construction materials. Moreover, a variety of roofing materials have been developed over the last 100 years which can be tricky to date. Do not assume that the roofing material is original to the house. The oldest remaining *original* roofs are of slate or tile and date from the end of the 19th century. These original roofs exist only in a fraction of the houses dating from that time.

There are other aspects of roofs that can contribute significantly to establishing their date of construction. Notice the pitch of the roof. A steeply pitched gable, for example, appearing to hang just over the heads of the windows on a one-and-a-half story house, probably was built prior to 1770. If a roof has a lesser pitch and ends two-and-a-half to three feet above the heads of the windows, this places the house after 1770. The side walls were elevated to allow more head room under a gable roof. (Illustration 7.)

NO. 7   DEVELOPMENT OF ROOF PITCH

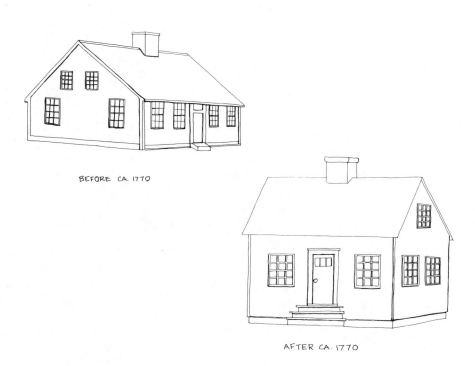

BEFORE CA. 1770

AFTER CA. 1770

Look under the roof line. Are there wide face boards on the wall following the roof line? This is called a frieze and was characteristic of the Greek Revival period (1820-1850). There may be decorative brackets supporting the edge of the overhang, or eaves typical of 1860 to 1900 Italianate houses. Is there a decorative face board following the pitch and under the edge of the gable roof? This is called a bargeboard or vergeboard. By its fancy cutouts it became known as the "gingerbread" look, characteristic of the latter half of the 19th century. (Illustration 8.)

ROOF EDGE DETAILS

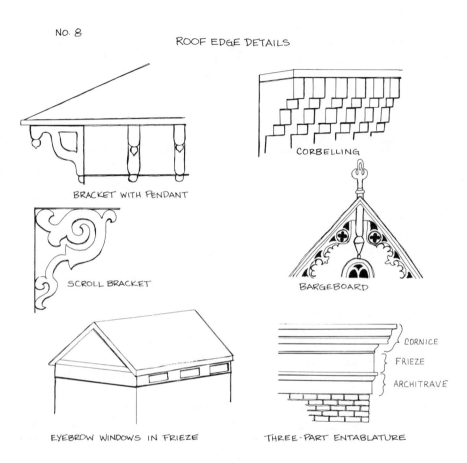

BRACKET WITH PENDANT

CORBELLING

SCROLL BRACKET

BARGEBOARD

EYEBROW WINDOWS IN FRIEZE

CORNICE

FRIEZE

ARCHITRAVE

THREE-PART ENTABLATURE

Walls and Fabric

Walls enclose the house. They have an interior and exterior side. Most walls have a *fabric* covering and decorating their exterior. Many materials and methods were used to do this.

The earliest houses had either crude log or sod walls. Some were temporary, half-houses, built into a hill for shelter while a more permanent house was being constructed. Depending on the availability of materials, both stone and wood were used for the walls of 17th- to 19th-century houses. In the southwest, however, the scarcity of wood led to the use of rammed earth or adobe with wood supports for walls.

If the fabric is of wood, it may be clapboard, shingle, novelty (barn) siding, board and batten or a combination of these. Depending on the physical characteristic of the boards—whether the surface is split, shaved, sawed and/or planed—and depending on the size of the boards or shingles, estimates tentatively can be made as to the age of the siding. Generally speaking, wood, including shingles and siding, was:

- split before it was sawed ;
- left rough or hewn before it was planed or sawed ;
- used as larger boards or timbers or shingles before uniform smaller sizes of the same became standard.

From the 17th to 18th centuries, much of the eastern part of the United States was wooded with the massive trees of virgin forest. Although one tree could supply the lumber for a small house, usually different woods were used for various parts of a dwelling. In the 17th and early 18th centuries most settlers had only hand tools to fell and lumber such trees. Thus, much hard work was required to finish the surfaces of a house. By the early-to-mid 19th century sawmills had become abundant, so wooden siding with finished surfaces became more common on houses.

Both crude-shingle and-clapboard sidings were common on 17th-century dwellings. Few examples of crude-shingle siding have survived. Clapboard was used in the 18th-century Georgian and early 19th-century Federal and Greek Revival styles. Later in the 19th century, clapboard was used for the Gothic Revival, Italianate and Second Empire styles, among others. (Appendix B.) Plain or patterned shingles were common in the late 19th-century shingle styles. Patterned shingles were found mostly in Queen Anne and Folk Victorian styles, while plain shingles characterized Colonial Revival and Craftsman styles, to name some examples. (Illustration 9.)

Novelty siding and board and batten were fabrics typical of specific styles in the mid-to-late 19th century. Novelty siding often replaced earlier clapboards, especially on the side(s) of the house away from the street, where it was less visible to the public. Board and batten commonly was used in Gothic Revival structures. There are several good sources documenting the various exterior wall fabrics in the many diverse styles which appeared. The subject is too specialized for this book, but you will find other works describing such fabrics and styles in the Bibliography.

If the walls are of stone, they may be small cobbles or large stones. The large stones may be cut, rough or natural, coursed or uncoursed and laid end-to-end flat or with the wide side facing out. Assessing the combination of these characteristics may help place your house within a given era. For example, if

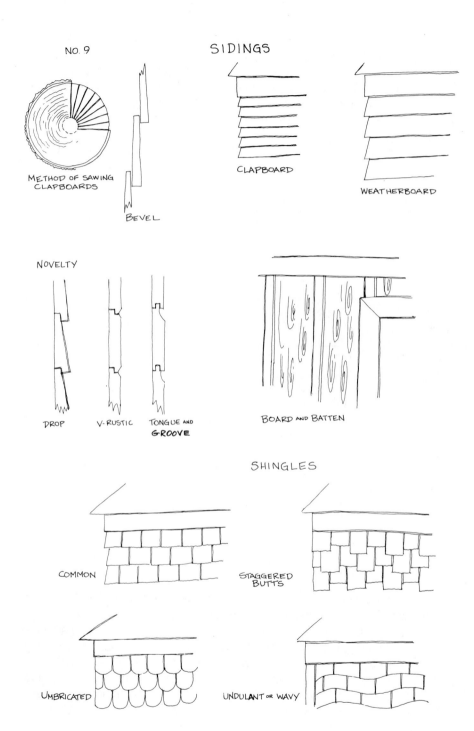

NO. 9

SIDINGS

METHOD OF SAWING
CLAPBOARDS

BEVEL

CLAPBOARD

WEATHERBOARD

NOVELTY

DROP

V-RUSTIC

TONGUE AND
GROOVE

BOARD AND BATTEN

SHINGLES

COMMON

STAGGERED
BUTTS

UMBRICATED

UNDULANT OR WAVY

fieldstone is uncut, uncoursed, dry-wall construction, it probably was built in the 18th to early 19th century. If the stone is ashlar (cut square or rectangular) with a thin layer of mortar between the stones, the house probably dates from the 19th century. Uncut fieldstone combined with uncut, relatively thin slate and round creek-bed stones, placed at random, with generous amounts of mortar, may indicate the work of an unsophisticated 20th-century mason. (Illustration 10.)

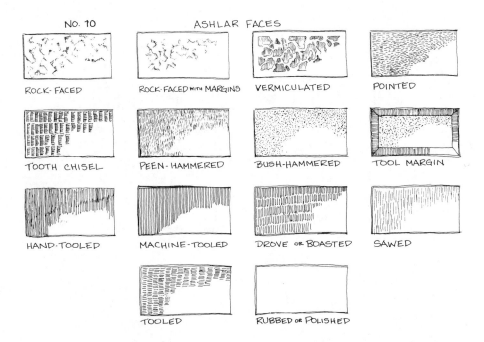

NO. 10   ASHLAR FACES

ROCK-FACED   ROCK-FACED with MARGINS   VERMICULATED   POINTED

TOOTH CHISEL   PEEN-HAMMERED   BUSH-HAMMERED   TOOL MARGIN

HAND-TOOLED   MACHINE-TOOLED   DROVE or BOASTED   SAWED

TOOLED   RUBBED or POLISHED

Brick houses depended on the development of brickyards and furnaces to manufacture the brick. Early bricks were fired at lower temperatures than they are today, and the mortar was more porous, so brick often was painted to preserve and water proof it and the mortar. If your house walls are brick, note whether it is painted, or if there are traces of paint to indicate that it once was painted. Painting was a late 18th- to mid-19th-century method of preservation and waterproofing. Notice the bond or pattern in the brick. It may be Flemish, English or one of the variations, which can indicate the ethnic origin of the builder and answer other questions about the structure. (Illustration 11.)

SOME COMMON BRICK BONDS

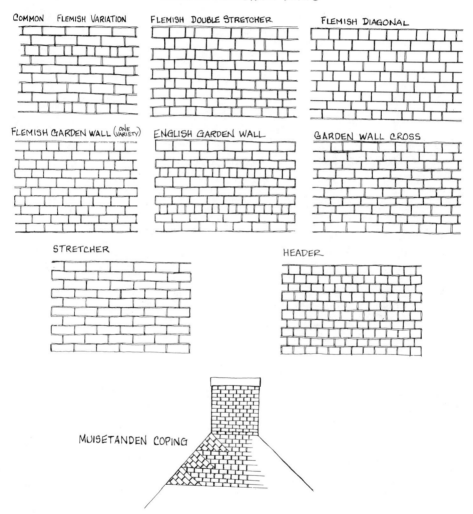

COMMON   FLEMISH VARIATION

FLEMISH DOUBLE STRETCHER

FLEMISH DIAGONAL

FLEMISH GARDEN WALL (ONE VARIETY)

ENGLISH GARDEN WALL

GARDEN WALL CROSS

STRETCHER

HEADER

MUISETANDEN COPING

Are there wide face boards that abut at the corners of the house? These are called pilasters. If they are made of boards four to five inches wide, they are typical of the Federal style (1790-1820). The considerably wider ten- to eleven-inch boards were found in Greek Revival homes, as well as in the late 18th-century Georgian. For stone or brick houses, there was an alternative to wood pilasters. These were corner quoins—large, rectangular, cut, corner stone blocks placed alternately so that the mortar joints did not coincide vertically. Such quoins are the Greek Revival pilasters done in stone. (Illustration 12.)

NO. 12   GREEK REVIVAL CORNER DETAILS

CORNER PILASTER
DORIC ORDER   QUOINS

CORNER PILASTERS
IONIC ORDER

Doors

Exterior doors are located within bays. A house can be described by these bays. A bay is that section of a house between the columns or piers within the wall—that is, between the upright posts supporting the structure. A window or door often is located between these vertical supports. Thus a five-bay by three-bay house has five openings along its long side (width), with three openings along the shorter side (depth). One or more of these openings may be a door ; the rest are windows. (Illustration 13.)

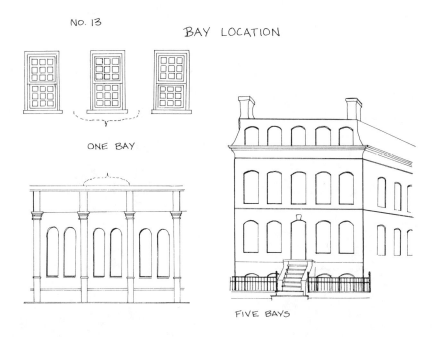

NO. 13   BAY LOCATION

ONE BAY

FIVE BAYS

The main entrance usually was placed in the front of the house, in the main section, but it may have been in a wing. If your target house has its main entrance in a wing, try to determine if this entrance originally was in the main section. If, for example, a house has a gable end facing the street, with only two bays, then it is likely that the original front door was parallel to the gable peak along the length of the house. This original entrance may have been buried when the wing was added, so a new front door was incorporated into the wing. Indeed, this was a common Federal adaption.

Sometimes a house was built with two symmetrical wings flanking a two-story center section whose gable end faced front. These houses therefore could have two front doors rather than one center entrance. In a later variation, the entrance was placed in the end bay of a usually three-bay Greek Revival house. Although some earlier houses were built with side-hall entrances, they became commonplace after 1820. Throughout the remainder of the 19th century, front entrances were either centered or off-center depending on the style in vogue, as well as on zoning requirements in urban centers. (Illustration 14.)

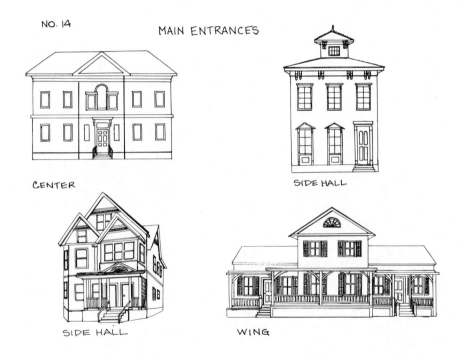

NO. 14 MAIN ENTRANCES

CENTER

SIDE HALL

SIDE HALL

WING

With certain stylistic exceptions, almost all porticos, porches and verandas were added in front of entrances after the house had been standing a while. Thus, porches often show characteristics of a later style than do the houses, and are not an accurate way of dating them. (Illustration 15.)

NO. 15

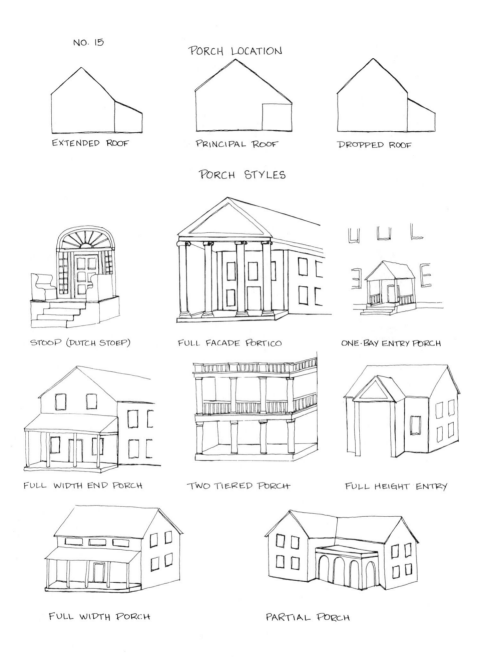

PORCH LOCATION

EXTENDED ROOF   PRINCIPAL ROOF   DROPPED ROOF

PORCH STYLES

STOOP (DUTCH STOEP)   FULL FACADE PORTICO   ONE-BAY ENTRY PORCH

FULL WIDTH END PORCH   TWO TIERED PORCH   FULL HEIGHT ENTRY

FULL WIDTH PORCH   PARTIAL PORCH

Examine the front-entrance details. Although the door may not be original —doors, like windows, were a common way to modernize—its wooden setting may be. The entrance might be dated by its transoms and wood detailing.

ENTRANCES

GEORGIAN (NORTHERN)

GEORGIAN (SOUTHERN)

GEORGIAN

GEORGIAN

FEDERAL

FEDERAL

GREEK REVIVAL

GREEK REVIVAL

GOTHIC

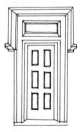

GOTHIC

ITALIANATE

ITALIANATE

An 18th-century solution to lighting a hall was to place a transom—a series of lights (panes) separated by muntins (wooden dividers), in the wall across the top of the door. By the latter part of the 18th century the transom had become a fanlight. The Adamsesque sidelights were introduced, with lacily designed leaded glass, and the fanlight became a delicately leaded ellipse. By the 1820's, in the Greek Revival period, the entrance acquired more elaborate woodwork, with wide board entablatures running across the top of the doorway and pilasters down the sides. Rectangular transoms and sidelights were typical. The emphasis was on the rectangle, so fanlights were out. Beginning in 1840 the trend led away from the rectangular emphasis and to pointed arches over entrances, as in Gothic Revival, or to inverted U-shaped arches, as in the Italianate style. These transom and woodwork styles may help you to date the door. (Illustration 16.)

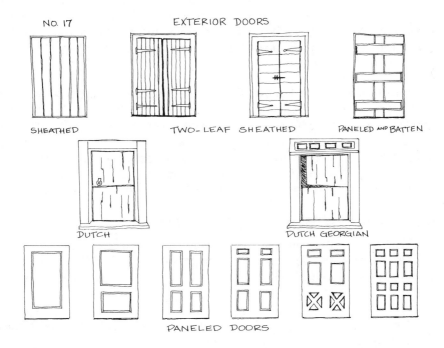

No. 17   EXTERIOR DOORS

SHEATHED   TWO-LEAF SHEATHED   PANELED AND BATTEN

DUTCH   DUTCH GEORGIAN

PANELED DOORS

During the rest of the 19th century a multitude of styles proliferated side-by-side, employing multiple combinations and variations. If your house is late 19th century, you may need to consult specific sources to determine the style of an entrance. (Bibliography.)

The earliest exterior doors in the 17th to 18th century were plank doors formed of two layers of thick boards. The planks on the exterior side ran vertically, the interior ones horizontally. These doors were called "sheathed" when the horizontal planks often were placed next to each other. The heads of the nails joining the two sets of planks often formed a pattern on the exterior surface of the door. Such exterior doors were placed flush with the outside wall of the house, not recessed as are later doors. (Illustration 17.)

By the 18th century, paneled doors were being made with two, three or four panels. They had progressed to six and eight panels by the end of the 18th century. Frequently they were sheathed on the inner side. During the various architectural periods in the 19th century, the number of panels varied, as did their styles, which usually followed window styles.

Doors at first were built relatively narrow, but were widened, during the course of the 18th century, to about three feet. Dutch doors—divided horizontally into a top and bottom section and of either plank or panel—sometimes exceeded three feet by as much as four inches or more. By the mid-18th century, double (or two-leaf) panel doors become common. Each leaf was two feet wide, for a total of four feet.

When trying to date doors (or the house by reference to its doors), keep in mind that people modernized houses by changing doors. It is not unusual to find fancy panel doors in the front section of a house, with homlier or older sheathed or Dutch doors placed in the back. For appearance sake, the prominent front door was replaced more often than the less visible back door. Since doors wore out from use and weathering, they may be much later than their surrounding trim. Other clues throughout this book will help you spot door changes.

Placements of Windows: Fenestration

Fenestration, the window arrangement or grouping—especially of the front elevation, visible from the road—can provide valuable clues to the dating of a house or to changes. The window size, shape, number, hardware or placement may be helpful.

Before the Georgian period, windows were small and sometimes irregularly placed. During the Georgian period windows were larger, standard-sized, and regularly placed. The common arrangement was three bays—the five window plus door front facade. By the late Georgian, two more windows were added on each floor. These were placed next to the "outside" windows—that is, those windows closest to the corners of the house facade. (Illustration 18.)

FENESTRATION

IRREGULAR — 17TH CENTURY

EVOLUTION DURING GEORGIAN PERIOD

THREE BAY

FIVE BAY

FIVE BAY

FRONT ELEVATIONS

ONE BAY

THREE BAY, FIRST STORY

THREE BAY

SIDE ELEVATIONS

When shutters and exterior blinds came into vogue at the end of the 18th century, these four windows had to be placed farther apart in order to permit the shutters of each to fold back against the house. After 1800, shutters also were used at the front entrance. (Illustration 19.) Whether shutters had fixed louvers or were paneled, shutter fasteners were needed to prevent them from blowing in the wind, and this hardware sometimes can be dated. (Illustration 20.)

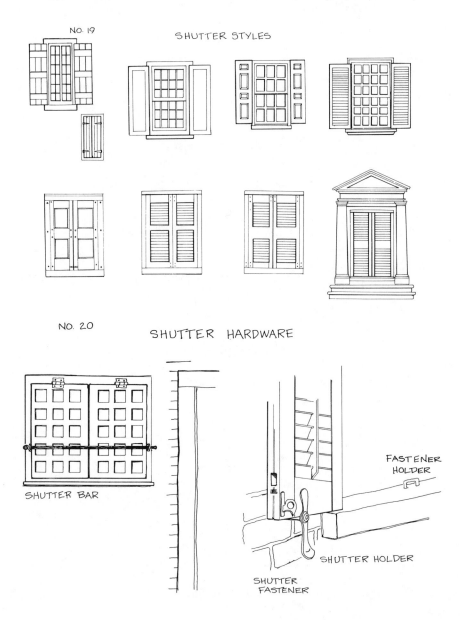

NO. 19   SHUTTER STYLES

NO. 20   SHUTTER HARDWARE

SHUTTER BAR

FASTENER HOLDER

SHUTTER HOLDER

SHUTTER FASTENER

After about 1850, however, the tendency to group windows in twos or threes with mullions between became common and eventually culminated in the multipaned ribbon or row windows of the 20th century. Separated fenestration has continued through the 20th century, often with decorative nonfunctioning shutters. (Illustration 21.)

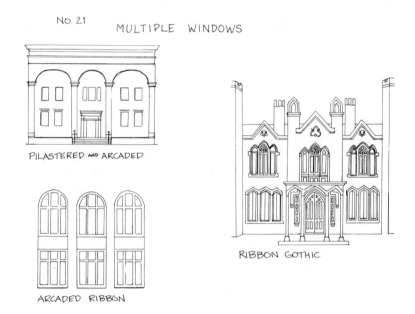

No. 21   MULTIPLE WINDOWS

PILASTERED AND ARCADED

ARCADED RIBBON

RIBBON GOTHIC

Windows

Rough dating may be done from the style of window sash: casement (swing out); single-hung (do not open); or double-hung (the top and bottom sections slide past each other vertically). Small casement windows were made from the 17th to the mid-18th century. Concurrently, single-hung windows were used exclusively to provide light, such as in a transom over a door. After 1730, the double-hung window was used. Its bottom section was raised next to what was originally a fixed upper section. Now ventilation was provided without the problem of having casement windows slamming in the wind. (Illustration 22.)

WINDOW EVOLUTION

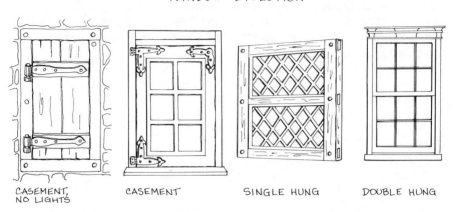

CASEMENT, NO LIGHTS   CASEMENT   SINGLE HUNG   DOUBLE HUNG

Typically, the earliest (17th-century) houses of the common man were one-and-a-half stories high. If there were any windows in the half-story (attic), they were small and placed in the gable end(s). Traditionally the upper half story was used as a storage and drying area. When the living space on the first floor became cramped, the attic was converted to additional living space. Often it became a sleeping area for children and servants and a weaving room, so better lighting was needed. Dormers provided this lighting. Gabled dormer windows appeared in Virginia by the mid-17th century, about the same time as did shed dormers in the Dutch houses in New York. (Illustration 23.)

NO. 23

WINDOWED DORMERS

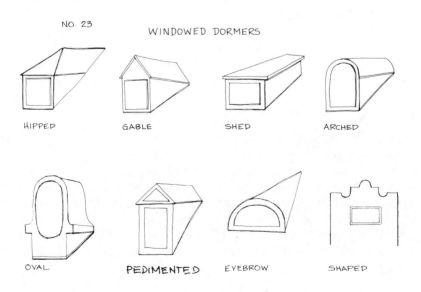

HIPPED   GABLE   SHED   ARCHED

OVAL   PEDIMENTED   EYEBROW   SHAPED

Some eras produced unique window treatment as an element of a particular style. Palladian windows—three adjacent windows, the center one with a fanlight heading it—graced the late 18th-century Adams style. With the appearance of cheaper domestic glass in the early 19th century, people added small "eyebrow" windows on the second floor of one-and-a-half story houses. This occurred during the Greek Revival period. These windows were placed below the roof edge to improve lighting and ventilation. Bay windows came into vogue in the 1840's and often were used as means to enlarge and better illuminate an older style house. (Illustration 24.)

NO. 24

VARIOUS WINDOW TREATMENTS

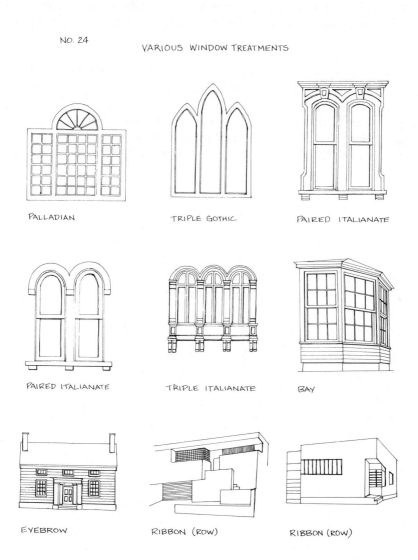

PALLADIAN

TRIPLE GOTHIC

PAIRED ITALIANATE

PAIRED ITALIANATE

TRIPLE ITALIANATE

BAY

EYEBROW

RIBBON (ROW)

RIBBON (ROW)

As the 19th century progressed, windows came to be paired, as in the Italianate style, then tripled or quadrupled as in the Queen Anne style. By the late 19th century, glass covered more and more of the house facade.

The window trims (surrounding woodwork) for different periods were similar to door-entrance trims and were likewise varied in style. Compare your window and door trims to see if they seem similar in design. Similarities indicate that there probably have been no changes since the original. Also note the window trims on each side of the house. The southern and/or western window sills and trim may be different from those of the northern and eastern facades, having been replaced due to weathering with those from a more recent era.

Count the number of lights (panes) in each section of a double-hung sash. Are there 12 lights over 12 (6/6, 2/2, 1/1)? Notice which facade has the window(s) with the most lights in each section. Generally speaking, the smaller and more numerous the lights, the older the window. Because you usually cannot get close to all of the windows to measure the lights, you will have to wait until you are inside the house for more window analysis. (Illustration 25.)

No. 25   EVOLUTION OF WINDOW LIGHTS

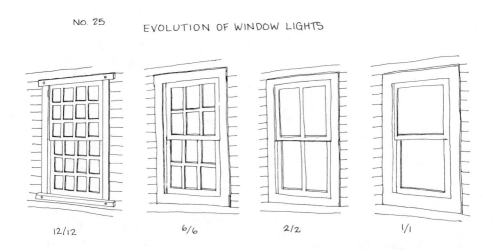

12/12   6/6   2/2   1/1

Number of Stories

One-and-a-half stories were typical of the pre-Revolutionary homes of the common man. Full two-story homes were built only by wealthier people. These two-story homes had a half-story attic above, which sometimes was made into third-floor bedrooms, with windows smaller than, yet complementary to, the windows of the first two stories. In the post-Revolutionary 1790's, two-and-a-half-story homes became more commonplace, although still representative only of the homes of the more affluent. (Illustration 26.)

NO. 26

FACADE HEIGHT (STORIES)

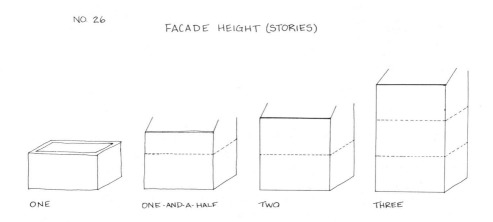

ONE   ONE-AND-A-HALF   TWO   THREE

Full three-story homes were built in the Greek Revival style beginning in the 1820's in New York City, but this style was primarily a local variation, developed because the city had standardized building lots divided into narrow 20' or 25' x 100' plots. Besides New York and a few other urban exceptions, such as Philadelphia, Charleston and Cambridge, Massachusetts, full three-story homes did not appear until the late 1840's, with the Second Empire (1840-1900) style, when a mansard roof — really a half story — topped a sometimes already existing two-and-a-half story house. (Illustration 27.)

THREE STORY HOUSES

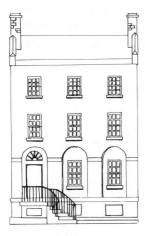

1820'S THREE STORY

LATE 1840'S THREE STORY

   Are there wings or ells added onto a main section of your target house? How many stories do they have? The center section may be two-and-a-half stories (built later), the wings or ells one-and-a-half (built earlier). If a two-and-a-half story ell is placed perpendicular to a two-and-a-half story main section, compare their window styles, lights and siding. Are they similar or different? Are there vertical breaks in the siding, indicating where additions were tacked on? Note where the "back" door is located. For example, is it opposite the front entrance? If not, this probably is not its original location. Use these comparisons as clues to deduce which section of the house came first.

   Although the main section may be the oldest part of the house, it also may have the most modern or decorative details on the facade(s) facing the road. Usually, the most recent windows and doors— like the more decorative fabric, shutters, windows, roof and door trim— are those that can be seen from the road. A rear ell or the back of the main section may show older or less decorative elements, such as small window lights or novelty siding. The owners usually felt that this view of the house would be seen mostly by family members or close associates, so they were less concerned with how it looked. This back facade of the main section is the one to which you should pay particular attention, because it will exhibit the earliest elements and give you the best idea of the actual construction date.

You have completed the circuit around the house and property and have a good idea of the setting and of the exterior features of the house. You have snapped complete pictures of the house and outbuildings and any other interesting elements, and have taken notes on what you think are unusual features (perhaps unique to the builders) or deviations (variations in the specific style). You have taken measurements and sketched the outline of the house. Now you are ready to give the same attention to the house interior.

3

Interior Clues:
Walls, Paint, Wallpaper,
Stencils, Metal Ceilings and Walls

To inspect a house interior, you examine the different elements that make up a house. The walls, floors, ceilings, woodwork, windows and doors usually can be dated because they show characteristics of a specific architectural era. As you try to assign a stylistic period to the various elements of the house, you may find there are characteristics of several styles and periods among them. Your job then is to establish whether a specific style (era) is found only in one or more rooms or wings. From these observations, you should be able to decide which rooms are original and which are later additions. The material in this chapter will explain what to look for.

Walls

What covering is on the interior walls of each room? Paneling, wainscoting and plaster, plaster and paint, wallpaper? Although the dating may overlap slightly, the order in which these are given here reflects the order in which they commonly were used, starting with the Colonial period. Wide boards placed vertically the full height of the room and horizontal wide-board wainscoting with plastered walls above it, are two wall treatments which were prevalent in the second half of the 18th century. (Illustration 28.) Plastered and

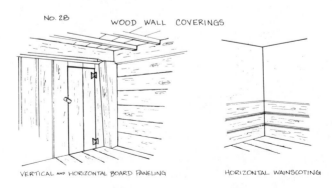

NO. 28   WOOD WALL COVERINGS

VERTICAL and HORIZONTAL BOARD PANELING   HORIZONTAL WAINSCOTING

EVOLUTION OF WALL TREATMENT

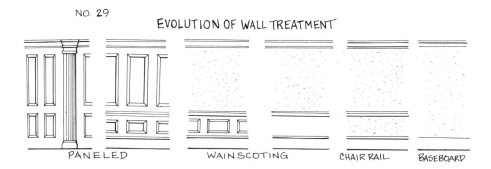

PANELED   WAINSCOTING   CHAIR RAIL   BASEBOARD

painted walls followed, beginning in the late 18th century. (Illustration 29.) Wallpaper came last, in the 18th to 19th centuries. The reasons for these changes in wall treatment were the usual ones of advances in technology and changes in taste and style.

Where lime was available locally in sufficient quantities to merit establishing a kiln or furnace, plastering became more common. Plastering also probably developed as an alternative wall covering concomitant with the deforestation of the early settlement areas along the East coast. Eighteenth- and early-19th-century plaster consisted of lime, sand, water and animal hair. The most common hair used was horsehair. On occasion other binders were used, such as dung, straw, brick dust and gelatin. By the late 19th century, modern plaster had evolved. This usually consisted of lime, sand, water and gypsum although, on occasion, other substances were included. Generally speaking, this later plaster was considerably harder than that found prior to 1850. Plaster usually was placed over lath in layers, the whitest and finest being the last coat. Gray plaster was coarser, and often the only coat affordable.

Early lath was sawed in broad sheets 3/8" to 1/2" in thickness, then split along the grain with a hatchet, stretched out to produce a zigzag effect, and nailed to the studs. In the 19th century, as sawmills became more commonplace, lath was usually cut to the standard size of 5/16" x 1 1/2" x 4' and nailed horizontally to the studs, leaving spaces in between the pieces of lath. Thus, the style of lath can indicate the age of the walls—the zigzag lath being earlier than the sawed, and used until the mid-19th century. (Illustration 30.)

Spaces between the pieces of lath provided a mechanical bond—a seat for the plaster to "sit" on. They also allowed for expansion and contraction during warm and cold, or wet and dry seasons, to avoid cracking the plaster. Plastered surfaces were durable and provided a smoothness ready for further treatment, such as the application of color.

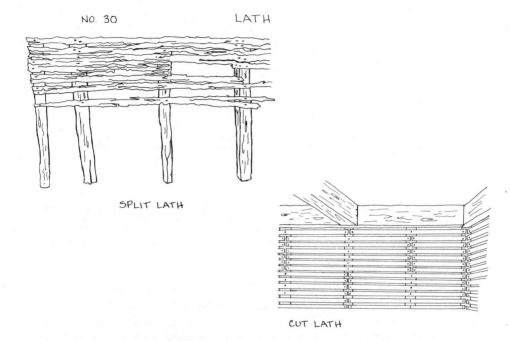

NO. 30   LATH

SPLIT LATH

CUT LATH

Paint-Chip Analysis

It is unusual to find large surfaces either inside or outside older houses still painted with the original paint. Inside, look for traces of old paint in window sashes or under moldings. Their colors may help to identify and date them.

Because of weathering, exterior paint may peel, enabling you to break off a paint-chip to find out what the original color was. If whitewash or milk paint, it probably is imbedded into the wood and may be readily visible. Or, if all of the paint layers are included in the paint-chip—that is, there is only bare wood under it—you might consider taking the chip to an expert to identify the original color microscopically.

A paint-chip analysis is a means of determining which colors were applied in a room over a period of years. This analysis will establish the original paint color, and should be done by an expert. The technique is so refined that a paint sample can be less than an inch square. The paint layers are peeled back with a surgical scalpel or a laser and analyzed under a microscope. Early, hand-ground pigments contain particles that are not uniform in size, while the particles found in later, machine-ground pigments are regularly-sized and fine. A paint-chip color analysis may help date a house, and may be especially helpful if other methods of dating are inconclusive.

Paint: Exterior and Interior

Whitewash, a creamy mixture of slaked lime and water, was a common method of covering wood—both interior and exterior—and plaster, beginning with settlement in the 17th century and continuing in use through the 20th. The lime helped prevent insect infestation and rot in the wood. With repeated coats on wood over the years, a plaster-like build-up occurred, smoothing out imperfections and filling in cracks.

Seventeenth century wooden house exteriors were not painted but rather, allowed to weather. By the early to mid-18th century, houses in New England, if painted at all, were dark colors, often with a buff trim. In the mid-Atlantic states and farther South, houses often were off-white with dark colors, such as green, black, ochre and umber, as trim. Mid-Atlantic shutters, however, often were painted white, in contrast to the trim. By the late 18th to early 19th century, during the early Federal era (1790-1820), pale yellow or gray, gray-blue, and pinkish tan were popular with white trim. The Greek Revival period (1820-1850) was characterized by houses painted white with dark green shutters. Often sand was applied directly to the white paint to imitate stone.

In the 18th century, pigments used for paint were imported and expensive. *The Builder's Dictionary*, published in London in 1734, gives us some idea of what colors may have been available to the colonists. It lists a combination of Spanish Brown, Spanish White and Red Lead as exterior primer colors and recommends "a fair White, made of White Lead and about a Fifth Part in Quantity (not in weight) of Spanish White" as the finishing coat. In addition to white lead paints, sometimes timbers were painted "with a Timber Colour with Umber and White, or a Lead Colour with Indigo and White." (Such stone and wood colors also were listed as being exterior paints used during this Georgian period.) Whenever such pigments were used in the United States, they would have been rather expensive, especially since various forms of processed lead were used.

One of the earliest publications written in the United States that describes paint colors common during the Federal period was a pamphlet written by a house and ship painter. Describing pigments in use in 1812 in Connecticut, the author notes the following colors as exterior oil paint: white, cream, straw, orange, pea-green, parrot green, grass green, red, slate and black.

Both the 1734 and 1812 listings contain many more interior colors than exterior colors. Perhaps it was common to use a wider variety of interior colors. While both listings note the same general colors for inside the house, the exterior colors in the 1812 publication seem more colorful than the exterior listings of 1734. Of course, because these are listings only, it is not possible to determine from them which colors were the most commonly used.

Homemade pigments sometimes were substituted for expensive, imported pigments. For example, lampblack was obtained be scraping out the powder from the insides of lamp chimneys. Red pigment was obtained from brick dust or red clay. "Paris green" was made from arsenic and copper. Most pigments were limited by their materials—you cannot tint brick dust or lampblack—and generally did not produce gradations of the color.

During the 19th century more and different pigments—both exterior and interior—were developed. By 1830 ultramarine was available as a cheaper substitute for the ground lapis lazuli, which made a rich, deep blue-purplish color but was extremely expensive and rarely used. Zinc white became available in 1850 and viridian, a bluish-green, in 1860. As new colors were developed, they also were assimilated into the various architectural styles that appeared after 1840. By the last quarter of the 19th century, a wide range of exterior colors were used, depending on regional influences and the style of the house.

In the 19th century, a commonly used substitute for regular oil paint was milk paint. A mid-19th-century recipe for this "Farmer's Paint" included: skimmed milk; slaked lime; linseed oil; white Burgundy pitch (which was developed in France from the pitch of a species of spruce brought there from Norway) and Spanish white, the pigment. In 1866 the 10th edition of *Dr. Chases's Recipes* included the "Painter's Economy in Making Colors," giving ten recipes for water-based colors. By this time the homemade pigments combined various chemical compounds, which could be purchased readily since they now were manufactured domestically. He also listed "Whitewashed and Cheap Paints," one of which was a "Paint-To Make Without Lead or Oil." It included whiting, skimmed milk and fresh, slaked lime.

Wallpaper

Wallpaper was imported from England between 1700 and 1780. It was so expensive that it usually was found only in homes of the wealthy. Wallpaper often was flocked, and by its style imitated the silk, woven damask that adorned the walls of English homes. Festoon borders with garlands of leaves, flowers and ribbons were common, and outlined windows, doors, fireplaces, wainscoting and ceilings. Wallpaper came with a selvage on the edges. One selvage was cut off and the paper was overlapped, not abutted as it is today.

A fledgling American wallpaper industry started about 1780. At that time dainty floral papers were popular, as were bold allegorical scenes proclaiming independence from England. During the period from 1780 to 1840, there was an increase in the importing of papers from France, England and China.

Papers popular in the early 1800's included floral patterns enclosed within concentric circles or double ogees. Festoon borders also continued to be widely used. By the 1830's, multicolored French wallpaper with a rainbow-shaped background and an overall pattern of stylized flowers, some within geometric shapes, was used extensively. French Gothic Revival paper, a new style inspired by cathedral spires and pointed arches often was used to modernize an older home. This wallpaper predated the American Gothic Revival, which began in the United States after Andrew Jackson Downing's popular book was published in 1842.

In the 1840's, the wallpapers imported and used in America were inspired by Louis XV designs from France. Typically these were naturalistic flowers surrounded by C-scrolls. Domestic wallpapers with American designs were developed throughout the century to complement the various architectural styles that appeared after 1840. From 1840 to 1870 wallpaper became an almost universal method of brightening walls as mechanization increased production. Widths became standardized and, during the printing, colors were not laid on as thickly—because the paint had to dry faster. Also, because of mechanical restrictions on the print roller, the repeated design became more regularized than in hand-produced wallpaper.

One particular style of wallpaper originating in France in the early 1800's was imported throughout most of the century. These wallpapers depicted a variety of scenes, from views of Switzerland to hunting scenes in Alsace, to battle scenes from the American Revolution. Often a dado, such as one simulating porch balusters and handrail, covered the lower section of the wall, a *trompe l'oeil* technique common in the naturalistic style rampant in such French papers. Highly praised, these papers were imported from Boston to New Orleans and used by those who could afford them.

Wallpaper can be identified by its paper and pattern, but usually only an approximate date can be given for its manufacture. Occasionally extra rolls are found in an attic with the manufacturer's name in the selvage that usually would have been cut off before applying the paper. By looking up the manufacturer's dates of operation, you will be able to estimate the general time-span during which the paper was manufactured. Two recent books identifying wallpapers by era are listed in the Bibliography. These books are by no means exhaustive —the miles of different wallpaper manufactured from the mid-19th century on is mind-boggling—but they may help you narrow down the date.

Wallpaper often was a means of sprucing up a house. It commonly was added, layer upon layer, in the late 19th century to the present. When you walk into a house and see wallpaper that looks old or with a design that seems to be from a previous century, it probably is a reprint. There are ways of establishing this. Dyes used in the 20th century are different from 18th- and 19th-century dyes. The chemistry is different, as also is the composition of the paper. Modern dyes appear brighter and would not be as muted or subtle-looking as dyes that have been faded or altered by light for a century or two. If you think it likely that the wallpaper is original, but are not sure, call in an expert to advise you.

Even if the wallpaper is original and you know the dates of production, be cautious. You still can be deceived as to when it was applied, and such a mistake could affect your house dating. Sometimes people saved expensive imported rolls for years before applying them, especially in rural areas, where paper-hanging was not a common trade. Look underneath the paper, if possible, for any other clues.

When wallpaper was laid on crude plaster, newspapers sometimes were used first as a cushion to smooth out the surface. From the newspaper dates, you know approximately when the wallpaper was applied irrespective of its date of manufacture. Weigh other factors which might be helpful. For example, finding older wallpaper in a room with modern molding could indicate that the room was added long after the wallpaper had been purchased.

In some houses wallpaper was used as a means of making an early house appear *structurally* modern. For instance, Georgian and Federal style houses were built with corner posts and ceiling beams exposed. When such beam exposure became old-fashioned, plaster and wallpaper sometimes were used to disguise this support system stylishly. Each time this was done, a layer of lath, plaster and wallpaper was added, resulting in a new wall or a lowered ceiling. If this was done several times, the structural members disappeared behind multiple layers of lath, plaster and wallpaper, and the homeowner was happy with the new style. In this process, the dimensions of the room became more than a foot shorter in width and depth, and the ceiling ten inches lower. In addition to style, warmth was gained, as the layers acted as insulation.

By peeling off each layer of lath, plaster and wallpaper, you expose the various times that a house was "improved." If you are able to date some of these wallpapers, other changes in the house can be related to the rough dates of the various wallpaper styles. Maybe windows or moldings were changed or added. If you have a window that you suspect was added, remove the molding around it to see if any paint or wallpaper design, or both, appear. If only plaster is visible, the window probably was original with that room. If wallpaper or paint identical with what covers the rest of the wall is visible, the window probably was added later.

Wallpaper analysis can be fascinating, but like other elements of house history analysis, it must be considered within the context of the whole house. Always keep in mind that you are sifting through and sorting out a variety of factors in order to establish the proper sequences of building, remodeling and redecorating that have taken place.

Stenciling

In the early 19th century, wallpaper was too expensive for the common-man's house. Stenciling with homemade paints became a cheap substitute for wallpaper, especially from 1800 to 1840, before domestic papers were available. Red and green were the most popular colors for stenciling. Black was the third, and whites and browns were used considerably less frequently. The pigments used to make green, white and brown had to be imported, so it is noteworthy that green was a common color. Since various shades of green also were popular colors for painting the exterior of Federal houses, it appears that demand for the pigments needed to create these greens was high enough to require their importation in large quantities, in spite of the cost.

Some old stencils have been found applied to the grayish undercoat of the plaster common in the more modest houses of the early 19th century. Stencils have been found under coats of paint or under wallpaper. Although it is possible to find buried stencils, they are hard to detect because a stencil was not always applied over the entire wall. It was cheaper for the less affluent home owner to pay the itinerant stenciler to apply stencils as a border or "wainscoting" than to have him work over an entire wall. Thus, a paint chip analysis may prove useful in finding stencils only if the right spot is tested. Again, use a specialist and ask him where you should look. If you know that a stenciler was active in your area and in your style of home, it may be worthwhile to check for stencils.

Metal Ceilings and Walls

A wall and ceiling treatment similar to stenciling—that is, a pattern being repeated—was developed in the latter half of the 19th century. Metal ceilings made of corrugated iron had first come into use in 1868. By the 1880's, commercial and public buildings sported metal ceilings made of lightweight metal sheets stamped in decorative designs. From about 1895 to 1915 some houses were built with metal walls as well as ceilings, especially in the kitchens. Sometimes these metal walls and ceilings were put up as a repair job instead of replastering. They were touted as being less expensive than plaster or wood, and safer, since they could act as fire stops. Several sheet metal companies had catalogs, which offered more than 400 patterns. Such catalogs can be found in libraries and will enable you to date a particular pattern.

4

Interior Clues:
Staircases, Moldings, Fireplaces,
Doors, Hardware, Windows

This chapter explores some specific elements of the house interior. It explains what can be learned about the house from the construction, style and materials of these elements.

Staircases

Start with the main staircase, which usually was positioned near the front entrance. Mid-18th-century staircases were wainscoted or paneled up to the handrail, so that they were boxed in. Later in the 18th century, staircases were partially paneled along the wall line to the stairs and then had an open balustrade. By the end of the 18th century, plaster and a baseboard replaced this wall paneling. This style alternated with wooden paneled staircases into the 20th century. Paneled staircases usually were the mark of more pretentious homes. (Illustration 31.)

Early to mid-18th-century stairs wound around corners or chimneys, necessitating triangular treads at the corners. In Georgian-style houses stairs usually were placed against a wall in the center hall. In the more elegant Georgian houses with wide center halls, the stairs were sometimes placed centrally toward the back of the hall and raised to a landing, splitting into double staircases to continue up to the second floor.

During the Federal period elliptical stairwells, placed on one side of the center hall, were popularized by Asher Benjamin's *American Builder's Companion*, a pattern book for carpenters published in 1806. These stairs, attached along one side, appear to glide up into space with no supports. (Illustration 31.)

In the Greek Revival period, side-hall entrances became common. Thus stairs in these homes might have been placed on an inside or outside wall, depending on how close the front entrance was to the outside wall. So, from

STAIRCASE EVOLUTION

GEORGIAN MID-18TH CENT.

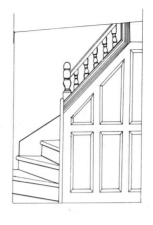

GEORGIAN MID-18TH CENT.

GEORGIAN LATE 18TH CENT.

FEDERAL EARLY 19TH CENT.

1820 on, stair placement varied, but usually corresponded to front-entrance placement.

The type of wood used for balustrade and treads may help date the stairway or house. In the late 18th century, oak handrails and newel posts often were attached to pine balusters. Cherry was a typical mid-19th-century balustrade wood, while walnut was a favorite in late Second Empire homes.

Back stairs are found in larger houses, especially in those that housed or had servants or slaves. These stairs usually were located toward the rear of the house near the kitchen, on a back wall. They were simpler in design than the front stairs and often were extremely steep, with narrow treads. Sometimes there was no handrail. Imagine carrying commodes down these stairs!

Moldings

The species of wood used in the stairs was not necessarily the same kind as that used in moldings. Stairs received heavy use and required harder woods than that in the moldings found around windows, doors and wall. Because moldings eventually became decorative pieces, they traditionally were made of pine, which was easy to plane by hand. Hardwoods came into use as moldings in the last quarter of the 19th century, when machine-driven tools and harder steels could produce moldings from chestnut or walnut.

Wood moldings were used decoratively to cover up the places where a plastered surface met another material, such as a wooden floor, a door jamb, or the casing that covered exposed posts and beams. These moldings also were functional in that they closed up cracks to diffuse drafts. The introduction of moldings as ornamentation coincided with the development of plastering and the cottage tool industry, especially plane-making, in the 18th to early 19th centuries.

Thousands of differently designed planes were manufactured to shape or smooth the wood for a variety of decorative or practical purposes. Some of these planes were developed specifically to produce the different molding styles that were in demand. The most common examples of molding made by such planes were simply adorned pieces with parallel double lines near the edges of the wood. Other, more elaborate moldings included the heavily pedimented Georgian window moldings. These contrast with the delicate Adamsesque moldings of the Federal period with their garlands, floral motifs or draperies. Label molds placed only across the heads of the windows were typical of the Gothic Revival, while hood molds—upside down U's—ex-

No. 32

MOLDINGS

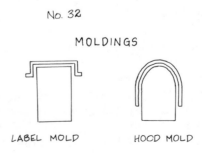

LABEL MOLD   HOOD MOLD

tending two-thirds of the distance down the windows, were Italianate. (Illustration 32.) Whatever the era, the moldings and the styles of windows and doors within each period were similar. Thus, if a house were constructed in the Italianate style with round-headed windows, the moldings would not have the drapery motif of the Federal period, but rather the arched hood of the Italianate style.

By 1800, when it had become common practice to plaster all other walls, paneling still was placed on the fireplace wall, probably because paneling did not show the soot stains that a plastered wall would. Often a cupboard was built into the paneling toward the upper half of the wall, where the chimney was reduced in size from the firebox. Moldings were used to cover up the edges of the panels. After 1800, the fireplace paneled wall began to be replaced by a plastered wall and a mantel shelf, supported by two pilasters on either side of the fireplace. (Illustration 33.)

NO. 33

FIREPLACE SURROUNDS

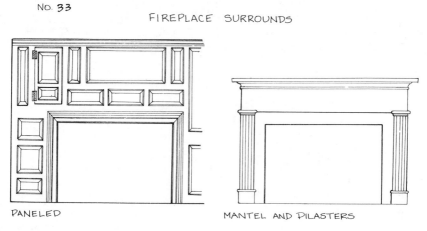

PANELED

MANTEL AND PILASTERS

Fireplaces

Generally, the older the fireplace, the larger it is. Fireplace dimensions had been defined earlier by the 16th-century Italian architect Andrea Palladio. The famous 17th- to 18th-century English architect, Sir Christopher Wren, considered Palladio as his master. Wren, in turn, influenced building in the American colonies.

Palladio's architectural treatise was translated into English in 1716 as *The Four Books of Architecture.* It was widely quoted in *The Builder's Dictionary* (1734), which was used in the United States as a reference for construction. One of the charts that Palladio created in his book included the dimensions of fireplaces. They varied from 4' to 8' wide, 4' to 5' high and 2' to 3' deep. An oven often was located on one side of the fireplace.

Some 17th-century American fireplaces were even larger, designed to offer warm working spaces next to the spot where the fire was laid. The fireplace was of stone or brick and the hearth usually of stone. The manteltree was a massive, hewn beam that extended across the width above the opening. A crane for cooking pots was built into the firebox. (Illustration 34.)

Sometimes these massive 17th- to 18th-century fireplaces did not draw well and smoked unless a draft was created. One way to do this was to crack the front door. Or, some doors lifted up. An old story recounts that an early settler neglected to put the door back down before going to bed, and in the morning discovered a bear soaking up the remaining warmth from the hearth!

There were several ethnic variations in 17th- and 18th-century American fireplaces. For instance, Dutch fireplaces—few of which can still be found—were end-wall fireplaces, characterized by a hood that was exactly 13 square tiles from the floor. Each tile was 5" to 5 1/8" on a side, so the hood hung about 5 1/2' off the floor. A good-sized fire was laid on a large stone, or stones, which projected into the room. Such fireplaces were large, without jambs, and enabled people to draw chairs close around all three sides of them. (Illustration 34.)

NO. 34

FIREPLACES

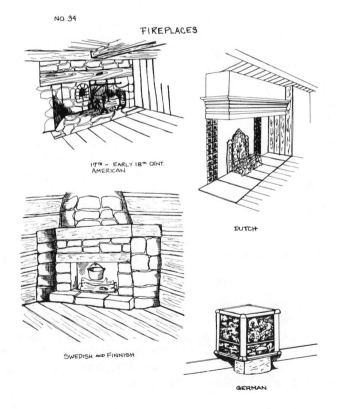

17TH - EARLY 18TH CENT.
AMERICAN

DUTCH

SWEDISH AND FINNISH

GERMAN

The Finns and Swedes who, in the 17th century, had settled in what is now Delaware, built corner fireplaces in their one- or two-room log houses. (In a log two-room house, however, there was only one fireplace, located in the main room.) Such fireplaces were usually of stone, until the Dutch took over the colony and introduced brick as an alternate fireplace material. (Illustration 34.)

The fireplaces of German immigrants added a new element. Their center chimney was off-center to accommodate the German all-purpose kitchen, or Küche, which was larger than their parlor, or Stube. These 18th-century kitchen fireplaces were of massive design and the stove in the adjacent parlor was backed into the center chimney. The stove was made of five metal plates—a top and bottom, two sides and a front. Its back was open to the kitchen fireplace where, periodically, coals were shoveled into it to warm the parlor. (Illustration 34.)

By the mid- to late 18th century, fireplaces in general had shrunk in size—partly because of the development of a smaller, more shallow design—and typically were made of brick. Small fires, laid in these shallow fireboxes with the flues angling up behind, reflected the heat into the room, rather than losing it up a large flue. A stone hearth still was used. After the Revolution these smaller fireplaces often were built into post-Revolutionary additions on Dutch houses. The Dutch fireplace was abandoned, probably partly due to the large space it had needed, as well as to the draftiness of the open flue.

Once fireplaces became smaller, they could fit into the corners of rooms. Often, several of these diagonal fireplaces were placed back to back in different rooms, sharing a common chimney. They occurred in end-chimney houses as well as center-chimney, and represented an economy of space. This change in fireplace location occurred in the last quarter of the 18th century and was found throughout the United States.

At the end of the 18th century as the forests were depleted, coal came into use and along with it coal grates, and eventually, more changes in fireplace design. Although coal was used increasingly in the 19th century, in forested, rural areas wood still was the more common fuel. Coal and wood stoves also were used increasingly in the 19th century, especially after 1830. A hole was cut into the flue over the mantel to accommodate the stovepipe, and the fireplace was closed up. Eventually chimneys became even smaller to accommodate the metal stovepipes used as flues for stoves. By the mid-19th century this change had occurred throughout the United States.

With fireplaces closed up, the alternative method of cooking was the coal- or wood-fired cooking range. Although cooking ranges were developed in the 1850's, it was considerably later—in the 1880's—before they came into general use. They were resisted because they changed the entire process of cooking. It was difficult for many cooks to shift from the methods and utensils of open-fire cooking to closed-fire, with the pot on a metal grate. If you find yourself in an old house with chimneys but without fireplaces or traces of them, suspect that stoves may have been used instead of fireplaces, for both heating and cooking, and that the house was built in the latter 19th century.

Doors

Doors provided privacy and helped keep rooms clean. That is why the parlor door was kept shut except when guests came. The earliest 17th- to 18th-century interior door was a batten door in which two or three boards were joined vertically with two or three battens placed horizontally. A simpler version did not have battens. (Illustration 34a.) Panel *interior* doors appeared about 1700 and developed much as did the *exterior* panel doors described in Chapter 3, becoming more stylized over the years. The number of panels and their shapes varied with each architectural style in the 19th century. For example, Gothic Revival houses sported interior doors with two vertical panels having pointed arches. (Illustration 35.)

Again, the front parts of the house interior, including the rooms most

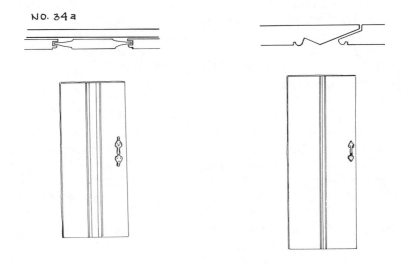

NO. 34a

CROSS SECTIONS OF PANELING SHOWING JOINERY

INTERIOR DOORS

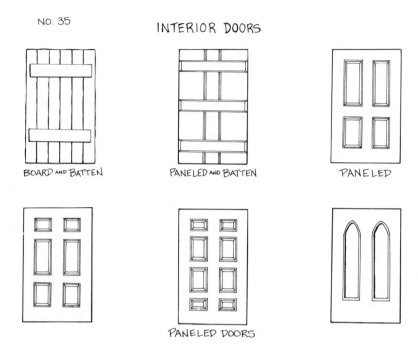

BOARD AND BATTEN   PANELED AND BATTEN   PANELED

PANELED DOORS

commonly viewed by the public, had the most recent doors, while the back of the house or the servants' quarters had the older doors. Because interior doors did not wear out, they were moved around as houses were added onto or modernized, and walls were changed. Occasionally, there may be an interior door that is older than the house. So, like most other elements found in a house, doors should be carefully analyzed and compared with the other elements before final conclusions are made about their origins or dates.

Door Hardware

Door hardware can be a general indicator of age, although dating houses by hardware alone is not recommended. Wrought iron hardware—hinges and door latches—was hand-forged in some rural areas well into the mid-19th century by local blacksmiths. Furthermore, because wrought iron was durable, not always plentiful, and somewhat expensive, it usually was removed from worn-out doors and placed onto new ones. Thus, some of its hardware could be older than the house, although this is not usually so.

Generally speaking, the commonly found large iron strap hinges, thumb latches and HL hinges date from the 18th century, but were widely manufactured by local blacksmiths into the 19th. Therefore, it is entirely possible that they predate the doors they are attached to. Door hardware made before 1860 is difficult to date with precision. (Illustration 36.)

The same dating problem arises with brass hardware. During the Georgian era in the late 18th century, brass hardware imported from England was a favored material for door hardware particularly in affluent houses. So, a large brass lock could be identified as post-Revolutionary Georgian (1780's) even if it is placed on an 1820's Federal house.

NO. 36

DOOR HARDWARE

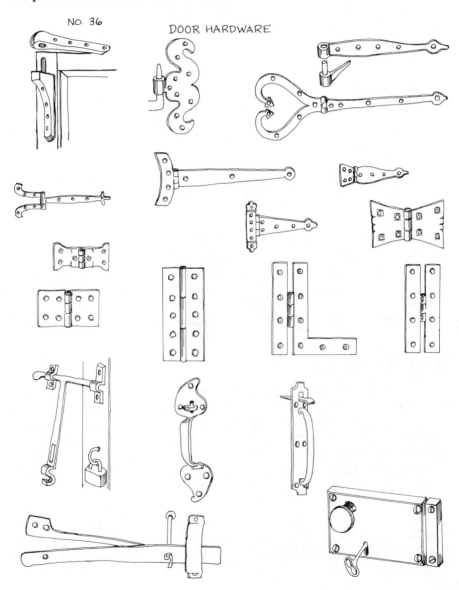

In trying to identify a specific brass lock, find out when brass, an alloy of copper and zinc, was first manufactured near you and where, and also where the particular item(s) in the house you are researching might have been purchased. If the item was not produced or sold locally, look for genealogical information indicating whether it might have been brought from the family's previous location during a period of westward expansion. Careful detective work may provide the answer.

Most kinds of brass and iron hardware manufactured after the Civil War were stamped with the name of the maker, so that it is possible to trace its date from the manufacturer's catalog or dates of operation.

Wooden latches (pintles and gudgeons) and some leather strap hinges—antedating wrought iron hardware—still can be found in houses throughout the United States, especially in old Spanish, German and Dutch areas. These are less likely than metal to have been changed—except for the replacement of rotten leather—because they might be broken when moved. Most probably date from the 18th century. They were created out of necessity, because the home owner could not or did not want to pay for commercial hardware.

Windows

Windows are easier to place than is hardware, because the technological advancements in glass manufacture and sash production can be dated more precisely.

Seventeenth-century glass was a fusion of silica (sand) and two alkaline bases — lime found in stone or oyster shells, and either potash leached from wood ashes or soda found in salt water. Most early window glass was imported, although a glasshouse was established as early as 1608 in Jamestown, Virginia. Later in the 17th century, small glasshouses appeared in Massachusetts, New York and Pennsylvania. Throughout the 18th century glassworks were started in various colonies or states: Salem County, New Jersey (1739), Brooklyn, New York (1754), Lancaster County, Pennsylvania (1763), Temple, New Hampshire (1779), Frederick County, Maryland (1785) and Pittsburgh, Pennsylvania (1795). After 1800 many glasshouses were built, but it was not until 1824, when the United States government enacted a strong protective tariff, that glass manufacturing became profitable. Thus, from the 17th to early 19th century, window lights (panes) were imported from England and were expensive. For this reason, and also because of Indian attacks and harsh weather, there were few windows in 17th-century houses.

The earliest 17th-century lights were diamond-shaped—about 4 1/2" x 5 3/4"—and were held together by lead bars. They usually were placed in casement windows, although early double-hung sashes, which appeared by 1730, also had diamond-shaped lights. By the mid-18th century the lights had become a standardized rectangle, 6" wide x 8" high. The double-hung sash was a standardized four lights wide, but its height varied, being two, three or four lights high in each half. One of the most popular window styles in the North was 12/12 (12 over 12) That is, twelve lights in the top half and twelve lights in the bottom. In the South, 9/9 (9 over 9) was the most popular. There were sashes throughout the colonies, though, that were 9/6 (three lights wide) or 6/4 (two lights wide). By the 1790's window lights had evolved to 8" x 10" and the sash had standardized to 6/6 (three lights wide) although there were many variations used through the early 19th century. (Illustration 37.)

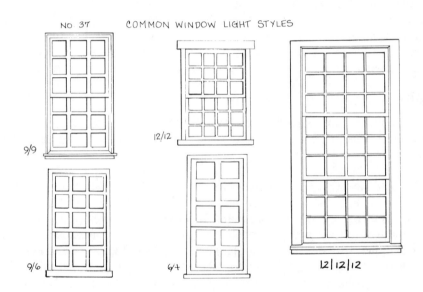

NO. 37   COMMON WINDOW LIGHT STYLES

9/9

12/12

9/6

6/4

12|12|12

Besides being imported and expensive, early glass was not very clear, and it broke fairly easily. As the 19th-century progressed several advances were made in glass technology, which can be seen today in the 19th-century window glass that survives in many houses. The most obvious change was the size of the panes (lights), which evolved from the usually imported, 8" x 10" light in 1790, to the domestic, 91/2" x 15" light in the 1850's, to eventually one or two large lights in each half of the sash by the 1890's. Also, the glass was clearer and less wavy than 18th-century glass.

Window *sizes* changed as well by the mid-19th century. The easiest and earliest method (ca. 1820 to 1860) of increasing window size was to add a third twelve-light double-hung sash. This made a triple sash, bringing the window closer to the floor. In some cases windows actually extended completely to the floor and could be walked through. The bottom two sashes were pushed up to cover the top sash, allowing enough head room to walk through the window— perhaps with only a little stooping—to the outdoors. In other cases, double doors were cut into the paneling beneath the double sash window, opening into the house.

When trying to date a window, measure the size of the lights. Then, count the number in each half of its double-hung sash. Before deciding the age of the window from this, make sure it is not a modern replacement of an old-style window. The modern window has clear, unwavy glass, a smooth or unmarked window frame and modern sash slide apparatus. Also keep in mind that variations in window styles or light sizes from room to room may indicate changes made in a house. As with other changes and additions, the more recent styles will occur near the front of the house.

5

Interior Clues:
Room Organization and Dimensions,
Roof Pitch, Cellars, Attics

This chapter explains how to explore and evaluate those other interior elements of a house which can tell something about its construction, dating, materials and alterations.

Room Organization and Roof Pitch

Note the room alignment of the house you are researching. Was the original house built one room deep or two? Seventeenth century houses were one room deep. Space was gained by adding a second floor or adding rooms along the lengthwise axis. The roofs were steep, with perhaps as much as a 60° pitch, because originally they were thatched and required rapid water run off. After it became apparent that thatched roofs could not withstand the rough American climate, wood shingles replaced thatch. Although this new roofing material did not require such a steeply pitched roof, it took about 100 years for roofs to evolve to a lower pitch. Do not assume, therefore, that a steeply pitched roof means that a house originally had a thatched roof. (Illustration 38.)

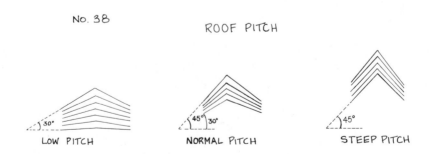

No. 38

ROOF PITCH

30°   LOW PITCH

45° 30°   NORMAL PITCH

45°   STEEP PITCH

By the early 18th century, houses customarily were expanded to one-and-a-half rooms deep by means of a half-room width added on the rear. The roof of this addition was an extension of the original roof (saltbox). In a one-and-a-half story house the roof extension retained the pitch of the original roof. (Illustration 39). In a one-story house the roof over the half-room addition was a shed roof attached to the original roof (catslide).

By 1750 houses usually were a full two rooms deep, and the roof pitch was lowered. This was necessary to accommodate a two-unit depth without adding excessive height. This massed (two-room deep) plan has been retained to the present day as a salient feature of American homes, and linear (one-room deep) plans still are used in rural and vernacular houses where there is adequate land available for a spread-out house. (Illustration 39.)

NO. 39

ROOM MASSING

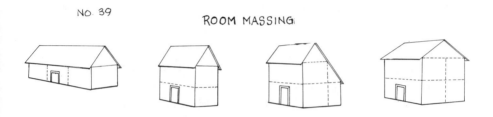

Measuring Rooms and Floor Boards to Detect Changes

Measure the interior room dimensions. Later you will want to subtract these interior dimensions from those of the exterior. By this comparison you may be able to determine—or guess at—the size of the house framing members.

In a center-hall house, note the width of each of the rooms flanking the hall; then measure the hall width. You may find that the width of the hall plus one room equals the width of the other room. This, then, was not originally a center-hall house. The hall probably was created out of part of one room when the second room was added. These flanking rooms will not be of equal width.

Another possibility is that one of the rooms was the original house and included at least part of the space that is now the hall. You usually can tell this be examining the flooring. Do the floor boards end short of the wall or beyond it, in another room? There may be lines or marks on the floor showing this. Or, there may be a narrow, 2" to 3" piece of wood inserted between the wider floor boards where a wall was removed. Many smaller houses were built a room at a time. Exterior walls became interior walls as the house expanded.

Notice the floor boards in each room. Is a floor near an outside wall pieced in small rectangles? Perhaps stovepipe was threaded through this floor, or large 19th-century iron grates were placed there for the central heating system. A large rectangle, the size of a stairwell, pieced into a floor may indicate the original position of the stairs. If the direction of the floor boards changes from room to room, the rooms may have been added at different times.

Of what species of wood is the flooring, and what are the board widths? Generally speaking, floor boards became narrower over the years. Although board width always was standardized in the better houses, wide-board, random-width oak or pine boards often covered the floors of less costly houses in the 18th to early 19th century. Wide boards were just as undesirable then as they are today, because their seasonal shrinking and expanding creates wide cracks that collect dirt. Whenever possible these wide boards were used in areas less likely to be seen, such as in subflooring or sheathing, or less public, such as flooring in kitchens or attics.

As these wider-board floors wore out or became insect infested, narrower (8" to 9 1/2" wide) boards replaced them by the mid-19th century. By the last quarter of the 19th century, standard 2 5/8" to 3 1/2" wide hardwood flooring was the norm. Sometimes combinations of woods were used to produce interesting patterns, such as parquetry or stripes, in which alternating maple and cherry strips were placed within a black walnut frame which edged the room. By the 20th century, 2 1/4" wide oak flooring was standard.

If you find exposed posts and beams during this inspection, note whether any notches are cut out of them near doors or windows. Notching next to a door or window frame indicates that larger doors or windows probably replaced original, smaller ones. The style of the sash or door, the number and size of the lights or panels, may give a clue to dating when the change occurred.

Cellars

Originally cellars were holes dug into the ground for the storage of foods. In the United States—unlike in many countries—they usually were found under the house. Cellar walls usually were the house foundation. However, some early foundations were built in trenches, dug where the walls were to be placed, but without removing the dirt and rock between the foundation walls. Because sills and floors rotted sooner if the dirt was not removed, and because it was more convenient to store food underneath the house rather than having to go outside, such cellars became popular.

Cellars are instructive in doing a house history, because it is here that much of the construction is exposed. Foundation, posts and beams can be seen in cellars—as well as in attics. It was not until the mid-20th century that insulation and concrete were added to cellars. When exploring the cellar, you may find concrete covering an uncoursed fieldstone foundation and dirt floor, metal jacks replacing rotted wooden posts, and insulation covering up ceilings and sills. Without disturbing these "improvements," look for exposed framing and note its characteristics. Are the main posts, beams and sills hewn, or are they separate, sawed pieces nailed together? Are the floor joists sawed or hewn? Each of these characteristics may give you a clue to dates or changes in the house. (Chapter 6.)

Are there—or were there—fireplaces in the cellar? Sometimes the 20th-century furnace covers up the remains of a center chimney. Look around the furnace carefully for obvious changes in the floor or foundation, or replaced beams. Fireplaces can be detected by their remains, by the presence of heavy construction on end walls which may cover up an original fireplace, or by replaced (newer) beams in the center of the cellar. (Foundations were thicker where needed to support a fireplace, or instead, timbers may have shored it up.)

A cellar may have been the original dwelling of the first owners, or a summer kitchen. Sometimes the cellar was the slave quarters. This was particularly true in the north, where it was cheaper for the owner to house slaves in a warm cellar, rather than in a crudely thrown-up house. Look for white lines —which may be parallel or zigzag—on the beams. This is where plaster came in through the lath, leaving traces after it fell or was removed. This, or a cobble-stone or laid-up-dry brick floor or remnants of plank flooring indicate that this space once was lived in.

Is there a small cistern or spring in the cellar? Some houses—especially German—were deliberately built over a spring. In other cases a spring was directed via piping from a hill behind the house to the cellar.

In the cellar you may be able to detect changes made in the house above. Does the cellar extend under the entire house or under only one section, with a crawl space under the remaining section? It is not uncommon for the cellar to be under what appears to be the main section of the house, or under part of it. From the cellar, establish where the foundation outlines the first floor. Does the flooring upstairs end part way across the room, with nail marks in a line along the break in the boards? This indicates that a wall was moved or removed. If this occurs in what appears to be a "center-hall" house, measure the widths of the two front rooms and the hall. Is one room larger than the other? The original room probably is the one found over the cellar, and this was not a center-hall house originally.

If there is a wing to the house, is the cellar or crawl space under it? Does this wing show characteristics of a structure older than the main section? For example, its siding, window framing and flooring may be older ; or, it may be one-and-a-half stories as compared to the two-and-a-half story main structure, and have smaller dimensions, all indicating earlier origins. While it is often true that the wing is the older part of the house, it may not have been the *original* house on the site. It was common practice in the 19th century to move structures and add them to newer ones.

The older wing, then, may have been the original house, constructed over a crawl space and later added onto with a larger, more elegant house over a cellar. Another possibility is that the house with the cellar was the original house on the site. An older, nearby structure could have been moved and placed adjacent to it after a crawl space was dug. Look for a nearby foundation. If there is one, measure it to see if its dimensions might fit the wing. If so, the wing may have come from this site.

There is still another possibility: that the wing came from another site. Many small, older structures were moved in the 19th century. The siding, lath and plaster were removed—often rotted anyway—and either the frame was moved on rollers or sleighs, or it was disassembled and moved. In trying to establish what was moved from where, keep in mind that foundation holes often had similar dimensions and so can be deceptive.

The author knows of several houses that were moved a few hundred feet, and others a couple of miles. One was added to a barn and converted into a cow stable below and a hayloft above. Another was raised to a full two-and-a-half stories and became a carriage shop. A third was moved and became a woodshed. Some houses were moved to more desirable sites and continued to serve as homes.

It was easier to move a hewn frame than it was to fell trees and construct one from scratch. By the time houses were being moved—a practice especially common in the latter 19th century—there was much less massive standing timber left. It also probably was cheaper to move an existing abandoned house than it was to buy lumber from the saw mill and haul it, perhaps a long distance, to the site.

Attics

The attic is the other part of a house besides the cellar where construction is visible. The first things to be examined there are the roof supports. As described in Chapter 6, there are various ways to support a roof, depending on the width of the structure, ethnicity of the builder, and the era when built. Are there sets of rafters pinned together, without a ridgepole, to form a gable? (Illustration 40.) Such a simple roof system was the most common one used in smaller structures before the 19th century.

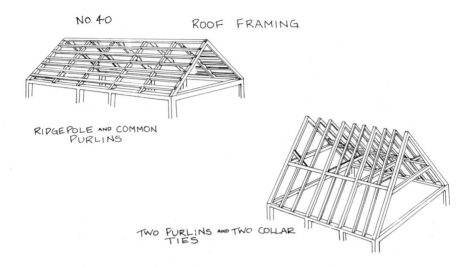

NO. 40   ROOF FRAMING

RIDGEPOLE AND COMMON PURLINS

TWO PURLINS AND TWO COLLAR TIES

When wider structures were built, some form of trussing was necessary to span a width that would have been impractical for a single timber. A truss is a framework of wooden beams, or metal bars, placed in rigid triangles to stiffen a roof. The rafters and collar beam of a simple gable roof system form a large triangle—a simple truss.

In these wider structures, the queen post truss was perhaps the most commonly used, because it afforded a center space between the posts, left open and available for use. A queen post truss placed two posts between the roof and the outside edges of the collar beam, and usually had no ridge pole. Another beam, between the heads of the posts at the roof edge, stiffened this roof system. Three triangles and a rectangle thus were formed. (Illustration 41.)

NO. 41

QUEENPOST

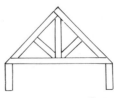

KINGPOST WITH STRUTS

Also used in wider structures was the king post truss, with one post placed from the collar beam to the gable peak, often in connection with a ridgepole. This formed two mirror triangles and prevented the collar beam from sagging. On occasion two additional diagonal struts were placed adjacent to the foot of the king post and reached to the middle of each side of the gable. Four triangles thus were formed. (Illustration 41.)

Ridgepoles were characteristic of buildings in Scandinavia, Scotland, Ireland and northwest England. A ridgepole was necessary to attach thatch to. When wood shingles became the preferred roofing material, the ridgepole became superfluous, since the shingles were attached directly to roofing boards. Since ridgepoles were a long-accepted way of building in specific areas of Europe, their use persisted through habit, with many ethnic groups who migrated to the New World. For example, ridgepoles were used in 19th-century houses built by Scotch-Irish settlers in New Hampshire, as well as other areas in which they settled.

In the latter part of the 19th century, once the typical joinery system changed from solidly pegged joints to the more flimsy, nailed boards, modifications had to be made in the structural system. Because nails alone could not hold two 2" x 6" rafters together, a plank ridgepole was used and rafters were nailed to it. This change from post-and-beam to board-construction occurred with the development of the balloon-frame system, which became widely used by the end of the 19th century. Thus, ridgepoles commonly were used in 20th-century buildings. (Illustration 40.)

Although some 17th-century houses were thatched, the most common roofing material in permanent houses was "shave" shingles. Look through the rafters and purlins (boards connected horizontally to the rafters) to see what the roofing material was nailed to. In the 18th and 19th centuries, roofing boards (the subroofing) of rough hemlock or pine—often with generous spaces in between—were nailed to the rafters. Roofing material then was attached to the roofing boards.

Roofs often were "raised" to add another full floor of living space. Glance around the attic. Can you see evidence in the roofing system that the roof was raised? For example, are there splices in corner posts, indicating that they were heightened? Are there breaks in the boards on the gable-end wall, indicating that the rafters changed pitch? The change may have been made from a late 18th-century one-and-a-half-story house to an early-19th-century two-story. Or, the roof may have been raised from a two-story to a late-19th-century three-story.

It was relatively easy to increase the length of a house by simply adding more paired rafters. Evidence of this also may be seen in the attic. Are there different kinds of rafter material? In a roofing system without a ridgepole, the rafters at one end of the axis may be sawed boards (newer), while the majority of the rafters are small trees (original).

Note also *how* additions were attached. Is there evidence of siding on what was the exterior peak of the original gable, and which now is under the eaves and perpendicular to the added ell? Was the shed addition an integral part of the roofing system or is there a break in the rafters, which indicates it was added later?

If there is a cupola on the roof, are there stairs leading to it from the attic or a second-floor room? If so, it may have been used for a specific purpose, such as ventilation, lighting, a lookout, an artist's studio or a bell tower. If it was for "looks" only and not functional, there would be no access to it, and it probably was a 20th-century decorative device. The cupola in the octagon house of the 1860's was a functional means of allowing hot air to escape up the circular staircase through the opened cupola above in summer.

Does the roofing system look new? For instance, is the whole roofing system made of band-sawed boards of the 1880's and later, while the framing system of the house is mortised and tenoned from the early 19th century? Perhaps the original roofing system was rotted, and a new one replaced it.

The attic may offer still other clues to dating the house or its alterations. Are there small, horizontal boards in the gable-end wall? This may be evidence of old windows, now boarded up. Two small windows on either side of a now non-existent end chimney—indicated by newer studs where the chimney had been—date this as 18th century. Or, there now may be a centered Federal-period leaded fanlight in its place. Look around the outline of any old windows to see if the sashes were pegged. This also is evidence of 18th-century construction.

What do the chimneys look like from the attic? Is there a massive center chimney, witth an extreme cantilever angling through the attic? This is 18th-century. Evidence that an old staircase was built into it would confirm this dating. (Illustration 41a.) Or, there may be end chimneys, which are an 18th- to 19th-century characteristic. Have the chimneys been repaired? Chimneys often were changed, and bricks replaced, because high temperatures eventually cracked their mortar. As they were modernized, they were made safer. There may be leftover replacement bricks stored in an outbuilding. If so, do they have the name of a brickyard stamped on them? It probably was local. Check for its dates of operation to help establish when the changes were made.

No. 41a

STAIRS BUILT INTO CHIMNEY

Before leaving the attic, look at the floor boards. Are they modern plywood or pressed board, or are they the original wide pine flooring? If the flooring is modern, a discussion with current or previous owners could tell you whether the attic flooring was removed and used in a first-floor room during restoration. Sometimes original wide-board flooring or wall covering was removed and sold to use in another house. By talking to previous owners when possible, you may find out about these and other changes.

As you conclude your interior on site inspection, make sure you have taken pictures of any of the house's oddities—elements that are different or unique or simply beyond your knowledge. You will use these pictures for comparison as you locate other records or information in your analysis.

You have just finished one of the most enjoyable parts of house history research. You have been privileged to poke about a stranger's house legitimately. It is fascinating to see how different people decorate and use the various spaces that similar houses offer. There never are identical interpretations. Because you do get inside so many houses, people sometimes will ask you for ideas of how others have solved decorating problems for their particular period house. This is one of the fun aspects of house histories and should be enjoyed to the hilt.

6

Inside the Walls of the Wood-frame House

If you are visiting a house to do its history, you are in luck if your visit coincides with renovation or restoration work. You may get to see what is inside the walls and under the 20th-century insulation. Although X-ray and sonar make it possible to detect shapes within the walls, nothing substitutes for actually seeing with your own eyes what is there. It is more likely, of course, that you will have to rely on observations of the exterior, and on explorations of the attic and cellar to get clues about the house from the wood-frame construction. This chapter will explain the ways that wood—its species, appearance and use in framing, can give information for your house history. To make the best use of this information, it is helpful to understand how a house is constructed, or framed.

Wood-frame Construction

A house has several systems—foundation, frame and roof—which are integrated so that it functions as a whole and does not fall down. The first system constructed, and the most important, is the foundation. Without a solid foundation, a house will tilt or rack.

Next, starting with the sill laid over the foundation, comes the framing system. One of the earliest permanent—as opposed to temporary—housing construction systems used in the United States is called timber frame or post and girt (beam). In this system of wood construction, the weight is borne by the frame. The frame starts with the sills and builds up from there. (Illustration 42.)

From the 17th century until the late 19th, sills were made of squared, hewn timbers. These were placed on top of the foundation, on all sides of the house, to support the wooden framing system above. Typically, they started to rot at their bottoms—the side nearest the foundation. As a sill deteriorated, the wood compacted from the weight of the framing members above the sill, and bowing or slanting of the floors resulted.

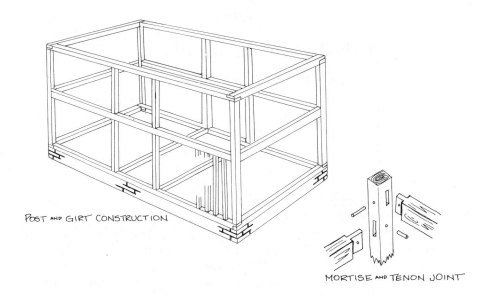

POST AND GIRT CONSTRUCTION

MORTISE AND TENON JOINT

Upright studs or posts supported beams and joists which carried the weight of the floors. Around the top of the first floor, a type of beam called a girt was placed on top of the studs and posts to support the second floor. At the top of the second floor studs and posts, two plates (beams) were placed on these studs to support the paired rafters, and two end girts were attached to the plates. Even if a house had a stone or brick exterior, the interior frame usually was wood.

The roofing system included the trussing, the rafter system and ridgepole, if used, as well as the sub-roofing and roofing material. The construction of the roofing system varied depending on the style of roof (e.g., gable, hip, mansard), its pitch, the span it bridged and the ethnicity of the builder.

Each of these systems—foundation, frame, roof—shows the characteristics of the different eras that influenced them, providing clues to the house's history. If the house is being restored or renovated, schedule a visit while the workmen still are there and any walls or ceilings opened up. You will find evidence to help date the house and may even see something unique. And there is always the possibility that the workmen may have found a coin, a bottle or letters in the walls or under a floorboard, which could help date the structure.

As you search between the walls and through the rafters, you will be looking primarily at wood in its various shapes, because wood often was used as the support system for houses. Even if house supports are of brick or stone, wood was used as lath or trim and also can be seen as floor joists in the cellar and roof rafters in the attic.

Slash and Burn

Sometimes the rounded edges of barkless timbers within the house walls appear scorched. Rather than indicating a house fire, this may be the result of the slash and burn method of clearing forest from the 17th through early 19th centuries. The colonists learned this particular method from the Indians. However, in other cultures—and even into the early 18th century in the colonies—some believed that one method of drying and preserving wood was to scorch the timber.

The slash and burn process began with cutting down small trees and bushes and stacking them around the trunks of standing large trees. Firing the brush then injured the standing trees by burning off their smaller limbs so the trees would not leaf out the next season. Dead or dying, these trees were dry and easier to use for timber because their sap had not risen. They also were not as heavy to remove as live trees. Finding such scorched timbers in a house implies that it was a vernacular house—that is, one probably not done by an architect or fancy builder, because the setting was isolated, or the owner was of modest means. Very early houses often were vernacular.

Dendrochronology

Dendrochronology, the study of the growth rings in trees to determine and date past events, can be useful in dating when timber actually was cut. This method can be applied only before the bark has been taken off a tree, such as in a rafter or a floor joist. A database of weather patterns and other verifiable influences on tree growth is being collected specifically to help date timbers. Although this information is not yet available, in the future it may prove extremely useful to house historians.

Hewn Wood

Always note whether the wood you are examining is hewn, split or sawed. Sawed wood is usually of a later date than hewn or split wood. Hewn wood is easily recognized by the adz cuts along the four faces of the squared timbers. (Illustration 43.) These timbers usually were reserved for the large posts and beams designed to bear loads. Hewn timbers were used from the earliest settlement in the 17th century to, in some instances, the last quarter of the 19th century.

In early (17th- to 18th-century) houses, or some of the more primitive houses of the 19th century, smallish trees, which had been hewn on one side

HEWING WOOD

only, often were used as joists and rafters. In northern areas it is not unusual to find the bark still attached to the rounded part of such joists or rafters. This timber was cut in winter when the sap was low and insects dormant, so it was not necessary to remove the bark.

Split Wood

In addition to the large hewn, four-sided supporting members and smaller supports (often rounded on one side), house construction required even smaller finishing boards and planks for walls and paneling, and for covering hewn beams and posts. These were either split or sawed.

With a froe and maul, wood was split along its grain. This split wood is characterized by the splintery quality of its surface. Splitting was a primitive, vernacular way to make finishing boards, shingles and shakes. Wood was split when there was no sawmill available. Thus a house with split wood was either early—17th to 18th centuries—or situated far from a sawmill.

Sawed Wood

Sawmills appeared at various times in different areas of the United States —the earliest in the 17th century. Before the appearance of water-powered sawmills in an area, logs were sawed with a two-man saw. Sawed planks and boards have either straight and parallel or crescent-shaped teeth marks, depending on the saw used. A pit saw, used in the 17th and 18th centuries, required two men, one on top of the log and one under it in a pit or under a hill, each grasping a handle of the long two-man saw. Pit saws produced *widely-spaced,* parallel saw marks. At times the angle of these might change, due to human error, and be less than absolutely perpendicular to the board edge. (Illustration 44.)

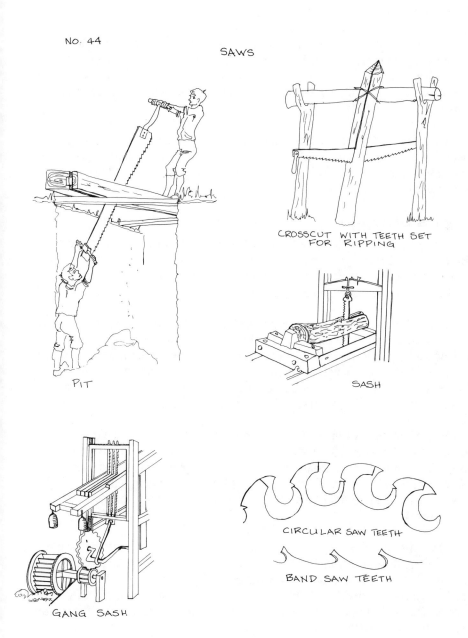

NO. 44

SAWS

CROSSCUT WITH TEETH SET FOR RIPPING

PIT

SASH

GANG SASH

CIRCULAR SAW TEETH

BAND SAW TEETH

The 18th- to early-19th-century sash saw was a water-powered, vertical saw blade clamped into a rectangular frame, called a sash, to prevent it from bending or buckling. Sash saws from these mills left widely-spaced, *consistently perpendicular* grooves that usually are deeper than pit saw marks. (Illustration 44.)

Water-powered circular saws were used in the shipbuilding industry in England in the latter part of the 18th century. Although there are records of their use in other countries in the early 19th century, circular saws did not come into general usage in the United States until the 1840's. Their cut marks are *crescent-shaped*. (Illustration 44.)

The band saw—an endless steel belt with a serrated edge running over wheels—came into use in the 1880's. The band saw produced *closely-spaced, parallel* saw marks. Often band-sawed lumber was planed to produce standard lumber sizes. (Illustration 44.)

Species of Wood

Identifying the different species of wood used in a house frame may provide some clues in your research, since use of a species or destruction of a species occurred within verifiable time periods. The characteristics of a species, and the history of its uses, also can help to date a house.

The primeval forest came about because there were large geographic regions with a temperate climate and abundant rainfall, peopled by a sparse, semi-nomadic population that had little need of felling huge timbers for ship's hulls and masts, wooden wagons, permanent houses or furniture. Nor did native Americans have large beasts of burden such as the horse or ox. Dogs dragged what the Indians could not carry, so there was no need of wide paths for wagons.

When the settlers arrived on this continent, they found a virgin forest with a canopy between 130' and 160' above the ground. Some trees grew even higher. The forest floor was darkish and relatively open, because the canopy did not permit much light through it. Because of the intense competition for light, trees grew tall and straight, with little branching until they reached near the canopy level.

Once the dense forest growth was destroyed, certain trees, such as the pitch pine never again attained such colossal heights with such straight trunks. Today the pitch pine is a small, scrub pine characterized by a crooked trunk. Yet pitch pine timbers—described as "a hard, dense, yellow pine"—still exist in 18th-century Dutch houses. Only recently were these timbers identified by microscopic analysis as pitch pines.

The settlers chose superior examples of these huge trees to fell. Because some of the species differed from the trees the settlers knew, they used what they thought was closest to the trees native to their homeland. Thus Englishmen used oak, while north central Europeans, including the Dutch, Swedes and Germans, worked softwoods, such as pine and fir.

Woods the English substituted for oak were beech, in the higher elevations where oak did not grow, and American chestnut. Pine and hemlock were used for framing by the ethnic groups used to working with softwoods. All groups commonly used saplings such as spruce as poles for rafters in vernacular houses. The abundant, easy-to-work pine, was used by all groups for woodwork, paneling and other decorative purposes.

Another abundant species, the American chestnut, underwent a serious blight in the 1840's and recovered, but it has never recovered from a later, more damaging blight in the early 20th century. Thus, chestnut appearing in a 19th-century house in an area where the blight occurred, would have to have been cut before the blight in the 1840's or after its recovery by the 1860's. (Again, when using this for dating, keep in mind that people sometimes cut wood intending to use it, but ended up storing it instead. It was not used until long after cutting.)

Variations in Framing Methods

If you do get a chance to look inside the house walls, take notes on the sizes of and distances between the studs. Also, note the saw marks and whether the wood is split or, rarely, hewn. This will help date it.

NO. 45

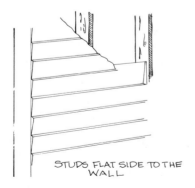

STUDS FLAT SIDE TO THE WALL

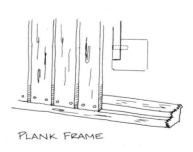

PLANK FRAME

If the studs are rectangular in shape, notice how they are placed in the wall. Is their flat side or their narrow edge along the wall? (Illustration 45.)

The answer to this question may help date the house, since stud placement changed over the centuries. One of the earliest (late 17th-century) wood-framing methods is called "plank-frame," in which 1 1/4" to 2" thick oak vertical planks 12" to 15" or more wide were placed, flat-sided, about 2" apart on the exterior of the sill and plate. Often these planks functioned as studs. A nogging (filler) of clay and straw filled the 2" spaces. (These studs sometimes were set in a rabbet—a right angle cut out all along the exterior of the first-floor sill.) (Illustration 45.) The plank-studs above were extended two stories and attached to the plate (i.e., the beam on which the rafters rested). These planks had oak pins pegging them to the sill, girt and plate. The exterior siding then was fastened directly to these planks.

By the 18th century, studs placed in the *exterior* walls usually measured 2 1/2" to 3" wide and were placed flush to the outside wall, 20" to 24" "on center," which is the measurement from the center of one stud to the center of the next. At their tops and bottoms, they were framed into the beams — sills and girts or girts and plates—with mortise and tenon joints. The exterior fabric, such as clapboarding, was nailed directly to the studs.

The studs between 18th-century *interior* walls usually were similar in size and spacing to the studs used in exterior walls, unless smaller 1 1/4" to 1 1/2" oak planks were used to nail lath to. Since the interior walls were not weight-bearers but space dividers, they did not have to be massive, because they did not support the floor above.

Half-timbered Houses

A 17th- to 18th-century variation of the post-and-girt construction method was the half-timbered house, which exposed the framework. The spaces between its supporting members—the posts and girts—were filled with brick, clay and straw, wattle and daub (woven sticks and clay) or cordwood. This mixture was covered with stucco, an exterior plaster composed of water, lime and stone dust. (Illustration 46.) Or, sometimes the complete exterior was covered with wood siding. If a clapboard siding or other material was added on the exterior, over the infill, these houses were well-insulated by the infillling materials.

There were ethnic variations to this framing method. Half-timbering is found in areas of 17th-century English settlement, as well as even later German settlement, such as Old Salem, North Carolina, or Bethlehem, Pennsylvania. Germanic migration patterns to the Midwest in the 19th century can be traced by the half-timbered houses they left behind, many of which have been buried behind clapboarding or another more modern fabric. Half-timbered houses are found in Missouri, Texas, Wisconsin and North and South Dakota.

INFILLS

BRICK

WATTLE ᴀɴᴅ DAUB

A curious infilling method appeared after the Civil War and was used into the 1920's. Cordwood, or stove wood, was used as infilling materials in houses found in the upper Midwest: Wisconsin, Michigan, Minnesota and Iowa. It was a cheap way of building a house using lumber yard rejects or the tops of trees. Round or split stove wood was mortared together so that the cut ends were perpendicular to the timber frame and could be seen both inside and outside the house. It formed the walls of the house and usually was covered with stucco or clapboard on the exterior ends of the cut logs and plastered on the interior. Curiously, this infilling method appeared simultaneously in several different places, crossed ethnic lines, and had no model as a precedent.

In the Northeast in the 18th century, certain groups—Dutch, Palatine and Huguenot—employed another variation of post-and-girt construction. They placed their comparatively small—4" x 4"—posts four feet apart. Each post had a corresponding girt attached to its head and another post across the room. Common infillings were soft, sun-dried brick nogging glued together with clay, or split planks dropped into channels placed on the sides of the studs. Usually the infill bricks were placed only in the exterior walls of the first floor. They provided insulation and minimized drafts. Split plank infill was found on the second floor as well as the first and was not nearly as efficient an insulator as brick. (That some people in the 18th century were concerned with filling in the air spaces within walls is interesting considering that insulation only became a heating priority in the late 20th century.) Infill probably was a way of eliminating housing and breeding grounds for rodents, as well as closing up drafts and insulating. Traditionally the second floor had no fireplaces and the board flooring there had no subflooring. Heat filtered up through the cracks.

This second floor was used for storage and drying and as an extra sleeping area, so a few drafts could improve air flow and speed up drying as heat came up from below.

Log Houses

Swedish, Finnish and German settlers—to whom this method was indigenous—built the first log houses in the United States in Delaware and New Jersey in the 17th century. Later, log structures became a common way of providing immediate shelter. Scotch-Irish and Germans built them in Maryland and Pennsylvania. By the late 18th through the 19th century, the log house was found north, south and west of this four-state, Mid-Atlantic area. As westward expansion heightened in the mid-19th century, log-house construction was utilized by several more ethnic groups as a relatively quick method of building shelter.

During this period, there were at least two methods of log construction. The principal method used long logs or squared timbers placed horizontally, one on top of the another, outlining the rectangular frame of the building. Although this method originated with northern European Germanic groups, the Scotch-Irish later incorporated this method of creating almost instant housing.

The second method was more characteristic of French houses and some Spanish houses (in Louisiana, Missouri, Illinois and California), in which logs were placed vertically, palisade fashion. In both methods timbers were either hewn or left as barkless logs, and clay nogging was stuffed in the cracks. Both methods were used concurrently, although the horizontal method was the most widespread.

In this first method the timbers placed horizontally along wall lines were notched at the ends to form the corner joints. Various notching systems were used. The saddle notch was the most common for round-log homes. For squared timbers, the full dovetail was the superior method, although the half dovetail, half notch, square notch, diamond notch and V notch all were used and were contemporary with each other. (Illustration 47.) The strength of these log houses depended on the fit of the corner notching and the weight of the timbers.

The Finns developed a unique method of strengthening log houses. They not only notched the corners, but they joined the logs in an additional way. The lower length of each log was hollowed out to match the rounded upper curve of the log below it, in a saddle notch, so that the logs fitted together. As the logs dried, they became tighter. No chinking was necessary using this method. In non-Finnish log houses, the length of the logs was limited by the corner notching, since bowing or twisting could occur in longer timbers which were not mortised and tenoned together other than at the corners. This, plus human limitations—a man could lift only a certain weight—restricted the size of log houses to walls that usually were not longer than 20'. There are occasional records of houses slightly larger, by a few feet.

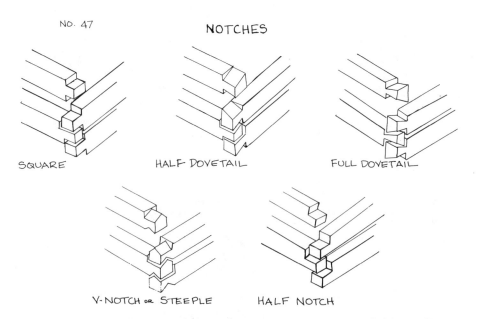

NO. 47

NOTCHES

SQUARE   HALF DOVETAIL   FULL DOVETAIL

V-NOTCH ᴏʀ STEEPLE   HALF NOTCH

Because any doors and windows cut into the logs reduced the strength of log walls, there were usually only one door and one or two windows. One way to make these openings was to cut out a piece of log and bore a hole into the log below. A wooden pin or peg, called a treenail, was pounded into the pinhole to secure the two logs together. This was done on both sides of the opening before the next lower log was cut out. Then an upright plank about 3" thick was pinned to the ends of the logs with pegs which were pounded into holes bored lengthwise into the log ends. Windows were similarly made. The most primitive windows were sliding boards or skins to cover the "wind hole" (later evolved to "window"). By the late 19th century, stock, milled windows reflecting contemporary styles were used. The style of such a window can be very helpful in dating a log house. Log houses were considered temporary structures, so their windows and doors usually were not replaced, as the structure was not modernized nor could their occupants usually afford it. (Illustration 48.)

The log house was roofed with rafters and split-oak slats on which pine shingles 3' long were attached with wrought nails. In some, oak shingles were used. And, in Swedish log houses, overlapped boards laid vertically held down a layer of birch bark. In the northern United States, black ash bark was the easiest roofing material to obtain. It was peeled into long strips and flattened with weights until it dried. Then it was placed, rough side out, and secured by poles that ran the length of the roof and were notched into the end timbers.

NO. 48

LOG HOUSES

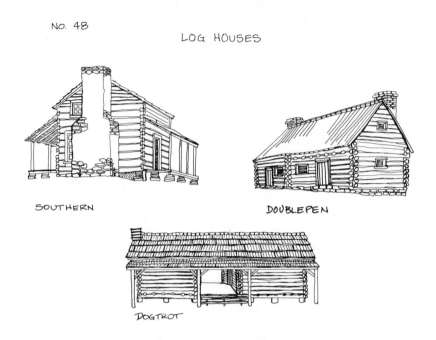

SOUTHERN

DOUBLEPEN

DOGTROT

Inside there often were ladderlike stairs placed against the chimney and leading to the loft above. Sometimes a root cellar was dug into the dirt floor. In those uncommon cases where the house became a permanent dwelling, wood or brick exterior siding was added, with plaster on the interior, covering up the log frame. A plank floor was laid with a trap door leading to the root cellar.

The Finns were the first to make log houses with more than one room, which became the model for expanding the one-room log home. Because the size of the one-room log house was limited structurally, the primary method of expanding the house was to build another house next to the first one. Each one-room house was called a "pen." There were three methods (models) of expanding the house by adding another log pen. In each method a door commonly was added to the outside and the two pens did not necessarily have a connecting door between them. (Illustration 48.)

One method was the "saddlebag," in which the chimney became central between the two pens. The second method was the double pen, with one or two end chimneys. The third was called a "dogtrot," in which the two pens were separated by a path which commonly was enclosed as a center passage and ultimately as a center hall. (Illustration 48.) Many log houses eventually were buried beneath modern siding and may not be recognized as being of log construction until additions or renovations are started.

As you can see, log-house construction did not vary much from century to century. Settlement and immigration dates, ethnic differences in construction patterns of house and chimney, and the use of stock windows and doors, are your main clues to dating a log house.

Poteaux en Terre: Posts in the Earth

Vertical logs placed palisade fashion was the other method of log construction, representing only a fraction of the log homes extant. Those still existing are found in Ste. Genevieve, Missouri, and Cahokia, Illinois, an area along the Mississippi River which was settled by the French in the first third of the 18th century. Most of these houses, however, date from the last quarter of the 18th century because Mississippi flooding destroyed the earliest of them. (Illustration 49.)

No. 49

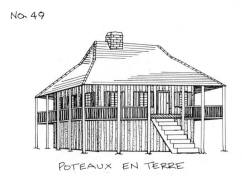

POTEAUX EN TERRE

The palisade method of log-house construction was called poteaux en terre, (posts in the earth), or poteaux sur solle (posts on a sill) — in this case, the sill is on a stone foundation. Usually cedar or oak logs were placed vertically next to one another about 3' into the ground and 5" or 6" apart. Long, floor-to-ceiling diagonal corner braces stabilized the vertical logs, so that they would not rack sideways. *Bouzillage* (clay with a binder of twigs, hair, straw or limestone gravel) or *peirrotage* (broken rock in lime mortar) was placed between the logs, and the whole wall was whitewashed to prevent rot and insect infestation. It was difficult to maintain the whitewash exactly at grade level on the posts that entered the earth, and so this was the Achilles Heel of palisade construction. Oxidation combined with moisture to rot timbers just above grade. Wasps also tunneled through the wooden posts and weakened them.

The first floor was raised off the ground so that it was necessary to ascend stairs to enter the house. A poteaux en terre also is characterized by a dually and steeply pitched hip roof extending over the galerie or verandah, which often encircled the house. In Southern Tidewater areas, raising the house off the ground was a means of avoiding water problems as well as insects. It also improved air circulation by allowing air to pass under and through, as well as over, the house.

Transitional Framing

As the 19th century progressed, sawmills became abundant, and more lumber was available for construction. By the 1840's a mixed timber-frame/sawed-lumber method had evolved, replacing the heavy timber-frame and log construction. This method used a combination of heavy timber frame with sawed two-by-fours in the walls as studs, sawed planks under the floors as joists and in the ceiling as rafters. This "transitional" framing method continued until balloon framing took over by the Civil War period in the 1860's. (Illustration 50.)

Balloon Framing

This new framing system was invented in the early 19th century. It revolutionized two-story house construction. Standardized sizes of sawed lumber were used instead of individually hewn and sawed lumber that varied in size. To create larger, weight-bearing members such as corner posts, sills and plates, the smaller, standardized sizes such as 2" x 4"'s were nailed together. Furthermore, no girts (beams) were used to support the second floor. Rather, *the studs now were two stories high.* Placed with the narrow edge perpendicular to the foundation sills, studs extended from the sills to the top plate under the rafters, spaced 16" on center. The second-floor joists (floor supports) were supported by a 1" x 4" ribbon strip which had been let into the inside edges of the studs (i.e., the studs had a cut out to match the 4" width of the "ribbon"). This method was called—derisively—"balloon" framing, because of its seeming lack of solidity. People thought that because a house now was framed with long, skinny, small framing members, it might warp. In fact, this method was found to be superior to a heavy timber frame when a brick or stone fabric was desired. There was less likelihood of movement between the two-story continuous wood frame and the masonry veneer, since each stud spanned both stories. (Illustration 50.)

Although balloon framing was invented in 1833 in Chicago, it was not universally used until the 20th century. Its employment of relatively small-size standard lumber—often softwoods—relied on the abundance and availability of cheap wire nails, since thousands were needed to fasten together the many smaller pieces of wood involved. Until the process of manufacturing

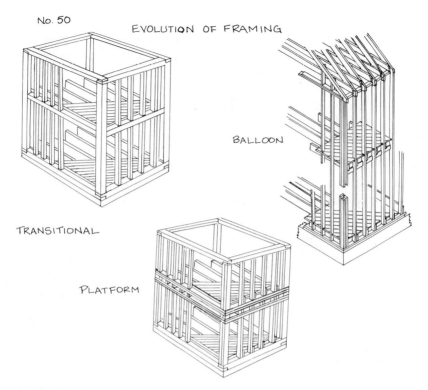

EVOLUTION OF FRAMING

BALLOON

TRANSITIONAL

PLATFORM

mass-produced wire nails was perfected, balloon framing was fairly uncommon in a structure.

Platform Framing

Platform framing, sometimes called Western platform framing, was the method of wood framing that largely replaced balloon framing. Like balloon framing, it used relatively small-size lumber and required abundant nails for fastening the multiple pieces together. It was developed in the West, particularly for one-story houses, but also was used for two-story homes. Essentially, platform framing varies from balloon framing in that each story is an entity unto itself. The structure is built one floor at a time. The studs are only one-story high and rest on the subflooring of each floor. The subflooring extends to the outside edges of the building to provide a platform for the studs. This method provides a ready work surface on which to assemble each wall-framing unit and then to tilt it into place. Because shorter lumber is used, platform framing is more rigid than balloon framing (the longer the two-by-four, the more it can move or bend). Platform framing continues to be used to this day in frame houses, sometimes in combination with some balloon framing techniques. (Illustration 50.)

Nails

Nails can help date a house. Crude nails had been used in most countries for centuries, but it took the Industrial Revolution and developments in metallurgy for wire nails to become commonplace in wood construction.

Nails and other fastening devices can provide valuable evidence to add to the collection of data that you have been accumulating on the house. Taken alone, however, nails are not a definitive means to date houses. They must be evaluated in relation to the context in which they are found.

Wooden pins—treenails—were the forerunners of metal nails. They were employed in America and elsewhere until the late 19th century to peg wooden timbers and planks together. By then, iron and steel bolts were replacing these wooden pins. Although hand-wrought nails were known and used from the 17th to the early 19th centuries, they were relatively scarce, and so were used selectively and carefully. These wrought nails were considered superior to the hand-headed, machine-cut nails that were manufactured after 1790. Finishing work, such as woodwork, however, mainly was fastened by wrought nails after that date.

A wrought nail was made by a blacksmith. A nail rod—a strip of metal the diameter of a specific nail size—was cut and heated, and the tapered shank was shaped and cooled. The top of the shank was heated, the shank wedged in a heading tool, and the head pounded on. Heads assumed various shapes after they were secured to the shanks, depending on the shape of the metal used. The most common were called rose heads; another common type were T-heads. Finish nails also were wrought with small L-heads and were called sprigs or brads. Lack of uniformity may help identify wrought nails. An expert can make exact identification. (Illustration 51.)

Cut nails, which appeared after 1790, were made by pushing a plate of iron into a shear blade that was suspended from above. The iron plate was either moved horizontally back and forth at precise angles to cut the tapered shanks or was flipped over and back for each succeeding cut, to insure the correct taper. Originally the heads were pounded on, much as the wrought-nail heads were attached. Later they were cold-headed by a machine heading tool which fused the head by displacement of metal through great pressure. Burrs and shear marks identify cut nails. (Illustration 51.)

The manufacture of steel wire nails was exhibited at the Philadelphia Centennial Exposition in 1876. It was not until the 1890's, however, that wire nails became widely used, and many builders still used cut nails well into the 20th century. Just as wrought nails were considered superior to cut nails, the latter prevailed over wire nails for many years after wire nails first were manufactured in New York in the 1850's. (Illustration 51.)

When using nails as *one* guide to help determine the age of a house, several specimens must be secured from various sections or wings. It may be determined from the nail selections that a wing was added at a later date or simply that repairs or alterations were made. For example, the presence of some wire nails in a section with predominantly cut nails could indicate when an

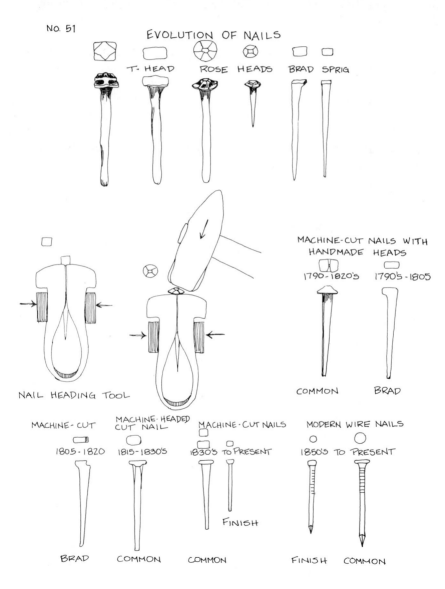

NO. 51

EVOLUTION OF NAILS

T- HEAD   ROSE HEADS   BRAD SPRIG

MACHINE-CUT NAILS WITH HANDMADE HEADS
1790-1820's   1790's-1805

NAIL HEADING TOOL

COMMON   BRAD

MACHINE-CUT   MACHINE-HEADED CUT NAIL   MACHINE-CUT NAILS   MODERN WIRE NAILS
1805-1820   1815-1830's   1830's TO PRESENT   1850'S TO PRESENT

FINISH

BRAD   COMMON   COMMON   FINISH   COMMON

1890's mansard roof was added to an 1830's two-story house.

Yet another factor must be considered in dating: before wire nails became abundant in the early 20th century, nails from old buildings were reused in new construction, much as hardware was reused. So, in using nails as a means of dating, you always must note their use in relation to other data—take them in context. For example, if wrought nails exist in band-sawed boards, they probably were from an earlier structure, since band-sawed boards did not appear before 1880 and wrought nails were used from the 17th to the early 19th centuries.

Since it has been estimated that 90% of most American houses use wood (at the least to support the upper floors and roof), it is worthwhile to analyze the wooden construction of your house and how it was fastened together. The method of construction and the fasteners (pegs and nails) will place the house within a general era, which then should be compared with the architectural styles evident in the house. The data usually mesh to allow you to arrive at conclusions about the times of the changes, as well as the time period of the original construction.

7

Mineral and Metal Building Materials and Construction Techniques: Earth, Sod, Adobe, Fired Brick, Stone, Metal

Although wood was used in some parts of all houses, mineral building materials were used as the *primary* housing material in areas where such materials were abundant, or where wood was scarce, or when people settling the area were more familiar with them than with wood as a building material. Earthen houses—sod or adobe—were constructed on the Great Plains and the desert, where few trees grew. Stone houses were constructed where stone was plentiful, but were built whether or not there was an abundance of trees, *if* a stonemason was available and stone was the preferred building material.

Dugouts

"Mineral" houses—of earth and stone—were built both as temporary dwellings and as permanent houses. As people moved farther and farther west, trees became scarce. Such trees as cottonwoods could be found near creek beds, and were used to construct half dugouts. These shelters were dug into hillocks, and wood was used for their log walls on the exposed sides of the hill. If stone was available in surface bedrock, it was used instead of wood for the walls. Often, the flat roof was a framework of poles and brush holding up sod. Sometimes rags were attached to poles, as flags, to identify the hillock home from afar. This temporary dwelling could be constructed quickly, and was common during the westward expansion in the 19th century. States as far apart as Montana and Oklahoma had their share of half dugouts. (Illustration 52.)

Sod Construction

Another method used for temporary dwellings was sod construction, in which damp, rectangular, sod building blocks were stacked like bricks to form four walls. Sometimes these "soddies" also were half dugouts with two or three walls. The sod blocks—"Nebraska marble"—were cut by a special plow which kept roots in the cutting, so that the roots acted as mortar between the blocks. Milled wood was needed for the one or two window frames and a door. Often settlers brought window frames and a door with them from back East. Rafters of sticks and brush for the roof framing supported the sod roof. These roofs were notorious for leaking during wet weather. During dry weather, cloths often were hung over the furniture to catch the dirt and insects which sifted through the roof framing. Although dugouts and soddies were intended to be temporary housing, a very few endured until the last quarter of the 20th century. (Illustration 52.)

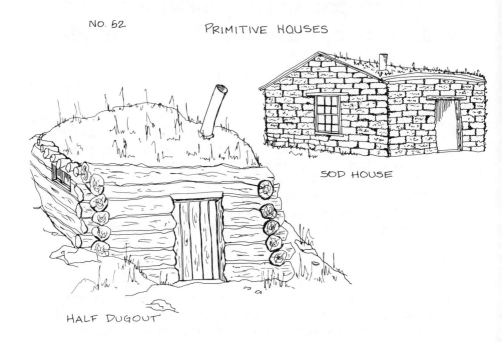

NO. 52   PRIMITIVE HOUSES

SOD HOUSE

HALF DUGOUT

Adobe

"Adobe" is an Arab word meaning "unburned brick." This brick construction method was brought to Spain by the Moors in the 8th century. The Spanish, in turn, brought it to the New World in the 16th century. It offered a more permanent method of mineral housing construction than did sod. The adobe made by the Spanish, from western Texas to California, consisted of a mixture of earth, sand, clay and straw or other binder and water. The bricks were shaped in wooden molds about 1 1/2' long, then left to sun dry. (Illustration 53.) When dry, they were stacked to make walls typically one-story high. A final smooth coating of mud was applied to both inside and outside of the house. This exterior coating had to be replastered continually or it would melt in the rain. The rounded exterior lines of adobe houses are due to the constant weathering by wind and rain.

92

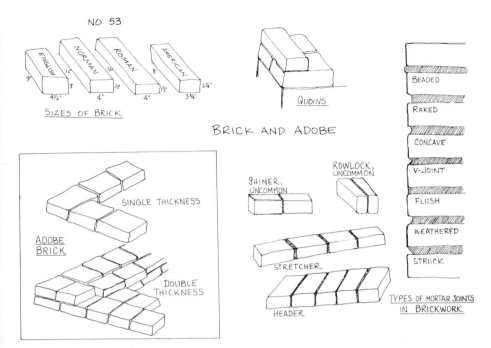

NO. 53

ENGLISH 9" 3" 4½"
NORMAN 12" 4" 1½"
ROMAN 12" 4" 1½"
AMERICAN 8" 2¼" 3¾"

SIZES OF BRICK

QUOINS

BRICK AND ADOBE

SINGLE THICKNESS

ADOBE BRICK

DOUBLE THICKNESS

SHINER, UNCOMMON

ROWLOCK, UNCOMMON

STRETCHER

HEADER

BEADED
RAKED
CONCAVE
V-JOINT
FLUSH
WEATHERED
STRUCK

TYPES OF MORTAR JOINTS IN BRICKWORK

The adobe house had two principal styles of roof: the slightly pitched gable roof and the parapet, flat roof. In a parapet the house walls were higher than the roof. By the early 19th century, the Spanish living in Florida and California had opted for the gable, tile-covered roof, because the flat roof had proved to be impractical in heavy rains. The Spanish living in Arizona, New Mexico and Texas, however, favored the parapet flat roof, which functioned well in the arid, desert climate. In making the parapet roof, pine poles or *vigas* were placed horizontally across the width of the house just under the roof line. Split-cedar or aspen *latillas* were placed perpendicular to the vigas to form a mat on which mud or tamped earth was placed to make a flat roof. When adobe houses were abandoned, the vigas usually were removed and used elsewhere, because of the scarcity of wood. (Illustration 54.)

The length of the vigas determined the width of the adobe room. Most vigas were 13' to 15' long, so the widths of the rooms were slightly smaller, because the vigas extended beyond the exterior walls. The length of the room theoretically was unlimited, because vigas could be added continuously in parallel lines. In practice, however, houses were built room by room as needed, with each room having a door and sometimes a window. Rooms often were arranged around an inner courtyard, with windows and doors opening onto it. A portal or porch, attached to the house around the courtyard, connected the rooms. This room arrangement was particularly well-developed in New Mexico, where protection from Indian attacks was necessary.

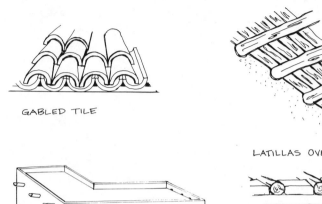

No. 54 SPANISH ROOFING STYLES

GABLED TILE

LATILLAS OVER VIGAS

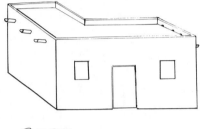

PARAPET

VIGAS

Before the Spanish introduced adobe construction, the Indians had developed a rammed-earth, mud-wall construction for their pueblos, called "puddling." In this method, walls of clay mud were built up in layers, each layer being dried by the sun before the next was added. Plank forms were placed on either side of the wall, filled with clay mud and straw, tamped to remove air bubbles, allowed to dry, and then moved up the wall for the next layer. Although "puddling" was not a commonly used construction method, there are homes still extant which were built that way. Fine examples of puddling are earlier Indian pueblos. This building method was adapted in the 19th century by later settlers.

Sod and dugout dwellers in the Midwest and Southwest had available one of the best building materials—clay—yet their bricks were not fired, but sun-dried, because of fuel scarcity. The only readily available fuels in the Great Plains or the Southwest were buffalo or cow chips, bushes such as sagebrush, corn stalks and cobs and prairie grass, none of which was capable of keeping a kiln hot long enough to fire bricks. Even after the railroads came through, the more isolated midwestern settlements did not have easy access to brick. Most of the 19th-century fired-brick homes in these parts of the United States are found near railroads or water routes. Both bricks, and coal for firing brick kilns, were brought to the site from elsewhere.

The windows and doors in Spanish adobe construction were made of wood. Before 1850, if there were windows in such houses, they were casement or fixed. Often there were iron bars set into an opening, but no window as such. If there were lights in the windows, they usually were of selenite instead of glass. (Selenite is gypsum in its colorless, clear, crystal form.) Heavy plank doors were common, often with unusual carvings. (Illustration 55.)

No. 55

WINDOWS

EARLY

AFTER 1850

AFTER 1860

NO GLASS, POSSIBLY SELENITE

GREEK REVIVAL

GOTHIC

ITALIANATE

DOORS

EARLY

AFTER 1850

AFTER 1860

PANELED

GREEK REVIVAL

GOTHIC

ITALIANATE

After 1850 Greek Revival doors and windows were popular, with Gothic and Italianate styles appearing by the 1860's. They usually were brought from the East, as there were few millworks in the Southwest.

In southern California, after 1815, the one-story, linear, gable roof "ranch house" appeared. In middle to northern California, by 1835, the Monterey style had evolved. With this style, the one-story ranch house was made into a two-story house. A second-story porch wrapped around at least three sides of the house and was supported by a cantilever of the second-floor joists. Sometimes the gable roof became a hip roof. Occasionally posts were placed under the balcony for additional support. (Illustration 56.) With a few modifications the Monterey style evolved into what became, from the mid-20th century on, the two-story-motel style that spread throughout the United States.

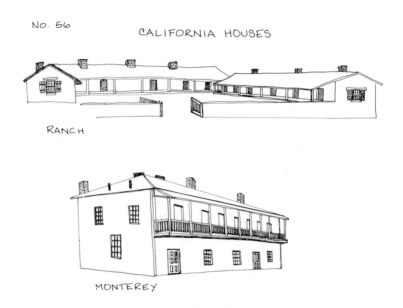

NO. 56

CALIFORNIA HOUSES

RANCH

MONTEREY

If you are researching an adobe house, pay particular attention to the windows, doors and woodwork to note whether there are characteristics of different architectural eras. Or, if you suspect a porch was added after the initial construction, compare the architectural style in the columns or the brick coping along the porch parapet to see if it matches the coping along the parapet edge of the house. If the styles do not match, they were built at different times. Are the rainspouts which drain the water from the flat roof all the same height from the ground? If there are variations in height, look for vertical divisions in the adobe. These show where the house was enlarged. If there are rainspouts and also a low hip roof, the house originally had a flat roof. (Illustration 57.)

Are there fireplaces? Very early (late-17th-century) adobe houses did not have them. When there are fireplaces, where are they located and what is their material and style? In adobe houses of the 19th century, fireplaces were built in the corners of rooms. Again, if they are of brick, they were built after the advent of the railroad.

ADOBE HOUSES

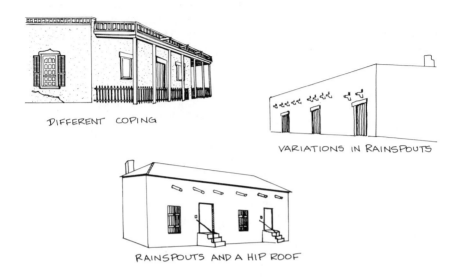

DIFFERENT COPING

VARIATIONS IN RAINSPOUTS

RAINSPOUTS AND A HIP ROOF

Fired Brick

In the East, particularly in the Southeast, fired brick was used as a building material in the 17th century. It was rarely used in the lower Midwest and Southwest because fuel was scarce, and not as much in the Northeast as in the South because limestone was not as abundant for mortar. The South was blessed with generous limestone deposits, so within a few years of settlement, brickyards were established. Several fine 17th-century examples of fired-brick houses still stand in Maryland and Virginia, and there are 18th-century examples in these states and in North and South Carolina, with a sprinkling in Georgia.

Building houses of brick originated in Flanders. Flemish brick construction techniques were exported to England during the 16th and 17th centuries, simultaneously with the disappearance of native timber in England. As the English became more experienced in working with brick, they developed their own variations, including making different sizes of brick for different uses. For example, "fence-wall" brick was larger than house brick. (Illustration 53.)

The establishment of brickyards in the colonies primarily occurred under English, Dutch, Huguenot and German tutelage. There are 18th-century brick houses extant from all four ethnic groups scattered throughout the original Thirteen Colonies.

Brick houses had a wooden frame which supported the floors. Wall anchors and wrought-iron bolts connected the wooden gable-end girts (beams) through the brick fabric. Often, the exterior ends of these anchors had decorative designs, such as numbers dating the year that the house was built, the initials of the owner, crosses or trefoils. (Illustration 58.) The roof also was framed and sometimes had wooden dormers poking through the roof line.

No. 58

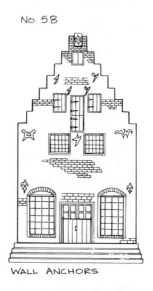

WALL ANCHORS

When researching a brick house, follow the same procedures as for a wooden house. You are trying to establish, for instance, the architectural periods evident in the various sections of the house. There are also questions that are specific to brick houses. What are the dimensions of the brick, its color(s) and its hardness?

The dimensions of the brick varied with its purpose. Paving bricks were larger than house bricks. Private houses had bricks smaller than the bricks of large public buildings.

The proportions of length, width and thickness of bricks varied with the style of bond, which ultimately reflected the ethnicity of the builder. English bond was based on the idea of alternating courses of headers and stretchers in a variety of pattern rows so that the joints were staggered. In Flemish bond, this was accomplished by alternating headers and stretchers in *each* course. In order to do this effectively, it was convenient if the width (the header) was one-half the length (the stretcher). Thus Flemish or Dutch bricks came to have the proportions of 6 x 3 x 1 (for example, 6" x 3" x 1"). In contrast, the English bonding patterns did not require such precise proportions, because what mattered was staggering the joints. Thus English brick proportions often were 6 x 3 x 1.7 (or, for example, 9" x 4 1/2" x 2 1/2"). (Illustration 53 and 59.)

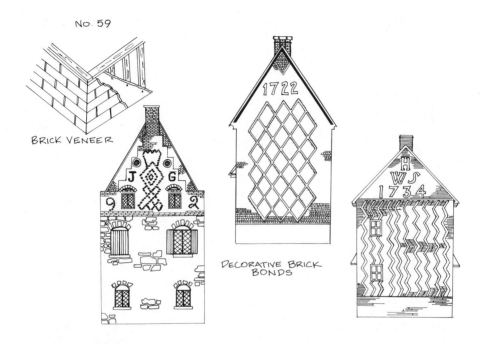

No. 59

BRICK VENEER

DECORATIVE BRICK BONDS

The color of the brick depends on the makeup of its clay as well as on kiln temperature. Bricks placed closest to the center of the early kilns fired the hottest, and some of the faces turned dark brown or black. Bricks around the periphery of the kiln did not reach consistently high temperatures. Their glazing was superficial and did not penetrate into the core of the brick. These are the bricks that, having already lost their glazed surface, appear to consist of crumbly—usually red—dirt. (Commonly these bricks were painted—often a cream color—to protect the glazing.) It is only with late-19th-century kilns that bricks were evenly fired.

Your next question is: where did the brick come from? Check local historical sources to see if there were any brickyards in the area. If there are any loose bricks, examine one to see if a brickworks' name was designed into the molds. Check incorporation ledgers at the courthouse to find out if there were brickyards on or near the property. In one case the author located a brickworks on the property itself from examining deeds 130 years after the half-timbered house was built, using bricks as infill. (Chapter 6.) From this information I concluded that the brick nogging (infill) for the house was manufactured on the site.

The brick bond—the patterns made in laying the brick—can be significant. It may help determine dating, architectural style or the ethnic origin of the builder. For example, if the brick is only a veneer one brick thick, the pattern

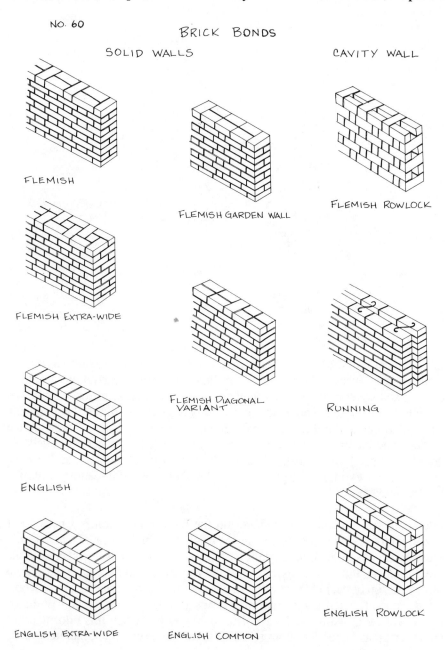

NO. 60

BRICK BONDS

SOLID WALLS

CAVITY WALL

FLEMISH

FLEMISH GARDEN WALL

FLEMISH ROWLOCK

FLEMISH EXTRA-WIDE

FLEMISH DIAGONAL VARIANT

RUNNING

ENGLISH

ENGLISH EXTRA-WIDE

ENGLISH COMMON

ENGLISH ROWLOCK

will consist of stretchers only, since there is no need for alternating headers to create the true bond necessary for a supporting wall. (Illustration 60.) This probably indicates balloon framing underneath and a date after 1860. Complicated brickwork, such as the zigzag "Muizetanden" or "mousetooth" edging of a gable wall was shared by both 18th-century English and Dutch. In the early 19th century, Flemish bond was a popular brick pattern. Sometimes colored bricks were used to form a diamond or a zigzag pattern, or to write out the year the house was built. Also, wall anchors varied from era to era and can be identified by their style. (Illustration 59 and 60.)

Besides brick size, color and patterning, the mortar also may give you a clue to dating. Note the consistency and the shape of the joints. (Illustration 53.) Early mortar will appear crumbly; later mortar was harder, of better quality materials. Early joints were wider than later ones because as mortar quality improved a better bond was formed, and less mortar was needed.

Mortar consisted of a variety of soil compounds. Clay by itself was the usual mortar used in primitive construction, in adobe houses and between sun-dried brick nogging. Once lime was located and processed in quantities—in the late 17th century in the South and 18th century in the North—the ideal mortar was sand, lime and water and sometimes clay.

Along the seacoasts, shells often were mixed with this lime mortar to make it harder. In St. Augustine, Florida, some dwellings were built of "tabby," a mixture of oyster shells, lime and water to form a type of concrete. Some of these dwellings remain from the 18th century. Cooking stoves there were made of coquina shells in mortar. Throughout the United States, stucco—a combination of water, lime and stone dust or oyster shell—was used to cover a variety of exterior surfaces. These included brick, stone, half-timbering combinations, clay tile and concrete block—the last two in the 20th century. The specific ingredients of these varieties of mortars differed with the materials available in any given area. Depending on the construction of the house you are researching, you may find it helpful to investigate when lime became available in your area. This will help to determine the age of the mortar. If you find Portland cement, variations of which are used as mortar, you can assume that it is probably after 1850.

Stone

While brick had to be manufactured, stone was available for the taking if the builder was satisfied with uncut fieldstone. From the 17th to the 19th century, all ethnic groups favored uncut fieldstone as a foundation material. For example, in addition to adobe, stone was a favorite Spanish building material. Some of the large churches in the Southwest have stone buried under the adobe. The same was true for chimneys, and cut stone was preferred by several ethnic groups for building the walls of houses.

In the 17th century, the biggest problem in building houses with stone was locating quality limestone and quarrying it in sufficient quantities. Even as late as the 19th century, in places where limestone was available but wood to make charcoal for the lime kilns was not, stone structures were put together without mortar. Sometimes clay, with a binder of straw, was used instead of lime as a primitive mortar. As settlement expanded, quality limestone was discovered here and there, burned in a kiln and transported to building sites for use as mortar. As a result, we have 17th- and 18th-century stone houses to enjoy today.

Some of the earliest examples of 17th-century stonework are the Rhode Island Welsh "stone-enders" with wood along the front and rear lengths, and one gable end. (Illustration 61) Often coursed, the fieldstone gable end, sheathed

NO. 61

STONE HOUSES

WELCH STONE-ENDER

FLEMISH

GERMAN

GERMAN

interior-end chimneys and walls served as a means of fire-prevention. The "stone-ender," a typically Welsh house, was unique to Rhode Island because Welsh settlers found a plentiful supply of lime there which was weather resistant enough to be used in mortar on the exterior of a house.

The Dutch, Flemish, Huguenots and Germans seemed to enjoy building in stone, especially in the rural setting. Because the first three groups all lived in Dutch New York and New Jersey, there was a great deal of borrowing of building methods among them in this area. For example, what traditionally is labeled as a Dutch-colonial house style—a gambrel roof with flaring eaves— is in reality a Flemish farmhouse style and can be traced as such. (Illustration 61.) In another example of borrowing, Huguenots and English, and Spanish via the West Indies, gradually combined to develop styles unique to Charleston, South Carolina.

The Germans, particularly, seemed to prefer stone to other materials. Whenever possible, stone was used in their foundations, cellar flooring and first-floor wall material—even if the second story was of brick or half-timber construction. (Illustration 61.) The German examples extant all date from the 18th century and are found mostly in Pennsylvania, Maryland and North Carolina. The traditional German stone house was built into a hillside, often over a spring. Water flowed through the cellar, which was used as a springhouse and provided not only fresh water, but refrigeration.

Other ethnic groups also sometimes built stone houses into a hill. (Illustration 61.) Usually at least one side of the house was flush with the ground at the base of the slope. An exterior door was located on this same side. A fireplace often was built into this first-floor, "cellar" level, so it could be used as the dwelling while work progressed above it. If this masonry work went too slowly to keep up with the growth of the family, a frame structure was erected and sided atop the uncompleted masonry to provide more rooms. This was easily accomplished by tying the frame story into the frame already in place for supporting the floors and roof. Sometimes this frame section became a permanent, full, second story. In other cases, the sheathing or fabric was removed from the frame as second-story masonry replaced it, in which case an obvious line still may be seen in the masonry. If there are stone lintels for the basement windows, but brick lintels on the first floor, it suggests that a local brickyard was established in the interim it took to construct the cellar level and the upper stories. These stone houses often were one-and-a-half stories high—or two-and-a-half including the live-in basement.

Although it was more difficult to change a stone or brick house than a wooden house, changed they were. Masons start laying stone or brick at a corner or at a window jamb. If you remove molding around a window frame—try any one that looks different from the rest, or try to remove a shutter—and you find slivers of stone or brick, or an extra-wide mortar joint, it is likely that the window opening was cut after the house was built. That is, this window was added in an existing, older part of the house. Such a clue helps you to determine which section of the house was built first.

If an 18th- or 19th-century house is of quarried stone (i.e., cut stone or ashlar), its stone most likely was obtained from a local quarry. A search for that quarry and its dates of operation might help establish your house's construction date. In much of the Great Plains, native limestone was buried deep beneath the surface of the fertile soil, with outcroppings found mainly along creek beds. Because it was difficult to reach, this limestone was not favored as an early building material. In places where the rock was found at the surface, however, stone buildings and even stone fence posts were constructed of it, as occurred in parts of Kansas. Later buildings in the Great Plains were built from deeper-lying stone, which had to be quarried.

Around the Great Lakes in the 19th century, houses were built of cobblestone—any stone that could be picked up in the hand. These stones were found in fields and along the shores of the lakes. Cobblestones provided a decorative face to uncoursed fieldstone exterior walls of houses. About 800 of these cobblestone houses survive.

Metal Construction Techniques

Some metals can be as hard as stone and sometimes as heavy, but are not as long lasting. Structural metals which were developed in the 19th century—especially iron and steel—rusted unless they were kept painted or were plated with nickel or zinc. Still, they were used in house construction because they were inexpensive.

In 1848 James Bogardus finished the first completely cast-iron building in New York City, heralding the "iron age" in architecture and eventually the steel age which produced skyscrapers. Almost immediately, prefabricated metal houses were designed. Manufactured in New York, they were shipped to California to supply homes for the "Forty-Niners" of the Gold Rush.

Developments in metallurgy from the mid-to late 19th century made it possible for iron to be used in a variety of ways, from reinforcing bars in concrete, to molded exterior trim, to bolts holding together the precut, pre-formed Sears, Roebuck and Co. frame houses that were ordered from catalogs and shipped via rail.

As a corollary of these advances in metallurgy and their many applications in manufacturing, the typical architect cum engineer became two separate professions: the architect and the civil engineer. A subsequent proliferation of architects was partly responsible for the multiplicity of house styles—ranging from Queen Anne to shingle style to stick style to Beaux Arts, and so on.

Although never employed exclusively, metal has had many uses in house construction. It has its advantages even in an older house. For its relative strength, metal is lightweight and trim, and when kept painted, will not rust. It is so easy to use that an amateur can handle it. For centuries it was used for nails in the structural system. After the 1840's it was used widely for terneplate roofs —seamed metal roofs. These were thin sheets of iron or steel, with a zinc coating. They were lightweight, weatherproof, long-lasting and inexpensive. From about 1895 to 1915, sheets or rolls of iron or steel were pressed to resemble stone, and used as exterior siding. After they were nailed to the surface, they were painted. Many of these still exist today, especially around foundations, painted gray to resemble stone. The use of metal ceilings and walls of corrugated iron to decorate, or to cover old plaster, has been discussed in Chapter 3.

Round metal posts and I-beams were used in the 20th century to support the house frame in the cellar. Often a metal jack—a post with a large screw in the center—has been placed in the cellar of an older house to replace a rotted wooden post or to support a sagging beam.

Section II
The Paper Search/ Written Records

8

The Deed:
The Basic Document

Now that you have inspected the house and examined its architectural characteristics, you can begin to tie in these observations with the paper records of the house. Deeds are the beginning point in your search for records. You will use them to learn the names of the previous property owners.

In most states, records of deeds, as well as wills and mortgages, usually are filed under the owners' names. When you "chain" a title—that is, go back through the various deeds to find out the consecutive owners of the property—you are compiling a time line of all of the owners. Thus the deed is the basic document by which you begin your "paper chase."

Why This Paper Chase?

There are three reasons house historians document the house's history in this way. First, architectural clues usually are not specific enough to establish precise dating. Second, you need to establish who the previous owners were in order to research the house. Third, if you want to achieve a landmark or historic register designation, historic commissions will accept only documented houses.

Although architectural periods fall roughly within certain years, some styles, such as the Greek Revival, can span forty years or more. There can be a considerable variation, within, for example, the Greek Revival style, if the house were built in 1820 rather than 1850. Furthermore, many rural areas experienced a new architectural fad or style fifteen to twenty years after it was commonplace elsewhere. Also, regional variations developed around each style. New England Greek Revival, for example, sometimes can look like a Federal house turned gable end to the street and given wide pilasters, a wide cornice and sidelights next to the front door. In contrast, the farther south one goes, the more often variations of the real Greek temple appear with a full facade portico facing the road. Thus, depending exclusively on architectural details for your analysis can be misleading. These details certainly will not present the full story of a house's history. Other records are needed to fill in information or to confirm datings.

A house exists because a person or family wanted it. Changes in houses usually were made because of the needs of family members. The family got too large and needed more space. Or, a rotting porch floor gave way when the elderly grandmother was walking on it. She broke her hip, which never healed properly, so her bedroom had to be relocated to the first-floor kitchen. Because the kitchen was small and too hot anyway, the wife lobbied for a new kitchen addition, so grandma could have some privacy. These are the kinds of personal things that initiate change.

Many people want their homes placed on a historic register or designated a local landmark. Only with documentation is it possible to apply for any of these distinctions. It is not enough to rely on a local tradition—for example, that Hessian troops were quartered at the farmhouse near Bennington, Vermont, before the Battle of Bennington in the Revolutionary War and that they killed the Quaker farmer because he was not cooperative. It is necessary to find out who the Quaker farmer was, when he brought the property and other specific facts before any historic commission will act on a request for historic designation.

What the Deed Will Tell You

As you go back through time from one deed to another, you will pick up a piece of information here and there which will help develop your comprehensive picture of the house over the years. A deed tells you who owned the property at a given time, how much it was bought for, a description of it and its size, and, possibly, if there was a mortgage (which may, in turn, give you more data). Sometimes a deed indicates whether the property was transferred by inheritance, a fact which can be followed up in other ways to give you further information.

On rare occasions the deed description may even mention the existence of the house and additions to it, or a barn on the property, any of which can help date the original building. You will find out *how* the property exchanged hands, which could lead you to further information.

The contents of the house at one point may be listed. You may even find out about the rooms in it, especially if a life estate was involved and an elderly parent claimed a room or two for his or her own use. Most importantly, you are now supplied with names to work with in looking up other documents, such as mortgages and wills, which will give you further information and help confirm some of your speculations about dates, additions and reasons. (In many of the states that were settled later, you may be able to find these names in an abstract of title. See Chapter 19.)

What Is a Deed?

Every deed is a document, signed, sealed and delivered by the *grantor* (the giver or seller) to the *grantee* (the receiver or buyer). It is a legal writing by which title to *real property* is conveyed from one person to another. The title usually is conveyed by purchasing the property with cash or a mortgage, but it may be conveyed by inheritance—through a will—or as a gift, or by a lien resulting from a mortgage default or judgement or tax foreclosure. A lien is the right to take and hold as security or sell the property of a debtor in payment for a debt.

The legal definition of real property is this: land, with all of its geological and botanical features of a more or less permanent nature. This definition includes any structures, because they, too, are of a more or less permanent nature. However, while a deed transfers all of the real property, which may happen to have structures on it, its houses or other buildings are not necessarily referred to in the deed. In other words, there may or may not be a house located on the property at the time, but you usually cannot tell from the deed description.

What you can do with deeds is establish the previous owners of the land and develop a description of the property's boundaries. It is only by knowing exactly where the property was located and who owned it that you can branch out to search for the other documents needed to verify the existence of a house on the property at a specific time. Deeds usually point the way.

Where to Find Deeds

Deeds are recorded—sooner or later—at the proper governmental office. Most contemporary deeds are found in the county clerk's office at the local courthouse, or, in the case of independent cities, at the city courthouse. (See Appendix B for a list of independent cities.) When doing a house history, most people usually will find what they need in their local courthouse. However, you may need to consult other repositories if you have a special problem or need a very early deed. Deeds do not have to be recorded, and sometimes are recorded only when the property is deeded out of a family. So there may be a lapse between their execution and recording dates.

Very early deeds and records—from the time each area was first settled— often are found in state archives, the National Archives, the Bureau of Land Management and in a variety of private repositories. The reasons for this are historic. Patterns of early settlement throughout much of the United States involved claiming the land, clearing it and erecting a house, sometimes without a valid piece of paper—a deed—giving the right to so do. After several houses were built, this new "community" petitioned the governing body (e.g., the Crown colony, patent holders, etc.) for a deed to incorporate as a town. So, learning who this early governing body was will help you determine where such early deeds might be. For instance, in the 18th century one state sometimes granted deeds for land that eventually fell under the jurisdiction of another state after early boundaries were clarified and legalized. The original deeds, however, would remain in the state granting them. You need to know about the early settlement and governance of your town.

There are other reasons that early records (including deeds) for many areas are not found in the "usual" place (e.g., the local courthouse). Sometimes records found at state archives are there for reasons of preservation. They are fragile and would be destroyed by handling, sun, moisture, etc. if they were left unprotected in local repositories. In other cases, during settlement the documents were granted by the colony or state, and the state thus has jurisdiction over them.

The National Archives contain property records of several states. Records pertaining to federal land grants given as pensions to men, and their widows, for participating in early wars— the Revolutionary War, for instance—also are there. Any documents for lands acquired from a foreign nation through treaty also would be located in these National Archives.

Another repository, the Bureau of Land Management, has records of 19th-century land grants given by the federal government before states were established. These involve much of the Midwest and Far West.

Private repositories include local historical societies or libraries that happen to accept documents, such as original deeds. Often these documents came down, through generations, into the hands of descendants who recognized their value and wanted to share their worth with others, yet did not want the responsibility of maintaining the documents properly and safely in their own homes.

Records also are found in repositories for primarily urban jurisdictions not subject to county authority, such as independent cities or metropolitan areas large enough to have city-county status, or more rural areas unorganized as counties. Beyond these independent cities and early records, there are only four exceptions to the general rule of finding most material at the county level. In Massachusetts, deeds were recorded at the town level until the creation of counties. Beginning in 1788, some counties were divided into districts, each with its own courthouse. In order to look up deeds, you must know which district to go to. In Connecticut and Vermont deeds are found at the town level; in Rhode Island at each city or town hall. If you are unsure of where to locate deeds, call your county clerk's office to find out.

Reading Handwritten Deeds

From about 1920 on most deeds were typewritten. Deeds earlier then that will be handwritten unless they have been typeset—something which has occurred rarely, and then mostly in large cities. Notice, in the handwritten versions, the stylistic attempts of the writer to distinguish the different sections of the deeds. Although prescribed legal phrases were used to set off the different clauses in deeds, it was left to the clerk or his superior to determine whether key words, signalling the changes in clauses, were to stand out, by using a broader tipped pen, or by printing or by using capitals. In reading these deeds it is easier to distinguish their different sections if the key words were made boldface or capitalized. Sometimes, of course, they were not, so becoming familiar with deed language will facilitate your reading of deeds, as you will know what to expect. Chapter 12, which familiarizes you with early handwriting, will also facilitate your reading of early deeds and also mortgages, wills, old church records, and other material you may need for your research.

The Language of a Deed

Reading a deed is usually straightforward, since it is made up of a few standard sections. In doing a house history, you need not comprehend all the legal jargon in the deeds. The next few pages will explain the typical clauses of a deed, so you will know what to look for. Once you recognize these various sections, you will easily learn to pick out the pertinent information.

The early style of deed language used legal formulas that are much easier to understand. Although this early style was used principally before the Revolution, it remained in use into the mid-19th century.

"To All People"

The deed begins with the phrase, "**To all People**" or "**To all**," often in larger handwriting. Following this phrase is the rest of the formula: "to whom these presents shall come." In some cases "**Greeting**" follows immediately, then is succeeded by the name of the grantor (giver) and his place of residence, but in others "**send Greeting**" follows the name of the grantor.

"Know Ye"

Usually, "**Know ye that I**" or "**. . . whereas I**" comes next, with a statement of the "consideration"—the amount of the money in the transaction. Then the listing of the grantee's (receiver's) name usually follows. Sometimes the date of the transaction is placed in this first paragraph, but it more commonly occurs before the signature of the grantor at the end of the deed.

Description

A description of the property will be included, if only to list the number of acres. The following is a transcription of part of this early style deed.

> To all People to whom these Presents shall come
> Greeting Know ye that where as I Ephraim Keys of
> Ashford in the County of windam and Colony of
> Connecticut near about Second Day of July 1765
> gave a Deed of three hundred acres of Land Granted
> by the general assembly of the Province of the
> Massachusetts Bay to be Laid in the County of Hampshire
> or Berkshire to Charles Goodrich of Pitsfield in the
> County of Berkshire the which Deed
> is Lost for Divers good causes and consideration . . .

The later style of deed language was more complicated. Prominent after the Revolution, it was riddled with stylized legal formulas. They are explained below in the order in which they occur.

"This Indenture"

It begins "**This Indenture,** . . ." *Indenture* simply means a formal written document or contract, in duplicate, between two or more parties. It was in duplicate, because of the early practice of cutting or tearing the document along an irregular line, so that the duplicate parts could be matched for authenticity at a later date.

Date

The date of the deed follows the words "**This Indenture.**" It is always written in the day-month-year order (e.g., "Made the twenty-first day of April in the year of Our Lord one thousand eight hundred and thirty-seven").

"Between"

Beginning with the word "**Between,**" the names of the party of the first part—the grantor or giver—follow the date. Their legal addresses follow their names. The party of the second part—the grantee or receiver—is than listed with the proper address. (A non-local address may indicate an inheritance; look for a will.)

"Witnesseth"

The next clause begins "**Witnesseth**, that the said party of the first part, for and in consideration of the sum of . . ." followed by the sum of money transferred: "Twelve Hundred Dollars lawful money of the United States, . . ." The dollar amount given may be the full purchase price or a partial cash payment, with a mortgage for the remainder, which latter will be found in a separate document. If the sum listed is "$1.00," this usually signals that the property was purchased with a mortgage. (In this case, you must look up the mortgage to find out how much was paid for the property.) If no sum is listed, the property was inherited directly. The sentence following the sum is legalese, a formula devised to establish that the property is being conveyed in good faith (i.e., the title is clear) and may be inherited forever.

"All" and "Beginning"

The next significant clause begins with "**All** that certain piece or parcel of land situate lying and being in the Town of Austerlitz, County of Columbia and State of New York. . ." and provides a general description of the location of the property: the city or town, county and state. It usually, but not always, is followed by the specific legal description, such as a written description of the surveyor's plat (map).

This description is signalled by the phrase "bound and described as follows" followed by the word "**Beginning** (e.g., at the Southwest corner of Said Farm on the North Side of the highway leading from the house of Aurillius M. Tracy) . . ." It then gives either the surveyor's *compass bearings* (stated in latitude and longitude degrees and minutes, such as North 80° East) or the *metes* (or measures) *and bounds* (such as, "thence along the land of said Smith three chains and six links to a brook"). These latter often name the boundary features as "lands now or formerly of" so-and-so.

This deed description is of particular value to a house historian. It usually establishes the size and specific location of a property and may designate markers, such as barns or houses. If the word "premises" or "farm" is used in this description, you can be pretty certain that a house was located on it.

In early deeds, especially when metes and bounds were used to describe the parcel, the word "**Beginning**" *may not occur*. Instead, the words "bounded and described as follows" occur directly before the metes and bounds description. Similarly the words "bounded and described as follows" will not be found in early 19th-century deeds if there is only a bounds description with no metes. In these two cases "**all**"—whether or not capitalized—is the key word signalling the physical description.

"The Same Premises Conveyed By"

Following the legal description there may or may not be a clause showing the previous owner in the chain of title. This clause may be signalled by "**Being and intending to describe and convey**," or "the same premises conveyed by . . ." or " . . . being the same premises conveyed to. . ." or slight variations of this wording. The phrase would be followed by "said (grantor) by (previous owner) by Deed dated (date) and recorded in the (name) County (or city) Clerk's Office on the (number) day of (month) (year) in Book No. (__) of Deeds at page (__)," or slightly different versions.

For a house historian, the finding of this clause is a boon because it speeds up the process of chaining the title. If it does not exist in a deed, then in order to chain the title from this grantee to grantor, you must look up, in the deed index, the grantor given in the first deed prior to the date of the deed you are using. There is no way of knowing what year to look in. You may have to search through several deed indices before you find who the grantor bought the property from. But, if the chain is given, as above, you simply go to the book and page mentioned to continue your search.

"Together"

Following this "chain clause" there may be a clause which often begins with the word "**Together** with all and singular the tenements, hereditaments and appurtenances thereunto belonging, or in any wise appertaining, . . ." This clause describes the legal rights, title and interest of the grantee. It is not important that you know what these terms mean; they are just "legalese." (Definitions of legal jargon are found in the Glossary at the end of the book.)

"To Have and To Hold"

Following "**Together** with" is the "**To have and to hold**" clause, in which the type of deed is defined plus any conditions connected with it. It is here that the type of "possession" being transferred is specified. For example, "fee simple" means that the property is transferred free from any and all types of conditions and encumbrances; the title is clear.

"**To have and to hold**" also is the section where conditions of sale or ownership may be specified, such as title to be given only if the grantor is cared for in "the same degree of style and comfort as . . ." he "has been used . . . to for . . . his natural life." (This latter deed condition was requested by an old man with no natural heirs who gave his house to his nurse provided she care for him properly and not hasten his death by neglect!)

"In Witness Whereof"

The final clause of the deed begins, "**In witness whereof**," and follows with the signatures of the grantor(s) and witness(es) and the date the deed was recorded. (Again, remember that recording may occur years after the deed was written.)

Although these various deed parts may seem, initially, strange and awkward in their use of the language, after a few readings your understanding of them will become easy, almost automatic.

Lease

In addition to deeds which convey real property, other types of deed also may offer information for a house history. Although these are not as common as regular deeds, you may run across them and should be able to recognize and use them.

The first of these uncommon deeds is a lease which involves the use, but not ownership, or real property. A lease is an agreement which creates a landlord-tenant relationship. Because a lease transfers some aspect of real property, its format appears very much like a deed. The difference is that the title transferred is less than "fee simple" and is subject to certain conditions, such as an annual rent, and the duration. Sometimes a lease begins "**This Indenture** of lease," but generally begins as a deed: "**This Indenture** made . . ."

The duration of the lease is stated in the "**To have and to hold**" clause. It may be for a lifetime, two lifetimes, ninety-nine years or forever, among other less common possibilities. The special conditions of the lease, such as rent, are enumerated in an additional clause that occurs last, after the "**To have and to hold**" clause and before "**In witness whereof.**" It begins, "**Yielding** and paying unto the said party of the first part . . ." In this clause the annual rent is specified, as well as any special conditions connected with the property and buildings on it, and the taxes to be paid.

In some cases, an annual quitrent was due, such as ". . . Perpetual annual rent of Eleven Bushels and one fourth of a Bushel of good clean merchantable winter wheat four fat hens and to Perform one day's service with carriage and horses. . ." A quitrent was a token payment, by the tenant of a freehold estate, to discharge him from any other rents or obligations to the landlord. It often was paid in the form of commodities. Although the tenant had the *privileges* of ownership, (e.g., voting), he still did not own the land. The terms of the quitrent varied and depended on the size and value of the property, and the wishes of the grantor.

In some leases the grantee was expected to erect a house, barn and outbuildings. In fact, he could lose the land if he did not construct the house according to the grantor's specifications. The buildings on the land were his property and were called "improvements." The lessee could sell the buildings, but the grantor usually took a percentage of the profit and maintained ownership of the land.

Leases also were set up as a means of avoiding inheritance taxes in life estates (i.e., an estate for the duration of a life). For example, in an 1837 deed an elderly father deeded his land to his son, who in turn leased the 204-acre farm to his father for two lifetimes—his father's and mother's—in exchange for $1.00 and $.06 a year payable annually on April 1. The terms included use of the dwelling house with no subletting of it. Although this procedure of deeding the property while the parents were still living was not commonplace, it assured the parents that their wishes were carried out, and there would be no haggling at the time they died. In exchange, they were assured of a familiar place to live until their deaths.

Hereditaments

Besides transferring real property, deeds also may pertain to other types of property, such as *hereditaments* (i.e., any kind of property that can be inherited). Such deeds often were written to specify transfer of real and personal property after a will had been probated. Usually this kind of deed specified in detail what may have been vaguely worded in the will. (For example: "My son David to receive all my real and personal property." became a specific listing.) These deeds verified exactly which real and personal property was devised and who the devisee—the receiver—was. You might not come across this sort of deed in your initial deed search. If you discover a will devising real property to a specific individual, however, then look in the deed index in the same or next year under grantee to see if a deed was written to that individual as grantee.

Chattel

Another type of deed transferred *chattel* (i.e., movable property). Movable property included removable fixtures, household goods, slaves and other personal property. An inventory of the contents of a house may be listed in a chattel deed separate from the house deed. (Inventories also may be listed with will papers. Chapter 10.) Or, there may be more than one deed—real property plus its contents—in, for instance, bankruptcy proceedings.

Inventories are very informative to a house historian. They give a fascinating picture of the house owner and his times and personal circumstances, and may indicate how the house was used and furnished at that period. For example, a judge who had overspeculated in real estate, gambling that the railroad would pass through his property, was forced to declare bankruptcy in 1854 after his town voted against the railroad being built there. In addition to deeding a house and thirty-eight acres, he also included his law books totalling 261 volumes, wagons, clocks, kettles, plows, one harrow, half the corn crop, a third of the oats, a pine table, chairs, fifteen fowl, one two-year-old spotted heifer, one lumber sleigh, two turkeys, one looking glass, two pipes of brandy (one a 137-gallon cask, the other 148 gallons), all worth $309.25 and cash amounting to $1,971 plus interest. In this instance chattel was used to help pay debts.

In another case, in 1802, Gabriel Ten Broeck owed four years and six months quitrent to William Van Ness. To pay this debt, he sold furnishings to Andrew M. Carshore. This transaction of chattel was recorded as a deed, because the potential loss of real property was involved. By using a public instrument—a chattel deed—to record his payment, Ten Broeck was insuring that Van Ness could not take back the property before the lease was up.

This deed was helpful to a 20th-century house historian researching a building once owned by Carshore. In 1802 Carshore recently had purchased this building, a tavern, which he had converted to house students. Carshore was the principal of a private academy. It was he who bought Ten Broeck's furnishings, probably needing them for his rentals. He paid £71 5 shillings to Gabriel Ten Broeck for six rugs, two sheets, one woolen sheet, one linen sheet, two feather beds, two straw beds, two bedsteads, one large dining table, two chests, six Windsor chairs, four matted (upholstered) chairs, one quilt, one large desk, two small tables, two iron pots, four new wheels and one sleigh. Some of these items represented good quality even in 1802. Upholstered chairs and a large desk were not the average man's furnishings, but rather the possessions of a middleclass man. Some of these items, such as the large desk, may have been used by Carshore himself at the academy. Although this chattel deed was not absolutely necessary in helping research the history of the tavern Carshore had bought, the information gleaned pinpointed the date of the conversion from a drovers' tavern to a dormitory, and also helped flesh out the deed and mortgage information.

Incorporation

In addition to deeds involving chattel, there are deeds of incorporation. Churches, libraries and other such institutions had deeds written for their incorporation. Although an institution's incorporation may appear to have little to do with a house history, the names of the trustees are always listed as are the names of individuals who donated the land. These names may correspond to names that you are researching and be of value to you in filling in some details.

For example, if one of the persons you are researching might have been a member of a nearby church, and the church was incorporated after the date that you think the house was built, check the incorporation deed of the church. You may find that your home owner donated the land for the church. Or, his house may be mentioned as a point in the deed description. Or, he may have been an original trustee, which meant that he had an income level above the average, a fact which also may be reflected in the house's design and construction.

Deeds for the incorporation of turnpikes also may mention, as incorporators, individuals you are researching. Their houses routinely were mentioned in these deeds as the survey of the roadbed was described. If you suspect that the road running by your target house was an early turnpike, it may be worthwhile to look up the incorporation of the turnpike.

Currency Systems

Although the Carshore deed noted above was written in 1802, twenty years after the Revolution, pounds and shillings were used in it as the means of exchange, not dollars and cents. This was not unusual. During colonial times, coins from most European countries were used as money in the New World, but the Spanish silver *peso duro* ("hard dollar") was the most prevalent coin. Furthermore, each colony produced its own currency based on the British monetary system of pounds, shillings and pence. Because the value of each state's money varied, it always was referred to, for example, as "five pounds lawful money of the State of New York," or "in Massachusetts currency," etc.

In 1792, Congress passed an act to establish the Untied States Mint and a national coinage system. Because of a few "bugs" in this legislation, universal acceptance of the new money did not happen immediately. Thus, until about 1810, it is not unusual to read legal documents with the consideration figured in pounds and shillings as an alternative, legal currency.

9

The Deed Search

Now you are ready to start looking up deeds. From this search you will learn the names of most of the previous owners, as well as the property descriptions and sale prices over the years, and will gain some hints as to the age of the house and its additions.

"Chaining" the Title

In a house history, to "chain" the title is to go back, from owner to owner —link by link—to the origins of the house. You begin by going to the local deed repository—usually the courthouse—and looking up the deed to the *current* owners. It will be filed approximately around the date that they bought the house, so you must know not only their names, but the month and year that they came into possession of the house. Ask the clerks at the main desk where the deed indices for that year are found. Also, ask how their indexing system works. Usually deeds are organized alphabetically by surname, and there are two deed indices for each year, one for *grantors* (sellers) and one for *grantees* (buyers). However, there are several different indexing systems in use in the United States. (See Appendix B.)

After you have found, in the grantee index, the deed book (liber) and page number where the specific deed is filed, locate the deed books or ledgers themselves. Find, by its number, the book you need and then look in it at the proper page number to find the actual deed. This deed will tell you who the current owners (the *grantees*) received the property from (their *grantors*), as well as some other pieces of information you will need later. In this way you start to work backward to chain the complete line of title. This first deed *may* tell you who sold the property to the people listed as the sellers, or givers (grantors) in this deed. However, if it does not indicate, in its "same premises conveyed by . . ." clause (see page 116), from whom the grantors themselves received the property, you then must go back to the deed indices and look up these grantors in the *grantee* (receiver or buyer) index. There you will find the previous deed listed and who *they* bought it from. This is "chaining" — looking up the seller or giver (grantor) and then going back to the previous deed, where the seller was the buyer or receiver (grantee). Using this method, you can chain a title all the way back to the date the property first was subdivided or sold, and to when the house appears to have been built.

What You Want from Each Deed

You will be abstracting specific information from each deed. Look for the date of the transaction, the grantor and grantee, the amount of the sale, and the property description, including the number of acres, in every deed you find. Keeping track of the amount of acreage as you chain back will help keep different properties (of the same owner) straight if someone in this line of title conveys more than one property with a single deed which included the property you are searching. The number of acres will help you identify your target property among the others described. And remember that your target *house* may not be mentioned in these deeds, even though it is situated on the property being transferred.

As you chain back, read each deed description carefully to make sure that you are working on the same property each time. Throughout the years, parcels may have been taken from or added to the original property. However, such changes will have been documented and should not cause you serious problems as long as you are attentive to the various property descriptions.

Neighboring Properties

Sometimes it may help chain your target property if you also chain ownership of the neighboring property, particularly when parcels were added to or deleted from yours. When a property is described by bounds, or even sometimes delineated in a regular survey, outstanding features of a more or less permanent nature on the edges of the property or near the boundary but on adjacent properties, are used as bounds and "landmarks." For example, the house or barn you are researching may be mentioned in a neighbor's deed description. The farther back you go in the 19th century, the more worthwhile it is to check neighboring deeds. Such information could help pinpoint the construction date of your target house.

You may have a lucky day and be able to keep chaining the title back to what you believe was the approximate date of construction of the house. More likely you will hit a snag and be unable to find a grantor for the last grantee you found. This is not unusual; do not be concerned. There almost always are ways around such snags, and they are explained in Chapter 10.

Abstracting or Photocopying Material

After you have found a deed, the quickest and most accurate means of recording its information is to photocopy it. Some people prefer to make notes, abstracting the pertinent facts instead of photocopying a whole document. (In many courthouses the general public has the use of at least one copy machine, so take some change with you if you are going to use the copier. It is a lot cheaper than having the clerk do the copying for you.)

I prefer to photocopy rather than to abstract. If I abstract only the information I think necessary at the time, I often find, while analyzing the chain of title back at home, that I have questions that need additional information. Frequently a fact that seemed unimportant in the first reading at the courthouse takes on a different meaning and should be part of the overall analysis. So it may be more efficient to have a copy of the deed that you can refer to later on at home when you are analyzing the chain of title rather than returning to the courthouse to look up the same deed again. If you are in business as a house historian, photocopying may save you time and your client money.

Before you return the deed to the shelf, write the book and page numbers on your photocopy or abstract, and check the photocopy for quality. Is all of the page copied? Is it legible? Write over the hard-to-read spots. Usually it is easier to read the deed book than the photocopy. Always note your source as well, for bibliographical purposes (e.g., Columbia County Clerk's Office, *Deed Liber 20*, Hudson, NY, March 21, 1820, pp. 570-571.).

As your research expands, you will be glad to have such source records. When you write up a house history, you must have accurate documentation. You and your client want proof that your content is accurate. Such source records also provide the documentation you must produce to register the house with a historical society or on a historic register should the case arise.

I always give the client all copies of documents I have made and pass the cost on to them. They usually enjoy having the copies for perusal, and it provides something tangible for them to hold in their hands to justify spending money on a house history. To many people research is an elusive concept. The only "product" is several typewritten pages and maybe some photos and maps. The resulting relatively small product may seem disproportionate to the number of hours needed to produce it. Thus, the more copies of sources you can present your clients with, the more obvious it will be how much research went into the final product.

Abstract and Outline

If you have found several deeds to analyze, you might want to call it quits at the courthouse for the day. Go home with your photocopies or abstracts all nicely marked with their deed book numbers and page numbers, and collate them. Once you have done this, list the pertinent information from each deed on a separate piece of paper which you will staple to the deed for easy reference. Remember that, at the minimum you want to learn from each deed:

- The date of the transaction
- The giver(s) and receiver(s)
- The amount of the sale
- Where the property is located
- How many acres were sold
- Brief description of the property

On each of these deed abstracts also make a crude drawing of the general shape of the property according to that deed description, and write in the names of the adjacent property owners at their approximate locations in the north-south (top/bottom) and east-west (right/left) directions. As you become more experienced, you may want to draw a more definitive property shape. (Chapter 15.) If there are no changes from the last deed, make a notation to that effect (e.g., "same as *Deed Liber 1,* p. 14)". Always compile this data for each of the deeds. These maps and information give you the bare bones of the data necessary for the time line.

Time Line

Now you are ready to do this time line—a chronological listing of the deed information, starting with earliest deed first and working forward. I organize the data as shown in the summary sheet below, but you may wish to adapt it to your own specifications. I like to see the facts in order, on one sheet of paper. You may prefer to use index cards or a computer. Whatever your method, leave generous gaps between entries so that you can add any deeds missed the first time around, or mortgages, wills, maps, assessments, tax-list information and other data that you may find as you do your research.

I write out all four digits of the year to keep me alert to the century I am working with. When your data takes you into the 19th and 18th centuries, a frequent and undetected mistake is switching dates—writing 1943 when you meant to write 1843. I list dates in the order of: month/day/year. You may be accustomed to ordering them: day/month/year instead, but be advised that records and documents other than deeds and mortgages will be listed in the month/day/year order. Choose one style and be consistent, to avoid mistakes.

L. = liber (deed book); A.= acres; w. = wife

L. 85, p. 482 5/7/1866	Caleb Forbes & Hettie, w., to Chester Tryon & Alice F., w. 122A. $1,050. Farm. Dwelling.
L. 296, p. 47 9/19/1922	Ernest Tryon & Helen, w., to John Novak. 122A. $3,250. Farm.
L. 453, p. 362 12/20/1950	John Novak & Catherine, w., to Joseph Niewinski & Sarah, w. 2A. $1.00. Formerly Novak Farm.
L. 507, p. 103 1/3/1952	Joseph Niewinski & Sarah w., to Ivan R. Fisher & Athena J., w. 2A. $1.00. Formerly Novak Farm.
L. 761, p. 322 2/13/1974	Ivan R. Fisher & Athena J., w., to Anthony DiNova & Guido Battalino. 2A. $32,500. Tract known as Abbey Subdivision. Formerly Novak Farm.
L. 1073, p. 534 4/5/1988	Anthony DiNovo to William Masek. 2A. $1.00. Tract known as Abbey Subdivision. Formerly Novak Farm.

Analysis

Once you set up your time line from your deed search information, study it to see what it tells you and what is missing. Learn to ask questions. Practice this by speculating on how things might have happened in the sample chain of title given above. First, note that the time line between 1866 and 1922 spans 56 years. This is an unusually long time for one owner to have had the same property. Further, there is a missing deed between Chester Tryon and Ernest Tryon. A good guess is that Ernest was Chester's son or nephew or grandson and inherited the property from him, but you should recheck your deeds. You then may have to check wills before you can verify how the transfer was made. (Chapter 10.)

There is a dwelling listed in the 1866 deed description. Is this the same house that William Masek lives in today? Or, does it refer to whatever had been built over the small foundation hole you saw close to the road? Or, was the 1866 dwelling incorporated into the back ell of William Masek's large house, which obviously has been added onto? More research may confirm one of these speculations.

In 1922, when John Novak bought the 122-acre farm from Ernest and

Helen Tryon, he paid cash. Twenty-eight years later when he sold two acres to Joseph and Sarah Niewinski, the deed shows he had a wife, Catherine. At some point the title must have passed from John Novak to John Novak and Catherine, so a deed is missing from this chain. When John sold the Niewinskis the two acres, was the farmhouse included or just the acreage? We know that the property was subdivided, because two years later it was called Abbey Subdivision. We do not know, however, if John sold other parcels to other people, or kept the 120 acres. If it was the latter, did he continue to live in the farmhouse or did he build a new home on the property?

Information is missing between 1974 and 1988. The title cannot have been passed by Anthony DiNovo to William Masek without some kind of document indicating what happened to Guido Battalino. Did Guido sell his interest to Anthony? Was he a brother-in-law of Anthony? Did Anthony inherit the property when Guido died? You must search for a deed from Anthony DiNovo and Guido Battalino to Anthony DiNovo. If, by chance, there is none— sometimes mistakes are made—you must go to the Probate County or District Court (depending on your state) to look up Wills and Letters of Administration. Further research is needed. (Chapter 10.)

These kinds of questions are typical of those you might find in an initial title-chaining. Most can be answered with some more research among deeds and wills. Or, you may have to try some other sources. But these questions must be answered to complete the house history.

Social History

The deed search will also raise other, more speculative, questions. If you find some answers to them, you will have even more details for your house history. For example, note from the 1866 deed that Chester's wife, Alice, has the middle initial "F." Did this stand for Frances, Florence or Forbes? Was Caleb Forbes her father, uncle or grandfather? Had Chester decided to settle down after the Civil War, so he married Alice Forbes and bought her family's farm?

Was John Novak unmarried in 1822? Was he a young man then, or had he recently emigrated from a Slavic country, forced out of his family home by the revolution there? Since he paid for the farm with cash, had he brought his life savings with him? Perhaps his wife had died in the old country, explaining why he had no wife when he bought the farm?

Notice that he sold the property to Joseph Niewinski, also with a Slavic surname. Was it a chance occurrence or were they friends? Had Joseph emigrated from a Slavic country after World War II, an escapee from the ravages of war? Or, was he the son of a friend of John, a second-generation American who was sick of living in an apartment with his new bride?

Why did Joseph and Sarah keep the property only two years? What happened to make them decide to sell? Did Sarah dislike her new surroundings? Did Joseph get a job transfer? Did they dislike the school district? Were they given an offer on their house that was too good to turn down? Was the house too expensive for them to maintain?

Notice that Masek and Fisher had mortgages, but Anthony and Guido paid cash in 1974, as indicated by the $32,500 figure. Do different life styles explain that fact? More research is needed if you or your clients want to know, in such detail, the social history connected with the house.

The answers to questions about social history may help explain a detail that is unique to a house—for example, heart-shaped motifs cut in or painted on woodwork, which are typically Czech. Research into social history almost always will tell you more about the house's history.   Indeed, a house's construction history can be considerably expanded and enriched by its social history, but this requires more research.

While social history is fascinating, you should avoid spending too much time on it unless you are sure that your clients will want to know as much about the previous owners as they do about the house. Before you do so check with them. Explain the difference in time spent and facts available, and the size of your bill. Of course, if you are doing this on your own it is a different matter. If you are willing to spend the time, there are many different and fascinating avenues for finding out more details.   Whatever you decide, you will incorporate all your data into a final, written analysis which addresses as many questions as you wish.

To conclude this chapter on title-chaining through the deed search, we must share a classic deed story. If you find deeds confusing at first, you are in good company. Even experienced deed interpreters get confused at times, including the Federal Housing Authority, as illustrated by the following:

> A New Orleans lawyer sought an FHA loan for a client. FHA advised him the loan could be granted if he proved title to the property offered as collateral. Since the title dated back to 1803, the lawyer spent three months verifying it.
>
> FHA wrote: "We compliment you on the able manner in which you prepared the application. However, you did not clear the title before 1802. Before final approval can be given, we must have clearance on the title prior to that year."
>
> The annoyed lawyer replied: "I note you wish titles further back than I presented them. I was unaware that any educated person was

ignorant of the fact that Louisiana was purchased from France in 1803. That title was acquired by France by right of conquest from Spain. Spain possessed the land by right of discovery in 1492 by a sailor named Columbus, who was privileged to seek a new route to India by the then reigning monarch, Isabella. The good queen, being a pious woman and careful about titles, almost as careful, I might say, as the FHA, secured the blessing of Pope Innocent VIII before she sold her jewels to sponsor the voyage. The Pope, as you know, is the emissary of Jesus Christ, the Son of God, and God is commonly accepted as having made the world. I believe it is safe to presume that He also made that part of the world called Louisiana. I certainly hope this information will enable you to grant my client's loan."

10

Mortgages, Wills and Letters of Administration

Mortgages, wills and letters of administration, because they each provide different information, can help fill in gaps remaining after your deed search. They may even provide names which will help you over some snag in title chaining, and can flesh out your documentation, further enlivening the house history. This chapter will explain what these records are and how to use them.

Mortgages

Creditors and debtors and mortgages have been around for hundreds of years and most likely ever since man conceived of the idea of land possession, The word *mortgage* literally means a "dead pledge." In English common law the mortgage developed from the Anglo-Saxon pledges of land for their debts.

A mortgage is a temporary and conditional pledge of property to a creditor as a security for the payment of a debt or for the fulfillment of an obligation. It may involve either real or personal property, but a house historian occasionally needs to know about chattel (personal property) mortgages. Most of the time you will be researching real property mortgages. In the 20th century, properties typically were purchased via mortgages, whereas in the 18th and 19th centuries this was a less common practice.

Although deeds sometimes were not recorded until the property was transferred out of the family, mortgages always were recorded in a timely fashion, because the exchange of money was involved with someone other than one's own family. Mortgages are the next step in researching the written documents connected with your target house. Mortgage documents can fill in gaps in your deed chain, giving additional information and, sometimes, revealing the existence of a house, which a deed usually does not.

Early Mortgages

Banks and lending institutions gave mortgages, but perhaps more significantly for the house historian, *individuals* —both men and women—in the 19th century and earlier, were the most frequent mortgage givers (mortgagees). These latter mortgages often were between family members. Thus, if a default occurred, the house often went to another family member. Or, if the mortgage holder died, another family member inherited the mortgage. Keep this in mind, as it may shorten your search.

Years ago, the length of a mortgage was much shorter than in the 20th century, often for only five or ten years. In 19th-century mortgages, more often than in today's, the interest was due on specific dates, with the principal due in five years. Or, the interest may have been due on specific dates with the principal due on demand, in which case the mortgagor never knew when he might have to produce the principal quickly.

After the parties concurred on the amount, collateral, interest and terms, a mortgage indenture was written and a *mortgage bond* was issued. A bond is a promise to pay principal and interest on a loan that is secured by a lien or title-conveyance on a property. This bond can be *assigned* to another mortgagee under prescribed regulations, which vary in different jurisdictions or states. In the past it may have been assigned to another individual upon the death of the original mortgagee. Upon payment of the mortgage, the *satisfaction* of the mortgage is filed, which formally acknowledges payment by the mortgagor. Any or all of these transactions—mortgages, assignments, satisfactions— could provide information you need for your house history, such as name of owners or the existence of buildings. Like deeds, they are indexed and available at your courthouse.

There are two theories of mortgages prevalent in the United States: the title theory and the lien theory. Most states now follow the lien theory of mortgages, in which the mortgagee, who is loaning the money, is considered as having a lien on, or a right to, the property as security for his loan to the mortgagor. The latter is regarded as the real owner of the property. In case of default, the legal process gives the *mortgagor* more leeway to negotiate a settlement. In states following the lien theory, it is more likely that alterations or additions to a house were made at the time that the mortgage was contracted.

However, it was common practice through the early 20th century, and still is in some states, for the creditor to hold the title until the mortgage is paid in full. This is called the title theory of mortgages. The *mortgagee* has the right to possession of the property, can collect rent, and is considered the real owner as against everyone else except the mortgagor. If a mortgagor defaulted and could not get a second mortgage to pay up the first, he lost the property without leniency. Thus, many 19th-century mortgagors, under title theory, did not want to sink any more money into improvements until the house was legally theirs. They postponed additions, alterations or wallpapering until they actually had the deed in their hands. They made changes only when the mortgage was satisfied. Thus, the question of whether title or lien theory governed a mortgage can hint to the house historian when changes were likely to have been made on a house by a mortgagor.

What You May Find Out from a Mortgage

Mortgages look and are similar to deeds in content and language. From the house historian's point of view, however, mortgages often contain more information. A mortgage indenture usually includes the same property description found in deeds, and also tells the amount of money lent and sometimes the terms of the payments.

From the mid-19th century on, most banks required fire insurance on the house before a mortgage was given. Because of this, a more specific description of the buildings and property was made in the mortgage—including dwellings, barns, "runs of water," orchards, etc.—than is found in the deed for the house at that time. Often you can judge the specific value of the house from the mortgage, because the amount of insurance needed is stated. Sometimes even the insurance company is named. In that case, you can contact the insurance company—or whatever company now owns its records—to see if they have a description of the house.

If, from this description, it can be established that the property used as collateral back then is the same property you are researching, you may have found the first documented reference to the house itself. By continuing to look up mortgages leading back to the probable date of construction of the original section of the house, you may be able to glean further pertinent information: the property's value over the years, whether it was remortgaged or lost through nonpayment or other information. (Do not assume, in this search, that the mortgage money was used to improve the house covered in it. It may have been used to finance a business venture, or for some other reason.)

Although it is recommended that you routinely check for mortgages—by looking up deed grantees (owners) in the mortgage index for that time—you will not always find one. Not everyone used a mortgage as a means of financing. Usually there will be clues in the deed wording as to the existence of a mortgage. The first clue is when $1.00 is listed as a consideration payment in the deed. This wording usually signals that either the purchase was financed by a mortgage, or the grantee was a relative and received the property as part of an estate settlement, where no mortgage was needed. You can tell from the way the deed reads whether an estate was being settled [i.e., "the grantor (name), Executor of (name) deceased . . . "].

The second clue to the existence of a mortgage is a consideration in the deed for substantially less than what the property previously sold for. For instance, if a property had sold for $3,050 and later then was resold for $1,000, then—barring national economic depressions, which sometimes affected the real estate market, or a natural disaster—it is possible that at least $2,050 was financed.

Looking Up Mortgages

Mortgage searching is different from deed searching, because you are not chaining or trying to connect one mortgage with another. Indeed, you often cannot do so, because the person giving the mortgage usually does not own the property. A mortgagee may be anyone who has money available to buy or sell mortgages as he sees fit. Thus no chain exists between mortgages.

When you realize—because of the wording in a deed—that a mortgage search might uncover further information, try to associate the deed wording with a specific mortgage. To do this, look up the grantee as mortgagor in the mortgage index for that year. There usually are both mortgagor and mortgagee indices. If you think that the grantor in the deed may have given the mortgage, look up that name in the mortgage index under mortgagee.

A mortgage obtained on property after it was bought would not, of course, be noted in the deed. For example, if a person wants to start a horticultural business on his property, he can use his real property as collateral to finance the greenhouses. Since he already has owned the property for ten years, there would be nothing in his original deed to indicate the existence of the mortgage.

Mortgage Language

Most mortgages begin with the same words as do deeds: "This Indenture Made (date) Between (mortgagor) of (legal address) and (mortgagee) of (legal address)." The "consideration"—the amount of the mortgage—is next. It acknowledges the receipt of a specific amount of money as well as the conveyance of title or lien against the property. Then either the property description follows or reference is made to the deed where the description can be found.

In addition to the description of the land, a reference often is made which confirms the existence of a dwelling house. The reference may be direct: "All that certain dwelling house, ..." Or, it may be indirect: "Being the same premises on which the said parties of the first part reside." If insurance was required, its provisions usually were written in after the description. Often the amount of coverage for the house and outbuildings was stated, which gives you a very good idea of how much the house was worth at that time. From this you may be able to guess at its size at the time and whether it had been "improved."

If you find that the property was remortgaged over several years, comparing the different valuations could provide clues to pinpointing when improvements were made, especially if you also compare them with the property value given on assessment and tax lists for the time. Use one or more of these latter sources to confirm any hints you may get from a mortgage about an addition or other change. (Chapter 16.)

Following the description or the insurance provisions, there will be reference to the bond in which the specific terms for payment are spelled out, even if they have been specified in this mortgage (indenture). Sometimes these terms were listed on both places—the bond and the indenture (mortgage). The mortgage then closes with the signatures of the mortgagor and, on occasion, of the mortgagee.

If a mortgage has been assigned, satisfied or foreclosed, look up such documents. While assignments and satisfactions generally are found with mortgages, foreclosures may be found under "Sales" (meaning, public auctions). They tell the final outcome of the loan: paid off, refinanced, foreclosed. You also may find details about the individuals involved, giving you a more complete story of the house and owner.

A mortgage may be the first or even the only document you find that actually mentions the existence of a house or its value. Such a mention could help you past a snag in your deed search. For example, if you cannot find a grantor for your last grantee, perhaps the mortgagee was the grantor. Look him up in the deed index. Or, the mortgage may be a remortgage and the original mortgagee was the grantor. Again, check the deed for the same names you find in the mortgages.

Photocopy any mortgages you find. Abstract the same information you did for deeds, including all references to the house, its value and insurance, and insert this information into your time line. You may be pleasantly surprised to see how it fills in some of your information gaps.

Public Auctions

A person may default on a mortgage—that is—not pay the required amounts on the dates designated in the bond. If over a period of time no payment is made, the creditor or mortgagee may request that the property be sold at public auction if the taxes have not been paid for a specified period of time. Usually the buyer obtained the property for a fraction of its real value. Such a sale may provide a clue for dating alterations, since houses often were "improved" by the new owner after a tax sale.

In public auction records, the court-appointed governmental agent is listed in the grantor's place as referee, with the person buying the property listed as grantee. The mortgagees are listed as plaintiffs—the parties instituting the court suit, while the mortgagors are defendants—the parties against whom the suit is being brought. Because it was the referee, rather than the previous grantee, who was listed as grantor, an unexpected name will appear in your chain of title. When you are working backward from the present in your deed search, this apparent break should pose no problem, because the buyer of the property is the grantee and becomes the grantor on the successive deed. However, if you have hit a snag and have tried to get around it by working forward from an earlier date, then you will have some difficulty, because the grantee's name on the earlier deed is replaced by the name of the referee on the public auction deed. So, when you cannot find the grantee as grantor, one possibility is that the property went for sale at a public auction. Start working backwards from the most recent deed, and you may find the link. It often happened that the same person held the job of referee over a number of years. In that case, the name may have become familiar to you as you have gone over various documents, and seeing it will signal a tax-sale transfer to you.

Wills and Letters of Administration

A will is a legal declaration of how a person wishes his property to be disposed of after his death. It is another way of transferring property—by inheritance. Like wills, but indirectly, letters of administration give authority to someone to act as executor and settle an estate. Usually they are used by the courts when someone dies intestate—without a will. Wills and letters of administration also are indirect records of three vital statistics—birth, death and marriage dates. Thus they are a tool in genealogical research—the study or investigation of ancestry—as well as a house history tool.

Wills and letters of administration, like mortgages, can be used to help you find grantors who are "missing" from the usual chain of title. They may give more specific information about a house, or explain a "gap" in the title chain. If the estate included real estate, you may find the name of the devisee—the person who received the gift of real property. The estate inventory also may list furniture or trade tools that the devisee received. Some of that same furniture may still be in the house you are researching. The tools tell you the decedent's trade, and possibly his heir's, and what the house was used for at that time.

Wills must be probated—legally presented to the court as the last will and testament of the decedent. A testament refers to the disposition of personal property. Probate comes from the Latin *probatum* and means "something proved"—in this case, that the will submitted is the *last* will. In American law "probate" has become a term used to encompass all of the matters over which a court of probate has jurisdiction.

Such courts have different names in different states, but they perform the same functions. Thirteen states or parts of them have county probate courts. Eleven states or parts of them use the name county court, while district court in the county is the name in eight other states or parts thereof. In the remaining states, probate occurs under twenty-nine different names, including "surrogate" court. Look for probate records under the designated court in your state. In some of the older states, early probate records have been compiled in one location for the entire state and can be found only there. If you do not know which particular court in your jurisdiction keeps will records, inquire at your city, town or county clerk's office.

Generally, will indices are organized alphabetically by surname in chronological, running fashion. For example, each surname beginning with "T" will be found in the "T" section of the index, with the earlier dates at the beginning of the section and the more recent dates toward the end. The wills themselves may be located in will ledgers or may be filed in boxes along with inventories and other legal papers necessary to probate wills. The will index lists either the will ledger and page number of the will, or the number of the file box where it can be located.

Finding a Grantor

In the 17th, 18th and 19th centuries it was very common for people to marry neighbors or townspeople and live on a family farm without a formal agreement as to their role in the ownership of the property. Eventually the owner died and someone inherited the farm. If the heir was a family member, while there may have been a will, often the deed transferring the property to the new owner within the family was not recorded. Or, it may not even have been executed until generations later. So if, while researching a title chain, you are unable to find a grantor for your grantee and you know that the house was built earlier than the date you have chained back to, look for a will.

A typical example of this kind of "jump" or "non-sequitur" in title chain is when you have found a grantor and grantee sharing the same surname, and there is no intervening deed. The new grantor probably inherited the property from a father, grandfather or uncle. It is particularly important to consider this possibility when a woman heir is involved, since you usually do not know her maiden name or family connection. A clue could be that her middle initial corresponds to the surname of the grantee. In either case, look up the will of the previous grantee.

The following example illustrates the process of using wills to locate the grantor of a specific property to Peter G. and Jacob G. Smith. First, in trying to locate the father as possible grantor, Smiths with either of these given names were looked up in the will index prior to 1841, the date of the last deed found in the chain. A Peter G. Smith who died in 1820, was listed. In his will, he left two-thirds of his farm to Peter and Jacob. The farm's location was not specified, so it cannot be compared with the deed description. To establish how this Peter G. Smith acquired the farm, a further search in wills was made of "G." Smiths, since G. was the common initial. George P. (Peter?) Smith's will then was located. He died in 1814 and left his "present chief dwelling" to his wife Maria, and to his sons, Peter and Jacob, he left the rest of the real and personal estate, of which Peter had already been given a farm and told to divide it with Jacob. The will of this Jacob, George P.'s son, also was examined. Jacob G. Smith had died unmarried in 1817 and left his real property to his brother, Peter G. Thus we have located three generations of Smiths:

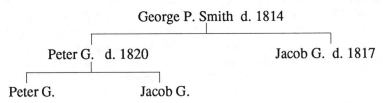

The two sets of Peter G. Smiths and Jacob G. Smiths all held property either in common or jointly, according to the wills, although the property's location still is not mentioned.

The next step is to look in the will file boxes or probate records to find any inventories of household goods which might mention the location of the real property. After exhausting probate records, search in deeds for Peter G. Smith as grantor to Peter G. and Jacob G. Smith. Then look for a deed with George P. Smith as grantor to Peter G. Smith. Such a deed might help establish whether or not the two properties are the same. In this case it was determined that they were not.

House Information from Wills

In some cases a will may provide specific information about a house. For example, after searching through deeds and mortgages and finding no direct reference to a certain house, the will of Johannes Hogeboom, Jr., the original lessee of a property, was searched. The will was long and thorough. In one of its sections he directs that if daughter Gertrude shall remain unmarried or daughter Helen remain separated from Squire Pixley and not remarry, that they are to live with brother Stephen or have the use and occupation of Johannes' "east uper room as they chuse."

This reference is not only to Johannes Hogeboom, Jr.'s house, but also to his "east uper room." So, from this will written in 1811, it was established that the main section of the house, a two-story Federal structure, was built before 1811. We can confirm this because our on site inspection showed that the earlier house was a one-and-a-half story with only one room in the upper half story. The "east uper room" could only have been located in the addition, which had bedrooms only on the east and west sides of a north-south aligned center hall.

When You Cannot Find a Will

If the person being researched is not listed in the will index, there are three possible explanations. The first could be that there was an informal or verbal or even written will but no contest among the beneficiaries, so that the "testator" —the person leaving the property—deliberately set up the inheritance to avoid probate taxes. One common way of doing this was to deed sections of the family farm to "heirs" before the death of the owner. Another was to set up a life estate in which the head of the family had life-time use of the house, yet already had deeded the property to the heirs. Disposing of property before death, to avoid probate taxes, occurred in the 19th—and sometimes in the 20th—century.

The second reason you cannot find a will could be that the individual died intestate—that is, with no valid will. In such cases the state settles the estate. The court appoints an administrator by filing a letter of administration, which you will find indexed under the name of the decedent. One of the first duties of the administrator is to make a complete inventory of the estate and file it with the court, where it is recorded and indexed in file boxes. Because the formula for intestate probate is established by law, all living legal heirs must be named there, and these documents must show how the estate was divided—that is, who got what from the total inventory.

Letters of administration usually are indexed separately from the will index. The letter itself will tell you only who the administrator is and, possibly, the heirs—information which may be a help in your search. To find the actual inventory and any other pertinent papers, you must go to the file boxes, under the name of the decedent.

The third reason you may have difficulty in finding a will is that the person died in another jurisdiction (town, county, state) and the will is filed there rather than being recorded locally. This can happen when a long-time property owner dies in a hospital or nursing home, or with relatives, over the line in another town or state. It also can happen if the person owned property located on both sides of a county or state line. If you cannot find the will in one jurisdiction, look in the other. (The author found a will filed in Berkshire County, Massachusetts, that had been probated in New York State by Martin Van Buren. He had written a note on it saying it should be filed in Pittsfield, Massachusetts, because the decedent also owned property there, and Van Buren was done with it. Yet there was no cross-reference in the New York files to indicate that the will had been probated.) Knowing who the relatives of the decedent were could help. Especially as they get older, people may go to live with relatives in another jurisdiction while still maintaining ownership of a property. Their wills may have been probated where they died, and filed there after it was returned from the jurisdiction in which they owned property.

Women as Heirs

Locating female heirs in your document search may present a particular challenge. Searching women's names can be easier in some states than in others. Whatever their property rights, married women in the English-speaking world were known by their husbands' names, a fact that always will plague genealogists. Because her maiden name is "lost," easy discovery of the "lineage" of a house is hindered if a married daughter, granddaughter or niece inherits the real property. This is one reason a house historian often must use genealogical methods in tracing the history of a house.

Until the latter half of the 19th century, women generally did not own property until they became widows. There were a few exceptions, notably in wealthy families. If a husband owned businesses, the ownership of the family residence sometimes was placed in his wife's name. If he lost his business interests, at least the family home was saved. Otherwise, ownership was by and large the privilege of men, whose voting rights hinged on property ownership. (Yet women who did own property did not have the right to vote, an issue which became basic to the women's suffrage movement.) A widow received a dower right, which was a life estate and one-third of the real property her husband had owned in fee simple during his life. This dower right usually was valid only if she remained a widow. So, she may not be listed on deeds. You must find her indirectly, through her husband, or through her maiden name. This situation generally prevailed in the eastern third of the United States.

However, in *community property* states—that is, states in which Spanish property law prevailed—the wife owned the property in common with her husband. Thus, there was no need for dower rights. These states are Arizona, California, Idaho, Louisiana, Nevada, New Mexico, Texas and Washington.

Because of this, searching in these states may be simplified.

In *public domain* states, which included parts of Arkansas, Florida, Illinois, Missouri, New Mexico, Ohio, Oregon and Washington, and the rest of the states west of Missouri and from Wisconsin south to Alabama, it was common for the wife to sign the deed as the co-owner. Thus the dower right did not need to be exercised because the wife already was the co-owner.

Many in these last two groups of states were not heavily settled until the latter half of the 19th century, when the tenor of American society was beginning to change somewhat to include women in traditionally male professions. Because of the Industrial Revolution, women had begun working outside of the home in mills and factories and were becoming more oriented to financial independence from men. Thus, it is understandable that either co-ownership of property or property held in common should occur in these newly formed states. Indeed, a precedent for female ownership was established in these newer states earlier than in the older eastern states, where more conventional laws already were in effect. So, keep in mind that women did own property, but it may be difficult to trace their ownership, depending on which states they lived in and the customs of their times.

Court Records

During the early years of the colonies, local courts were practically the only governmental unit with which everyone had contact. These early courts performed many of the functions later taken on by separate governmental departments. Records of these courts contain information that can be of great interest to the house historian. For example, these courts issued licenses for the various professions, as well as for taverns to sell alcoholic beverages. The home owner may be listed as a merchant, for instance, which could mean that the house's front rooms may have been used as a store. Or, if the owner was a tavern keeper, the house may have been an inn with a tap room in a corner of the first floor.

Courts also mandated that roads and bridges be built and maintained. In maintaining them the courts used home owners as road workers. In order to do this, they listed where the home owners lived on each road. The road list may mention your house owner. (Chapter 16.)

Courts also assessed and collected taxes, often basing them on property values. (Chapter 16.) They even built housing for the handicapped or indigent, on occasion in conjunction with the local churches. Your house may have been such a building.

These local courts had a variety of names, such as the justice court, mayor's court, or small claims court, among others. In some states, records of the court of common pleas may tell you more social history than will a deed search. Many matters brought before these courts would be considered trivial today—such as one woman swearing at another—but there also were serious cases, including property damage. We still can relate to someone's ire when a neighbor's farm animals broke through fencing and destroyed a kitchen garden or field crops. In rare instances, these records may explain such things as a property division which affects your house.

You may need to ask court clerks to locate such court records. When you do, you may find that some 17th- to 18th-century court records were placed in the town or district minutes, while others may have been squirrelled away in an archive. Or, such records—especially the 19th-century ones—may have been indexed, if not by the local jurisdiction, then by the federal Works Progress Administration (WPA) in the 1930's.

If there is no index, or it is incomplete, use the court dockets (bound books of court agendas) as an index. These dockets usually are organized chronologically, so you would look from year to year within the years you are searching. There may be one court docket covering all civil actions, or there may be several different dockets divided into categories designating the nature of the action. The dockets that may be valuable to a house historian are those which list the following actions:

- civil cases between individuals, which are initiated to recover monetary damages for injuries;

- equity (or chancery) in which "reasonable justice" or "common good" is decided, because following the letter of the law would be unjust, such as in real estate controversies;

- claims which creditors have against property and estates;

- miscellaneous cases, which include tax foreclosures, estate ownership, insolvency, etc.

These dockets can be used to help you locate court minutes, which actually contain all the details of the case. The minutes may offer an explanation, for example, of a tax foreclosure or a property suit not extant in other documents.

11

Genealogy

Genealogical research draws on vital statistics—records of births, deaths and marriages. These records can be used to link some of the information you find in a will or letter of administration with the present and past owners of the target property.

As past owners are researched, a house comes alive. This genealogical quest may help you to discover a family connection or event which could explain how or why a house was built or changed, or explain some unique characteristic of it. This chapter will describe various genealogical records and explain how to use them in your house history search.

Vital Statistics

Vital statistics were not kept on a systematic basis by city, state or federal governments until the first quarter of the 20th century. Originally, such data were compiled as medical statistics in an effort to control epidemics. The earliest large cities to require civil registration of births and deaths were New Orleans (1790), Boston (1848), Philadelphia (1860), Pittsburgh (1870) and Baltimore (1875). Later, vital statistics became important for tax-collection and military draft purposes.

By the 20th century, collecting vital statistics records was deemed by the federal government to be the responsibility of each state. This accounts for the different starting dates for recording data and the variety of data collected as different states put their own systems into effect. It was not until 1912 that all states had a system for recording vital statistics. Fortunately, there are a number of other sources besides town, state and federal records which offer such information.

Birth Records

There are a variety of sources in which birth dates can be found. In some towns these vital statistics were recorded in the town minutes. In other towns, churches were the keepers of birth and baptism records. In many cases, birth statistics were not kept on a regular basis by the local government until long after a town was settled. If you are researching before that time, check church baptismal records. Most churches practiced infant baptism of the children of church members. Or, the family Bible could be the ultimate resource. By the 19th century, the census data offered another source. There the ages of inhabitants were recorded, from which birth dates can be derived.

The example of the George P. Smith family, used earlier to explain the use of wills (Chapter 10) will be utilized again to demonstrate the use of other genealogical records. (Refer back to page 136.) Note that although Peter G. had been given a farm and told to share it with his brother, Jacob G., it is not clear which one was the younger son. Because his name is listed first in the will entries, and because his given name is Peter—presumably the middle name of father George P(eter)—and because Peter was given the farm before Jacob, it has been assumed that Peter G. is the older son. However, it may be that he married earlier than Jacob G. and hence had had an earlier need for independence, which the father recognized by giving him the farm. To resolve this question, a check was made of the baptismal record of the Reformed Dutch Church in the town where George lived. This showed a Petrus, son of George P. Schmit and Maritje (Maria), baptised September 1, 1794. Having established this, a search of some other records will help use this birth date to confirm which brother is the eldest.

Gravestones

Birth and death dates may be derived from gravestones. But you may not even have to search through a graveyard in your area. Many genealogists have compiled local tombstone listings and make them available to researchers, or have published them. Indeed, our local town historian has done such a book, and in it one sees that our Peter G. died July 19, 1820, at age thirty-five and Jacob G. died April 21, 1817, at age twenty-two. By subtracting their ages from their death dates, it becomes obvious that Peter was older than Jacob by about ten years, so our earlier speculation that Peter was older is correct. We now see that Jacob was only sixteen at the time their father's will was probated in 1814. It was logical for father to request older brother Peter to take Jacob under his wing and share the property that father already had given to Peter. Since Peter already was living on it, we assume he had a house.

A note of caution about lists taken from gravestones: when a person dies, the relatives, neighbors or friends who bury them may or may not know the exact birth year of the deceased, even if they are "sure" that they do. Dates and even names on tombstones may be inaccurate.

A cemetery may not necessarily have been associated with a particular church, even if it is located adjacent to the church. There are numerous family plots—and many of these are unmarked—as well as land set aside by philanthropic souls for cemeteries. Such land often was undesirable for farming, usually because it was on a stony knoll or not easily used. Family plots were not necessarily recorded on any lists unless there later was a formal incorporation of the cemetery with a board, a sexton or a caretaker to keep the records.

Another problem with gravestones is that the 18th- and 19th-century slate, marble or other soft stone or metal markers still standing have weathered so badly that it can be hard to decipher letters and numbers from them. Also, many markers have heaved from frost and have fallen over or are buried under brush and earth. The 20th-century lists that do exist for 18th- and 19th-century graveyards have been compiled by dedicated individuals who struggled to read letters and numbers so worn, in some cases, that they are almost impossible to decipher accurately. Thus, these lists also are subject to human error.

Church Records of Deaths and Burials

Not all churches kept death or burial records unless the cemetery was in the churchyard or was church-owned. Often there was no regularized way of recording deaths. On some church membership lists an individual's name was crossed off either after death or, after dismissal, when he left the church to join another because he had moved. More commonly, however, the name simply ceased to be assessed for attendance or voting purposes and finally was omitted when a new list was drawn. In spite of these variations in consistency, church records always are worth checking for death dates or confirmation of death.

Which church's records should you research? In the earliest settlements, there often was only one church in town. Regardless of the church they had been baptised in, if they were Christian, people usually went to the local church whether or not they followed all of its tenets. In some cases, however, religious practice was very important to the individual, so he drove or sailed several miles from his home for the important sacraments of baptism and marriage. It could help your search to know the religion or ethnicity of your past home owners.

How do you find this out? There are a variety of methods. The two easiest are checking in records of local churches or looking for clues in the person's surname. A German, for example, may be Lutheran, while an Irishman may be Roman Catholic. First and second names may be significant too. Since the Peter and Jacob Smith in our previous example both have a "G." as their second initial and their father's name is George, a calculated guess is that they were Reformed

Dutch. In the early Dutch culture the children were given a patronymic, their father's first name, as their second name. Thus their names would read: Peter son of George Smith and Jacob son of George Smith. Furthermore, George's second initial is "P.," so it is assumed that he was George son of Peter Smith. The Dutch had a tradition of naming their children with alternate paternal, then maternal given names beginning with the paternal grandparents. Thus, the elder son was named Peter for the paternal grandfather, son of George.

Name Variations

Establishing that George P. Smith was the father in our example now affords a more exact check of deeds and mortgages, maps, tax lists and censuses. (Chapter 16.) These show George's name spelled in a variety of ways in the late 18th century: Jurritje; Jurrejie; Jurrian and Jury. (Names ending in "itje" or "etjie" or "ejie" usually indicate a Dutch given name; these suffixes are diminuitives meaning "little," much like "y" or "ie" in English names.) Over the years George's Dutch name became Anglicized until he finally was known legally in deeds and mortgages as George.

Why was the name George used for Jurritje? Probably because George was the closest sounding English name to Jurritje, and it was easier for an English speaker to say and spell George.

How do we know that Jurritje and its other versions, and George, all referred to the same person? There are several reasons. Because of the "P." for the middle initial used with the various spellings. Because—as we see from tax lists—he was taxed for the same number of acres in the same district and town, under both Jurritje and George. Because the dates were logical ones fitting credibly into the time line being developed. And, finally, because the population of the district/town was so small at that time that all people were easily accounted for. There was no other George P. Smith anywhere in the county.

Similar spelling changes occurred with Smith. Note in the previously listed baptismal records that the surname is spelled "Schmit." The dominies, Reformed Dutch clergymen, often spoke Dutch and recorded in Dutch well into the early 19th century.

By the second generation of Peter G.'s and Jacob G.'s, we see that father Peter G. gave his two sons his name and his brother's rather than his father's and his wife's father's. Over time, he had become even more Anglicized.

The Dutch were very early settlers with many descendants. Because of this, Dutch names appear often in early records. Spanish nomenclature is perhaps the only other minority culture that has kept its distinctive naming customs until recently. Other 19th- and 20th-century immigrant groups which have patronymics (e.g., the Russians) or who maintain their own name after marriage (e.g., Chinese women), almost immediately assumed the English system. Since the Dutch and the Spanish were here in the 17th and 18th centuries, before the English predominance, there are many records in which their names occur following their own customs. It is helpful to understand these in order to best use such records.

Marriage Records

Marriages are of particular interest to a house historian, since the date that a house was improved sometimes coincides with a marriage date. Church records of marriages were consistently maintained. However, many marriages were civil, not church, and performed by a justice of the peace. Whether or not civil records were kept depends on how early the marriages were. That is, early J.P. records were not kept either consistently or at all, even as late as the mid-19th century.

Some marriage data is found on gravestones. In addition to "wife" or "wife of," a woman was married if her gravestone has the words *consort, relic* (widow) or *uxor, ux, vx* (Latin for wife).

Returning to our example of the Smith family, we find that after Peter G. Smith died in 1820, Nancy Smith, his wife, married W.E. Rowley some years later and died October 8, 1859 at age fifty-eight. This information comes from her gravestone, not from other sources. Note that if her age at death was correct, she would have been only nineteen when Peter G. died, barely old enough to have had the four children that she was left to support in Peter's will. This raises the question of whether she might have been Peter's second wife. Further investigation and some consultation with the town historian revealed that in 1807, Eleazer Andrews, who lived in the same town, willed money to "the natural children of my deceased daughter Sarah, the late wife of Peter Smith, heretofore of this place." Was this the same Peter Smith? Censuses, tax lists or assessments may answer that question. Since there were no other Peter Smiths in the county from 1785 to 1820, and if Sarah were about Peter's age (she would have been about twenty to twenty-four in 1807) it is probable that Sarah was Peter G. Smith's first wife. She had had at least two children before her death (which occurred before 1807), because her father's will refers to "children."

Why do we assume that it was some years later that she married Rowley? Because she was listed as head of household in the early 1820's on censuses and tax lists. We also know, from maps and deeds, that Rowley lived next door. By 1827, Nancy Smith's name disappears from the assessment list, yet Walter E. Rowley's name remains. The assumption is that they had married by 1827.

From all these bits of information, we learn that Peter G. Smith married twice, had several children by his first wife, and died, with four children, before his second wife, who later remarried. Putting various facts together has told us a great deal about these people.

However, in pulling together such pieces of information, always be careful not to assume too much. Ask yourself if there is more than one possible explanation to fit the facts. Use common sense, arithmetic and your knowledge of human nature, along with the facts you have uncovered, to try to arrive at the most logical interpretation.

Ethnic Variations

All ethnic groups have their own customs and traditions about inheritance. The above illustration—uncovering and working with the Smith family vital statistics—has involved a particular geographic location within an English/ Dutch heritage. Each locality, era and culture produces its own unique characteristics. For example, certain family names may predominate at a given time. If you are researching Spanish names in Colorado, for instance, be aware of which surname on either side of the hyphen to look up. Alfonso Díaz-Pérez's last name is Díaz. Pérez was his mother's maiden name.

In the English tradition, a will tended to follow primogeniture, that is, to leave the family property to the eldest son, cash to the other sons and much less cash to the daughters. Although this practice was abandoned by law by 1811, it continued under disguised forms much later than that date. Some English wills could be quirky by our standards. In one case, a husband left his childless wife the household furniture and his brother his real estate! Brother ended up marrying the wife, a common practice.

In contrast, Dutch wills left property and cash to both sons and daughters, apparently according to a pattern of equitable distribution and need. If a son or son-in-law had already received property or cash from the decedent, his inheritance was reduced by the value of the previous gift. If an heir had not been blessed with affluence through no fault of his or her own, papa tried to make that up at his death.

Genealogies

In addition to cemetery lists, vital statistics and church records, there are genealogies written for specific surnames (family names) and related other families. Check with your local historical society, genealogy group or in area archives for the surname that you are researching. Chances are that local groups have accumulated some information on a few families who were neighbors in a specific locale. Even if it is listed only in manuscript form it may be available to you.

Family names, like ethnic groups, are associated with specific geographic locations. Families usually arrived within a specific time period and settled near each other. For example, a group of Moravians from Pennsylvania moved to Old Salem, North Carolina, in the 18th century. The chances are that someone has done research on them at their point of entry or of settlement. Who does not associate the Lees with Virginia or the Roosevelts with New York? Families can lend their name to an area. When twelve out of seventy-five names on a town deed are Spencer, and they settle the town en masse in the 1750's to 1760's in eastern New York, even though sixty or more other families trickle in, the name of the town, not surprisingly, will be Spencers' Town. When a group of Spencers leaves this town in the early 1800's to move west to greener pastures, and they build a town at about the same time that the Erie Canal was being dug through the middle of it, the town is called Spencer's Basin. (Later it became known as Spencerport.)

Of course, not every surname has a genealogy written about it, and you should beware of books published as genealogies of everyone ever bearing a particular surname. Those books are about the *surname*, not necessarily about *families* with that surname. They are not always accurate and do not help the house historian. True genealogies are about people, not about names alone.

For example, there is a book about the Light surname which is written as if Light were exclusively an English surname. Most Lights were not English in origin, even though the surname Light is an English word. Most were German Lichts who translated their name for pronunciation reasons. Even so, not all were German. In the case of the author's surname, the origin was "Lloyd" which means "light" in Welsh. The oral history "story:" after the Revolution, two Welsh brothers jumped a British ship in Baltimore harbor, because they did not want to return to England. They changed their name to Light to avoid discovery. The "evidence" (oral history "proof", See Chapter 13) is that there is a Light Street in Baltimore. Whether or not this story is true, it points out how often American surnames were translated, shortened or otherwise changed.

Other Genealogical Sources

School records, social organizational rosters and civil-servant lists all are possible sources of ancillary data that can help make the individuals you are researching come alive as real personalities and flesh out your house history. And, if you are lucky enough to locate letters or diaries, you may have a gold mine of details. These writings often mention houses and barns that are being built. They also are fun to read and are guaranteed to add zest to your search and brighten your day.

The documents discussed in last these two chapters—mortgages, wills and letters of administration and genealogical sources—all contribute to the discovery of data about the house you are researching. In the majority of cases no one piece of information will supply answers to all your questions. House historians must dig and dig, like all researchers, whether they be in the humanities or the sciences. Eventually, there is the satisfaction of finding an answer— much like the story of the old man in the reading room of the New York Public Library. It was deathly quiet, everyone glued to a book, when suddenly the old man shattered the silence with a "Whooee!" The startled researchers just smiled and started clapping. Obviously he had found an answer to a question that he had been working on for years.

12

Reading Old Handwriting

As you have seen from the previous chapters, your house history search may lead you in pursuit of old records—wills, deeds, mortgages, letters. Because many of these documents exist in their original handwritten form, you will want to accustom yourself to reading 18th- and 19th-century handwriting. This chapter will demonstrate some of the most common variations in early spelling and handwriting you will encounter in your search.

Importance of Reading Older Documents

Even if some documents have been partially or completely transcribed, you will want, whenever possible, to have the benefit of reading them firsthand. Being familiar with old handwriting puts you in better control of the old material. This will enable you to dig out any information *not* transcribed that is of help to your house history. It actually is fun to work with such primary sources. Holding and reading an aged piece of paper written on by someone long ago personalizes the document.

Two very practical reasons should encourage you to go to original material rather than the typewritten (or handwritten) transcriptions frequently available from genealogists or town historians. The first reason is because our forefathers had a casual attitude regarding spelling, especially names. For example, there were a number of different versions of what might be the same name (e.g., Lovisa, Louisa and Lovinia). Furthermore, rarely used and unfamiliar first names (e.g., Staats, Nehemiah and Asahel) easily could be (and have been) transcribed incorrectly. Transcribers rarely made notations about whether a name was difficult to read, so the resulting, nicely typed lists appear "official," but may have mistakes.

Town, county, city and federal government ledgers are copies of the originals. Over the years, as ledgers wore out, and as many of them were recopied, mistakes were made. Nevertheless, they still may be more accurate than other transcriptions. Where possible, go to the original, or the earliest copy you can locate.

The second reason for learning to read the handwriting yourself is the extra tidbit of information that a transcriber may not have included, but which you can extract as you read the documents. Most transcribers are genealogists. The genealogist primarily is looking for dates: births, deaths and marriages. While that information can be useful to a house historian, what can be more important is *where* the statistics took place: *what* town, church or cemetery, for example. Or, it may be important to find out other details—for example a wife's maiden name. *She* may have inherited the house and property from her family. Because she is female, her married name, not her maiden name, appears as grantee in the title chain. Unless you know the maiden name, you have no clue as to how the property was acquired. For such reasons, it is helpful to read the original documents, rather than a transcription. You may find something that answers one of your questions, but which the transcriber did not think important enough to transcribe.

Most of the documents handwritten in English are from the 18th and 19th centuries. There are earlier records, of course, especially in Virginia, Connecticut and Massachusetts. There are also early handwritten records, in Dutch, French, Spanish and German, some of which have been translated into English. Because the primary language used in the United States was English and because most of these records were written in it, we are restricting our discussion of deciphering handwriting to those in English.

Although some of the examples given will illustrate letter and number formation earlier than the 18th century, we are using primarily 18th- and 19th-century samples here. Samples earlier than this are mostly for specific words that have a high frequency of occurrence in English, such as *the, and* and *that,* or are Latin legal terms still used today. Also, samples of abbreviations that were still being used in the 18th century will be given.

Reading 18th- and 19th-century handwriting could be the key to unlocking the reams of information found in old letters and diaries. Although it may take some time to get used to, it really is not difficult, and soon you will be amazing yourself (or your clients) by the ease with which you can decipher old documents.

Style

During your research you will encounter a variety of handwriting styles, including: beautiful yet undecorated clear script; beautiful, wavy, hard-to-read flourishes; square handwriting; backhand; sophisticated scrawls; childlike scratchings with inkblots all over—in other words, virtually all the various possibilities that exist today.

Some of these stylistic differences are explained by custom. For example, people who were naturally left-handed were not allowed to be. They were forced to use their right hands because of numerous superstitions. Children showing a preference for using the left hand were discouraged from using it. Some "lefties," however, did go on writing left-handed, using a pen with a chisel-cut angled to the left.

Another reason for stylistic differences was that many people, even though literate, wrote only on rare occasions, so their handwriting appears childlike, as if they were having trouble forming letters. They were! This style of handwriting usually will not be found in the text of legal documents, but rather in the signatures. You find this on original deeds, or in notes or letters, such as those found in orphan court records.

Styles of handwriting also were dictated by the writing tools used. Around the beginning of the 17th century the quill pen was changed from a squarish chisel-cut on the end to a pointed cut. This development permitted greater speed in writing, but at the same time the pointed nib made it easier to accidently stab the paper, creating inkblots. It was not until 1830 that the steel pen nib was introduced, and within several years it was used universally. This invention allowed for a greater increase in writing speed, but it was not as flexible as the quill. It also initiated the development of non-corrosive inks, as the steel nib— unlike the quill—would not long withstand the common ink made of copper sulfate, tree galls and iron salt!

The following penmanship samples illustrate a variety of writing styles common to the 18th century.

Robert Storm (1795)   Jacob Ford (1795)

Another signature of Jacob
Ford and one of Abraham Yates

said Timothy Brainard &
Elizabeth have hereunto set
their hands

Timothy Brainard
his Elisabeth X Braynard
mark
(1795)

Note Elizabeth/Elisabeth and Brainard/Braynard.

to exercise strict discipline. On the 24 of September 1789 The Rev. David Porter was ordained to the pastoral care of the church & congregation. The church from the Last mentioned date to the year 1799 had various cases of discipline, but all difficulties were harmoniously setled without one instance of Excomunication. Till this . . .

An excerpt from the heading of a town tax list:

A Tax List of the District of Kinderhook Pursuant to an Act of the Legislature of the State of New York Entitled an Act for Raising the Sum of Two Million & Five Hundred Thousand Dollars by Tax within this State Passed 23rd Day of October 1779.

Repetition

Repetition is the key to learning any new skill, and reading old handwriting is a skill. A simple way to ease yourself into reading handwritten documents is to first read some early 20th-century—sometimes typewritten—deeds and mortgages. You will soon be familiar with the language used in the various parts of these documents. Once you feel comfortable with this jargon, it will be easier to read these early documents. You will see that legalese has not changed that much in 200 years.

Capitals

As you peruse 19th-century records, notice that—compared with today—more words were customarily capitalized. For instance, the first two or three words of most documents were capitalized (e.g., "This Indenture Made . . ."). Months and proper names of people and places also were capitalized. Other than these rules, capitalization appears to have been random. The reasons for this are not readily apparent. Perhaps capitalization was haphazard or whimsical, as the writer fancied. Or, perhaps words believed particularly important to the context by the clerk or scribe were capitalized. Or, perhaps there actually was a system of capitalization, but, if so, it was so complicated that it would take a doctoral thesis to understand and explain its rules. Whatever the reasons for these varied capitalizations, they are unrelated to your research. Just remind yourself not to be put off or misled by capital letters unexpectedly appearing in the middle of sentences.

The next two samples are 19th-century handwriting with random capitalization. The first is from a deed, the second sample is the beginning of a survey description taken from a surveyor's field notes.

This Indenture, Made the nineteenth Day of July in the year of our Lord one thousand Eight hundred and thirty-seven Between Henry Hogeboom one of the Masters in chancery in and for the State of New York dwelling in Hudson in the County of Columbia of the first part, and Eli Mosier of the Same place of the Second part,

Lease Granted to Adam Dingmans October 22nd 1736. Beginning at a certain Rock of the East side of the Kings road that leads from Claverack to Kinderhook & Near a wing Gate that opens to go to the aforesaid Dingmans House & near a Small run of water to the North of said rock And Running from thence

Unusual "Ss"

As you look more closely at the script of the tax list on page 153, notice the unusual looking *f* with a small cursive *s* after it in *"Passed."* It is a double "s"

(ss): ✆

Sometimes you will find an "ss" that looks like a fancy *p*, other times like *ff*. The "ff" occurred when a writer was influenced by German script. Remember, spelling was not regularized in the United States until after 1783, when Noah Webster published what became popularly known as *Webster's Spelling Book*. Its universal acceptance was even later. So, you may run into

✆ 's

when there should only be an *s*, as correct spelling was not always used.

In addition to these ✆'s, some other letters were formed differently from today's. An *H*, for example, can look like

FC or TC: ℋ ,

but generally you can figure out the letters from the context.

Deciphering the Unreadable

Once you are familiar with the vocabulary used in deeds or other records, you often will be able to decipher odd letters and whole words, from their context. However, if you cannot decipher an individual word or letter, search methodically for a similar letter on the page which you *can* read. This should help you decipher the first letter. If the letter is still unreadable, try to form the bothersome letter yourself on paper. Sometimes that will spark recognition.

If it is an isolated letter with none comparable on the page, hold the page up at an angle as if you were using a drawing board. This gives you a different visual angle and may help you decipher the word. Or, if you are at the courthouse, ask someone else in the room—possibly someone more experienced at reading old writing—what it looks like to them. If it remains a mystery, go on to something else and return to the troublesome page a while later. By then it may be easier to recognize. Be assured, that as you gain more experience, it will become much easier to decipher such words and letters.

Sound It Out

If your eyes do not give you a clue to deciphering the letter or word, try your ears. Sound the word aloud, the way many of us were taught to read, keeping individual letters or letter groups together. Sometimes reading aloud the phrases in which the troublesome word is found can spark recognition, because of the context. Or, the word may have been misspelled, further compounding the problem. Often hearing a misspelled word spoken aloud will make it comprehensible.

Letter Formation in Early Records

The following list gives examples of the most common ways that letters were formed in the 18th and 19th centuries.

The letters that can cause the most confusion are *d, e* and *o:*

= dwelling; = one.

The next most confusing is the *s:* = said. An *L* can look like an *S:* = Large.

Occasionally *K* and *R* are hard to distinguish, but again, the context usually will help determine which it is:

= King; = Running.

On a few occasions a *Z* has appeared to be a fancy *T* or *L:*

= Zachariah. Again context is the main clue.

Interchangeable Letters

Another source of confusion in reading old handwriting arises from the fact that two major deviations from our modern alphabet are found in old documents. Until almost 1840, the differences between an *I* and a *J* were indistinguishable. Many Biblical names—such as John, Isaac, Joseph, Jesse, James and Israel—and their ethnic variations were popular ways to name children. Often it is impossible to discover a middle name because only the initial *J* or *I* is given, and the reader cannot distinguish between them. Either letter can look like a 20th-century *J*, or, at other times an *I*, because they frequently were made with the bottom half of the letter below the line on a page:

Your confusion may be compounded with an *s*:

Ǫßaac = Isaac or an *ss* spelling error *Ǫefe* = Jesse.

The other major deviation from the modern alphabet is found in the capital letters *U* and *V*. These often were written the same way, although the lower case *u* and *v* were different. Sometimes a wiggly line similar to an accent mark was placed over the *u* in order to distinguish it from a *v* or an *n*: *ũ* .

This diacritical mark is one of the few accepted ways of punctuating that you will see.

Punctuation

Punctuation as we know it did not exist on handwritten documents until the 20th century, so do not expect it to help in separating "ideas" or clauses within a sentence. Dots, dashes and sometimes commas or colons, all were accepted means of separating phrases and sentences, but they may or may not have been used. Dashes after a written number were used to list or itemize objects, much as we would use a comma today. The following are three samples from the 19th century.

> the bedroom on the second floor one half
> the front room on the first floor the
> dwelling house and the one half the sty
> or hog pen
>
> 1845

> Sept 11th we took a Line Boat at Amsterdam; for 1 1/2 cents per mile, meals extra, (it is worthy of remark that we had the extra along with us, in the shape of a chicken pie etc.). Well it was a dear little boat by the name of "Jackson" - the thing that they dignified by the name of "Ladies cabin" was about as large As our Mother's pantry, and the big shelf very much such a thing as they gave me to sleep on, and called a borth — The other Cabin might be a fraction larger than Dr. Foote's bedroom & served for Gents. cabin, sitting room, parlor etc.
>
> -1834

Dear Sir

    Your cider-brandy is now in our store - I have been offered 40 cents per gallon for it, <u>first proof</u>, which will probably bring it near 45 cents - It can remain here as long as you choose to have it, free of expense - or I will sell it at the highest price I can get -

        Yours Respectfully   J. Olmsted

                              1835

    Abbreviations of given names had a variety of punctuations. A "few rules" are listed below:

- a colon after a name indicated an abbreviation of the name (*Fran*: = Francis);
- a line through a name (*Ed* = Edward);
- a line under a final letter raised above the line (*Anc*^{w} = Andrew) indicated omission of part of a name;

- a line written over a letter meant that a letter had been omitted, often an

m, n or *an* (*Hanah* = Hannah).

Abbreviations

    Many frequently used abbreviations were developed by scribes to cut down on the time it took to copy, or on the amount of paper or parchment used. Being able to recognize these abbreviations is a great help in reading old documents. The following analysis explains many common abbreviations. Even these, however, were not standardized, and other variations were perfectly acceptable. (More complete lists are noted in Glossaries A and B, the former containing common names, the latter common words.) Some of these abbreviations still are used today, but always with periods following them. If more than one variation occurred, all are included here.

    By far the most common method of abbreviation used the first two to four letters of the word with the final one to three letters often raised above the others:

chh = church; *Orig*^{l} = original; *survd* = surveyed.

    Perhaps the second most common method of abbreviation employed the first two to four letters of the word:

Capt = Captain; *def* = default; *Inq*. = inquiry; *Mar* = March; *N*/° = north; *Test*. = teste or witness.

    A third method of abbreviating used the first and last letter of the word:

Cd = continued; *Et* = east; *m*^{r} = Mr. (mister); *pd* = paid; *sd* =said.

A more complicated method evolved using various letters from the beginning, middle or end of a word:

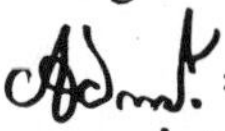 = administration;  = clerk;  = Mrs. (mistress);  = plaintiff;  = receipts.

Then, of course, there were abbreviations involving a combination of methods, such as

 = aforesaid.

There are several words that employed more than one method of abbreviation:

 and  = defendant;  and  = August;  and  and  = account;  and  and 

= September. Some of these and other variants are examples of dual spellings or spelling mistakes.

High Frequency Words and Latin Legalese

The final group of abbreviations deals with words that are high frequency words in English. That is, they occur frequently in common usage, or are words that are generally used, Latin legal terms. The following are examples in alphabetical order of these commonly occurring abbreviations.

The best example still in current usage is the ampersand for *and*: &. The following are other earlier variations of the ampersand, which itself is a contraction of "and per se and:"

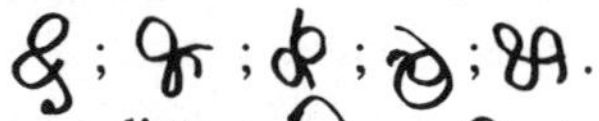

ditto = 

Locus Sigit, which means "seal place," replaced the seal of the testator. (It does not mean "legal signature," as commonly supposed.)

 or .

par-; per-; pre- was shortened to several variants: 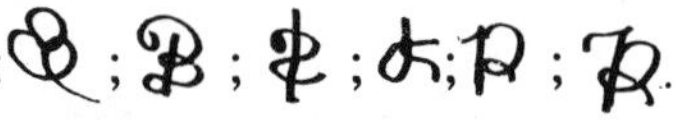

Here are some examples of its usage:  = presence of me; 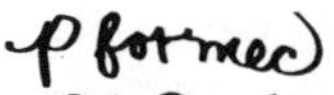 = performed; 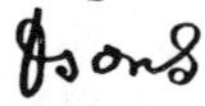 = persons; 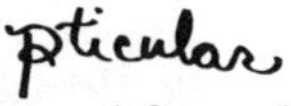 = particular; 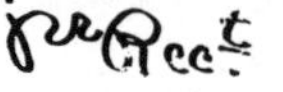 = per receipt. The modern % sign evolved from this.

Suprascriptum, which means "as written above," = .

that = *handwritten symbols* or *handwritten symbols*.

the = *handwritten symbols* ; *handwritten symbols* ; *handwritten symbols*

them = *handwritten symbols*

Videlicet, which means "namely" or "to wit," is commonly known as viz=
handwritten symbols or *handwritten symbols*.

Numbers

Numbers, like letters, changed over the years. The following are samples of typical number shapes.

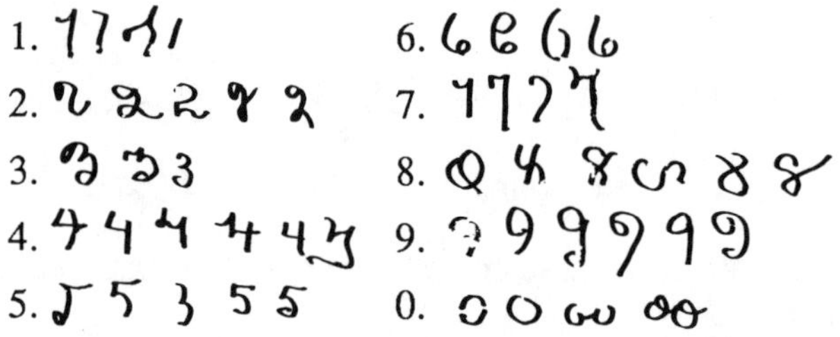

1. *handwritten numbers*   6. *handwritten numbers*

2. *handwritten numbers*   7. *handwritten numbers*

3. *handwritten numbers*   8. *handwritten numbers*

4. *handwritten numbers*   9. *handwritten numbers*

5. *handwritten numbers*   0. *handwritten numbers*

Although it generally is easier to decipher numbers than letters, you may have problems with certain numbers. The incomplete 5 with no "hat" on top can look like a 3: *handwritten symbol*

handwritten symbol . The 6 made with two strokes:
can appear to be a 0 if the right-hand stroke is almost the same size as the left. A 9 with the left-hand stroke going straight up:

handwritten symbol can look like a 4. The early 8 that looks like a circle with a line through it:
handwritten symbol looks like a 0 with an extra flourish. Some of these numbers resembled certain letters, but usually it is apparent from the context that they were supposed to be numbers.

You will be helped by the fact that the abbreviations for ordinal numbers traditionally used the last two letters of the word: *st*, *nd*, *rd*, and *th*, as we do today.
They looked like this: *handwritten* 67 *st*   42 *nd*   53 *rd*   97 *th*

Now that you are acquainted with early letter and number formation and have an idea how to approach reading early script, you are ready to tackle such documents at your courthouse. Until you gain more experience, spend only a couple of hours the first few times, or you may find it tiring. Soon you will develop the knack of reading old handwriting. As with all skills, time and experience improve the result.

13

Secondary Sources and Other Places to Find Answers

In previous chapters we have discussed primary sources available for researching your house. These primary sources are your very best, because you can draw conclusions directly from what you see and read. You apply to them your own analysis, and your perceptions are not influenced by the perspective of another person who has already interpreted these sources for you. This does not mean that secondary sources should be ignored. They can help *you* form conclusions, but usually should not be weighted as heavily as primary sources. This chapter explains pertinent secondary sources and how to use them.

Finding Secondary Sources

Because a primary source is a record made at the time of a transaction, the original legal document may be unavailable—stored in a lawyer's office or, if it is over 100 years old, probably long since destroyed. Thus, secondary sources often are easier to find than primary sources. More importantly, some of these used primary sources that since have been destroyed or disbursed. Prime examples of secondary sources are 19th-century county histories, written to celebrate the national centennial, and published ca. 1876-1880. Such county histories often include brief biographies of individuals prominent in the latter half of the 19th century, some of whom may have a connection to the house you are researching.

Other secondary sources are 20th-century town histories. These can be purchased from town historians for a nominal fee. They vary in their depth of research. Some are excellent examples of primary research, while others are a combination of factual material interspersed with folklore. The folklore adds color, and kernels of truth probably are buried within the tales, but their value may be primarily to impart a general "feel" for an area.

Oral History

Oral tradition stories have two elements, the "story" and the proof. The proof may be an isolated fact, but it later is associated with the "story," and sounds plausible. Actually, the story is a folk myth, such as the one that Dutch bricks commonly were used as ballast on ships coming to the colonies from Holland. In this case the "proof" is the Dutch-style brick house. However, although some small, pale yellow bricks were exported to New Netherlands by the Dutch early in the 17th century, they now are found only in archaeological sites, not in houses still extant.

Furthermore, bricks were relatively easy to make and, in areas where clay and lime were abundant, brickyards were established in New York by the mid-17th century. Also, incoming ships usually were laden not with ballast, but with articles that were not produced here, such as window glass, tea, china and hardware—expensive, not cheap, commodities.

Folk traditions, such as alligators or snakes in the city sewer system, the barred cellar window—"proof" of slave quarters; the paneled space next to the chimney opened by a "secret" means, where mothers hid children from Indians or abolitionists hid slaves fleeing on the "underground railway," a famous person who slept or ate here. Such stories are fun to listen to and to repeat, but they must be seen for what they are: stories. As you do more research, you will learn to recognize many of them and their variations.

How does one go about separating fact from fiction in such oral tradition stories? Certain key elements in any story are assumed to be true. Isolate each of these and ask questions about it. Weigh its probability, taken on its own. Get some perspective. The truth or distortion of each of these elements usually can be established.

Ghosts

There are houses which, when entered, spark an unexpected emotional, sometimes irrational, reaction. A certain house may elicit this reaction in more than one person who enters it alone. Although there has been little hard evidence of ghosts, it is generally conceded that they do exist.

If, on entering a house, you feel "spooked," be rational. Look around to see what it is that makes your hair "rise" or your footstep exploratory. Is it because the house has been abandoned for years and its rotted floors are dangerous? Is it the huge honeybee hive that is poking through the ceiling while hundreds of bees travel in and out through the broken pane in the window? Is it the breeze flowing through cracks in the door and window frames causing groaning or whistling noises that spook you? Is it the waist-high weeds that prevent you from seeing what you may be about to trip on or into? In other words, is it certain natural conditions resulting from the house's age or abandonment that make you fearful? These probably have nothing to do with ghosts, but rather with your own fear.

If you can return to the house when the conditions have changed—with a friend, for instance, or when the owners are in it or after it has been renovated—you probably will not have the same spooky feelings. It is probable that your initial reaction was the result of being frightened by your own apprehensions. If, however, under the changed circumstances, you still feel an extra presence or unexplainable phenomena, there may be a ghost. In this case, when doing your research, pay close attention to the cemetery records. If you can pinpoint the date of a death under strange circumstances, consult a newspaper from around that time to see if anything was reported. There may even be a local story about an unusual or untimely death, or even about a ghost.

Some people are more sensitive than others to ghosts, and some houses appear to be more susceptible to "unusual" happenings. If you feel such "vibes," go for it. Research your "hunch." You may be correct. However, before you report your findings to the owners, be sure that you have cleared with them previously —preferably at the on site inspection—as to how much they really want to know. Most people will want to know "all," but some do not want to know about something unpleasant which may have happened in their house. It could be as extreme as a murder, rape or some other devastating horror which they would be uncomfortable knowing about.

Church Histories

In addition to town histories, other local institutions, such as churches, may have produced a history to celebrate their 100th (or later) anniversary. In addition to listing the ministers and when they served, a church history may list other church officials, such as deacons and trustees, some of whom may have lived in your house. The church history probably will discuss how the church changed architecturally over the years. If there is a similar window, door, siding, etc. in your house, a church history may prove valuable to you for comparison purposes. At the least, it will give you a time frame in which the changes occurred in your house. Window changes, bay additions, exterior gingerbread and so on, often started as fads and caught on in an area at a particular period of time. If your house exhibits details that exist in other local buildings, the chances are that they were built or added on within a ten-year period.

Telephone Company Histories

Relatively small, independently owned telephone companies sometimes published the histories of their development from scattered "centrals," placed in several locations, to concentrated transmission from fewer locations. If you have a little building attached to your house or in your yard, or if odd wiring has been located in a wall—often in the kitchen area—your house may have been a "central" for your neighbors. In rural areas "centrals" sometimes were located in every eight to ten houses, depending on how far apart they were.

The local telephone company history may provide information with which you can confirm this. If no local telephone company history was published, call the phone company and ask for the person in charge of public relations. If they do not have a history, they may be able to tell you of someone in the community who has done research on it. Although being a telephone "central" played a small role in the histories of only a few homes, it will add local color to those which were centrals.

The Masons

Another possible local source for information on your home may be the history of freemasonry in your area. Your library may have such a history.

By 1733, Masonic Lodges had been established in America. Initially the local lodges met in individual homes or taverns, and always served refreshments. The minutes of the meetings listed the location of the meeting, such as "resolved, that we move to the house of Widow Abigail Swift . . ." and also disbursements, such as, "Paid Widow Swift thirteen shillings for refreshments. Also four shillings for use of room." Because of the houses and taverns mentioned, the minutes of local lodges can be useful in identifying who lived there and when. If the house or tavern had a room devoted to regular meetings, it is possible that various Masonic symbols, such as a square and compass, or the ark, were used as decorations on the walls and ceilings, or on the exterior of the house (e.g., cut-out bargeboards along the roof edge). By the last quarter of the 19th century, Masons were building temples and no longer met in taverns and houses. Masonic minutes often were compiled and published and can be found in local libraries.

Account Ledgers

Account ledgers from a neighborhood general store may provide helpful information. Often these have found their way to the local history division of your library or historical society. People relied heavily on barter and credit, so remarkably detailed records were kept, listing the person's name, date, item sold, and amount paid or credited. If the business sold such things as wire nails, stovepipe and other hardware, the account book may provide dates showing when such items were purchased for your house. You then may be able to establish not only who lived in your house at a given time, but date a change or addition to the house or barn.

Photographs

Nineteenth century photographs of your house may be found at a local library or historical society, or in the possession of a previous owner or neighbor. Local historians often request that older residents try to identify old photos before their subjects are lost to memory. Otherwise, unidentified photos usually end up forgotten in someone's attic or in the "to do" file of a museum. Thus it may be difficult to locate an old photograph of your home.

If you do find a photograph, in addition to showing what the house looked like at the time, it also may show how it was landscaped. If there is no date on the photograph, it can be dated by other means. Often you have to date a photograph by the details shown in it: dress of the subjects, type of conveyance shown, or a hotel sign. If a photography studio's stamp is on the photo, you can find out what years it was in operation by looking in a city or county directory.

You may be able to have a photograph analyzed by a cataloger specializing in photography. Such catalogers can be found in photography museums. Or, a photographer specializing in reproducing early developing techniques may be knowledgeable and willing to date a photograph. Such specialists can determine the photo's approximate date by its method of development, style of composition, style and type of mounting, the paper or metal used in the mounting, the colors used in the film and mounting and the revenue stamp which may be placed on it.

Photographs can give hints of exterior details that have been changed over the years. Sometimes shadings appear in photos that are not very noticeable when looking at the structure first hand. For example, in one old photograph, outlines of a no longer extant roof railing around the roof of a first-floor entrance porch were barely visible against the white siding of the second floor. Through computer enhancement, which enlarged the photograph, the detail of the railing post could be seen accurately. Computer enhancement and enlargement can show other details in photographs, such as the number of panes in a window or the decorative work in brackets.

Newspapers

Another local source—and often a challenging one—is the newspaper. Unlike photographs, they often are readily available. However, they usually are not indexed. Or, if indexed, they probably are subject-oriented, with people's names listed only if an article centers around them. An exception is the New York Times Index, which is indexed by name as well as by subject. In some localities there may be individuals as well as genealogical societies who have published newspaper indices which are name-oriented, usually with reference to vital statistics, not home-building. Check in your neighborhood library.

This library also may have microfilmed copies of the 19th-century issues of the local town newspaper, but they, also, rarely are indexed. You have to know what year you are looking for and then patiently weed through the local notices, gossip and advertisements to find a reference, such as, "Abraham Hogle commenced building his new house this week." Perhaps you might suggest to the local genealogical society that indexing the names listed in these old local papers would be a useful project, and might even be funded by private, local foundations or, in some cases, public, state funds.

Meanwhile, you may find yourself hoping that the crick in your neck which developed from reading a vertical microfilm screen through the lower level of your bifocals will not become permanent. If the crick lasts for days, you may find yourself fervently petitioning the library trustees for a horizontal screen.

Because of this prevailing lack of indexing by name, finding information —unless you have unlimited time or your client is willing to pay for hours of searching—is often a matter of luck. It can be done, though. The author verified her grandfather's date of birth by locating a reference to it in the society column of a local 19th-century Kansas newspaper, within ten minutes of searching in Topeka. Most 19th-century papers did not list births, deaths and marriages as is done today. Rather, the articles of small-town correspondents are probably the best place to look for local "gossip," such as "So-and-so finished painting his new barn this week."

Fire Companies

If local fire-company records exist, you may find from them that your target house had a fire, and that much of the existing house dates from after the fire. In some instances, you may even find yourself needing to research a house which completely burned and no longer exists. A new house may have been built on the old foundation, but you or your client may want to know what was there originally.

Early fire-prevention measures were taken in urban centers as early as 1648 when Peter Stuyvesant, the director-general of New Netherlands, appointed four fire-masters. The first paid fire department, however, did not appear until 1678, when the city of Boston hired thirteen men and purchased a hand-operated pumper. Although major cities established fire departments in the early 18th century, many, such as those in New York City and Philadelphia, were organized as volunteer systems. It was not until the middle of the 19th century that paid fire departments became an integral part of municipal administrations.

Because of urban population density, fires could be devastating to a large area. After such a fire, structures often were rebuilt with relatively fireproof brick or stone. If the building you are researching is of veneered brick or stone, and there are other similarly constructed structures in your urban neighborhood dating from roughly the same time, this may hint that there was a large fire there in the latter part of the 19th century.

In many areas, fire-company formation proceeded on the volunteer basis already in effect in New York City and Philadelphia. From the outset, the volunteer fire company was designed as a social, almost fraternal club, concomitant with its specific function as a fire-fighting unit. The reason for combining purposes was to build camaraderie and an esprit de corps, since the members had to rely on each other in firefighting. The clubhouse and its sociability provided a means of rewarding volunteers who constantly were put in life-threatening situations. In short, keeping records of fires was not the major aim or function of the volunteer fire company.

This lack of record keeping and difficulty of retrieval of existing records is the problem you, as a house historian, will encounter. Until the late 1970's in many states, volunteer fire companies did not submit "incident reports." Thus, records of fires were not kept on a *systematic* basis unless someone died in the fire or while fighting the fire. However, if you suspect that a fire occurred in the home you are researching, contact your fire company to find out if there is a record of it.

Records were kept in a variety of ways, usually by year or by general address. In some cases, they are filed by actual house number, since the likelihood of a building fire occurring at the same house number on different streets is rare. Because retrieval of information pertaining to a fire must be done by hand, page by page, most fire companies—both paid and volunteer—are reluctant to assign valuable personnel to such a low-priority task. In some cases, a mandate must come from city hall or the county seat, or a hefty donation be given, before anyone will be assigned to look up such information. If you come to a dead end at the fire company, there are other options.

Fire chiefs or firemen often kept unofficial personal scrapbooks of fires. Because fire-company membership rosters are carefully kept, it is relatively easy to contact a past fire chief or fireman and inquire if they have kept personal records. If you live within a paid municipal district, either the fire department or the archives room in your city or, in some cases, the sheriff in your county, may have the fire records—"incident reports" of fires, kept as official records.

Another method of confirming a fire, particularly a spectacular one, is a newspaper account. It may be hard to find such a reference, however, due to lack of newspaper indexing. If you do find a reference, it may tell how much of the house was involved—your clue as to which part of the house was rebuilt.

Fire Insurance

If, via your fire company, you are unsuccessful in your attempts to track down a possible fire, try to find out who the fire-insurance company was. Some fire-insurance companies keep archives which contain original blotters or records of insurance written, surveys, sketches and drawings or descriptive records, and, if there was a fire, fire-loss records.

Benjamin Franklin organized the first effective fire-insurance company in 1752. This company, The Philadelphia Contributorship for the Insurance of Houses from Loss by Fire is still in operation. Another major early company was The Insurance Company of North America, founded in 1792. Recently it merged with Connecticut Mutual and is now called Cigna Corp. Its records from 1841 to the present are complete, while those prior to 1841 are incomplete. These earlier records do not list as many details about a house and its construction. They are adequate, however, for historical purposes.

What we know as the standard fire insurance policy was not adopted until 1943, when New York State enacted the legislation which became a prototype for other states. By the mid-19th century, however, some sort of fire-insurance coverage often was a prerequisite for obtaining a mortgage. In fact, it was written on many mortgage indentures that the mortgagor—the person who mortgages his property—must prepay the fire insurance before receiving the mortgage money. Sometimes the fire-insurance company is named in the mortgage, giving the means to start your search for the original fire-insurance blotter. Your local insurance agent may be able to help you trace the history of this company to discover where its archives are located. Companies changed hands and names, mergers took place, and sometimes companies went out of business. In the last case company records may have been donated to a local repository, such as a historical society or library, or to local fire companies.

If you can locate the archives and the fire blotter, or other records, you will have found a gold mine. The records will show the number of stories and rooms in the house, the building materials and possibly a list of contents and furnishings. The records also may include sketches, drawings and street plans, and may mention outbuildings on the property. If you compare different records for the same house, you may be able to clarify changes in ownership, as well as changes in the appearance and furnishings of the house. If you are lucky, you may even find the date of construction.

Because fire companies did not exist in rural areas—often not until well into the 20th century—fire fighters had to travel a distance, sometimes even by railroad. Thus, it was difficult in rural areas to get insurance against fire damage. It was not until 1935 that rural fire insurance was offered to its members by the National Grange of the Patrons of Husbandry. This organization, which was founded in 1867 in Washington, D.C, was established to protect the social, economic and political interests of the farmers. It served to alleviate the isolation inherent in farm life, and the Grange, as it is popularly known, became a household word in rural areas, primarily in the northern states. The national headquarters and archives are located in Keene, New Hampshire. If the house you are researching had Grange fire insurance, contact this organization.

Although these other sources of answers are varied and scattered, connecting with one of them may provide you with the specific clue you need to tie together your house history. In addition, there may be other sources unique to your locale that may provide data pertinent to the house. It may be a business or industry associated with house construction, such as a millworks or a building-materials manufacturer, a glasshouse or a brickyard, a hardware or tool factory. Each area has at least one unique quality that may be reflected, in some way, in its houses, and also helps make researching houses a fascinating pursuit.

Section III

The Paper Search/
Graphic Records

14

The Surveyor's Plat: Mapping the Country

When you begin your deed and mortgage search, you will come across a written description of the property, probably done by a surveyor, and almost certainly using specific terms common to those who describe land boundaries. Describing property in ways that are universally accepted and in language that is universally understood is essential if land is to be bought and sold. The property changing hands must be identifiable to persons who have not seen it before. This chapter will describe the two kinds of surveys you will run across in the United States.

Using a Survey

The survey is a means of adequately and accurately describing the outside dimensions of the property. Usually, this means a description of its boundaries. You may not always be concerned with or need such a description when doing a house history. However, these descriptions, depending upon how complete they are, could be very helpful. Indeed, the more complete, *written* descriptions can be so clear that, if need be, a rough map can be drawn from them. A description may give you a clue as to where a house was located on the property. Or, it may show you that this property, although belonging to the same person, is not the property that the house you are searching is on.

If you can find a surveyor's *plat*—a map of the property made by a surveyor —it can show you the exact shape and size of the property and indicate who the neighbors are. It may locate geographic and man-made features: buildings, stone walls, dug ponds, etc. are shown. Thus, a plat can tell you a great deal about the setting of a house, or changes in the property boundaries over the years, especially if you are lucky enough to find several plats to compare. Again, you may not need them, or they may not exist, but if they do, they may be very helpful if you have learned to "read" them.

Variations in Land Descriptions by State

Depending upon which state you are doing your house history in, the description, or deed language, will conform to one or the other of two systems used to describe land throughout the United States. Why two systems? Because the United States is so large that westward settlement took centuries to accomplish, and during that time the land-surveying system was revamped the better to make wholesale descriptions of the federal government's vast landholdings. During the 17th and most of the 18th centuries, the English system of survey-description (indiscriminate surveys) was used as the more easterly part of the country was being settled. By the 19th century, a different system had been established. This latter was called the Federal Township and Range system, and was used to transfer quickly large tracts of land from the public domain to private ownership. Both the early system of indiscriminate surveys and the Township and Range system of surveying are still in use— sometimes in the same state. Thus, it may be helpful, especially if you are doing house histories as a business, to understand how each of them describes land.

State-land States (Indiscriminate Survey System)

Those states using the indiscriminate survey system are called state-land states. They include the original thirteen—New Hampshire, Massachusetts, Rhode Island, Connecticut, New York, Pennsylvania, New Jersey, Delaware, Maryland, Virginia, North Carolina, South Carolina and Georgia—plus Maine, Vermont, West Virginia, Kentucky, Tennessee, Texas and Hawaii.

In the original colonies land was granted by the monarch or his governor, or by certain private citizens by permission from the monarch. Later, when these colonies became states, the state granted the land. These grants were made to private individuals or groups of individuals on a request basis, as the lands were petitioned for. (That is, you asked for it and sometimes got it.) Thus the land grants often were surveyed independently as the need arose, and with little reference to other land grants being surveyed. Such surveys were *indiscriminate* because they were not tied into a larger survey grid (as in the Township and Range system), and each was done at a different time and independently of other surveys already done in the area.

These state-land states used either a simple bounds description, in which boundary features were named, or they used the more exact metes and bounds description or survey. (These descriptions varied in their complexity, and will be explained in greater detail in the next chapter.) A very *simple bounds description* might read: ".... and bounded on the West by lands of said Johnson ..." A more informative, *metes and bounds description* might read: "...then Westerly two chains to a white oak tree in the corner of lands of Johnson ..." An actual metes and bounds *survey* of the same property might read: "... thence

South 40° West two chains ten links to a white oak tree on the line common with lands of said Johnson . . ." The last description gives you the exact compass bearings along the property line, so there is much less room for error than in the other descriptions. Such a survey began at the edge of the property, usually at an easily recognizable point, a more or less permanent landmark, such as a road.

Public-domain States (Township and Range System)

Those states using the Township and Range system—the remaining thirty western and southern states—are called public-domain states. Here, the federal government, rather than individual states or colonies, had controlled and granted lands in the public domain from territories acquired of various foreign nations, such as England, Spain and France. These lands later were divided into the public-domain states.

This new survey system was adopted by Congress in 1785 and used a systematic grid pattern as a method of keeping track of the vast landholdings that the federal government owned. In the final count—excluding Alaska—over one billion acres of land were disposed of. The adoption of this uniform grid pattern provided a pre-established structure within which the government could more efficiently transfer ownership.

When the federal government granted land in these territories, it also recognized previous private land claims as a special category. They were incorporated into the system, and the township grid continued around them on all sides. Such private land claims usually had existed prior to the opening by the federal government of land for settlement. For example, in the territories acquired after the Revolutionary War, it was customary to recognize valid French and Spanish deeds in specific areas or villages, such as the French deeds in Vincennes, Indiana.

In contrast to the randomness of the indiscriminate survey already described, the Township and Range system superimposed a rigid "township" grid over the *whole* of each territory or state affected by it, dividing land into similarly sized *townships*. The land was surveyed wholesale—most of it during the same time period—rather than in irregular pieces as buyers expressed interest. Using the north/south meridians and east/west baselines as a guide, surveyors established township lines at six-mile intervals. These townships measured 6 miles by 6 miles, or 36 square miles in area. They then were subdivided into *sections* one-mile square (640 acres in area) and assigned *section* numbers. The section, in turn, was subdivided into four 160-acre *quarters* labeled NW, NE, SW, and SE. Finally, these *quarters* were further subdivided into 40-acre *lots*.

Although the Federal Township and Range system was mandated by the federal government, each individual territory or state was surveyed as a whole and not necessarily in relation to other adjacent territories. Also, within each territory it was decided by the surveyors, on location, just how far ahead to survey, keeping in mind the Indian threat. Thus, some states and territories were surveyed to a specific western point where the survey was stopped, and continued only at a later date when the problem was eliminated. Also, because surveys always started from some section farther east in any territory or state, there are townships on the western edges of some states that do not contain full mile-square sections, because the surveyor ran into the boundary of another territory and had to stop before the full township distance had been reached.

Boundary Problems: Irregularities and Exceptions

In contrast to the grid system in the public-domain states, in the state-land states often only a survey of town boundaries preceded the granting of a town deed. Only after it was purchased—by a group, or by speculators, or by an individual—was a detailed survey made for individual plats. Consequently, this latter survey often will contain references to houses or barns built by persons already living there. As with the township grid systems, these pre-existing plots were incorporated and worked around. However, this indiscriminate method of town planning resulted in many more oddly-shaped plats and town boundaries than occurred with the grid system. It also resulted in changes in town and even state boundaries as various jurisdictions haggled over ownership.

These discrepancies could affect a house historian's search if the jurisdiction—the town or county name—in which your target house is located changed sometime in the past. However, it is not difficult to find out if this happened. (Town historians usually will know.) If this is the case, then when using 19th-century or earlier records, you sometimes may have to go to an adjacent town to locate the town minutes or records for that particular period of time. They may contain survey references, road lists, or vital statistics pertinent to your house.

Also, in the late 18th century many older towns and counties in the state-land states surveyed still unalloted lands following or adapting the ideas presented by the 1785 Township and Range system. If your property was one of those adjacent to the line of change, then the adjacent boundary might have changed. This will be indicated in the deed.

Tract Indices and Indiscriminate Plat Indices

Because they were done in different ways at different times, Township and Range surveys (the grid system) and indiscriminate surveys may be filed differently. Indeed, the latter may or may not be intact and available anymore.

If your deed description makes some reference to a survey and a surveyor (e.g., ". . . according to a survey done by David Burr in 1841"), this only establishes that a survey was done. It does not mean that it still exists. If the plat was a subdivision of a large property, for example, and this plat was one of many completed at the time by the same surveyor, the maps may have been preserved at the courthouse or removed to an archive. If the plat is of an isolated property, however, the chances are that its map never was filed and is lost, or may exist in private hands somewhere.

Proceed, however, by assuming that it was filed. Generally speaking, indiscriminate plats were not required to be filed consistently until the 20th century, varying by state according to statute or banking rules for mortgages. (In many areas, it has only been in the last ten years or so that banks required surveys for home mortgages.) Inquire how such maps are filed at the courthouse you are using. They may be listed under surveyor, grantor, grantee, town or road name. You may be lucky and locate the plat. If so, it may be in map form or on microfilm.

In contrast, Township and Range tracts of land are indexed somewhat differently. After massive surveys were completed to set up the Township and Range system in any given area, local federal land offices were opened to sell the land. Since the land was surveyed and lot records established and indexed by number even before the land was sold, the deeds in many of these territories were in two indices. One was a listing by tract name or number. (A "tract" varies in size. It can refer to an area as small as a quarter of a section, or as large as all the townships in a county.) The other was by deed grantor/grantee in which all former owners were recorded under the title number of the tract, rather than under the individual grantors and grantees. Thus, when searching in these indices, you must search each page to find the grantor/grantee, unless the legal description—the section, township and range numbers—is known for the individual. For instance, in identifying a 40-acre lot (that is, 1/16 of a section of 640 acres), you need to know whether it was NW, NE, SW or SE of the NW, NE, SW or SE quadrant within the mile-square section. If, for example, it was in the southwest corner of the southwest quadrant, it was called SW quarter of the SW quadrant.

Township numbers may not always follow the geographic order you would expect. In the previously cited instances where, because of the Indian threat, some far-western lands in each territory were surveyed much later than the rest of the territory, the township numbers of adjacent lands may not be in sequence with adjacent tracts surveyed earlier. Furthermore, a town may, in some cases, overlap two or more *township* boundaries because the grid surveys were not coordinated to natural geographic features, while settlements sometimes were, For instance, a town may have been founded on a creek for convenient water supply. The grid however, simply was superimposed irrespective of the creek, so that two townships could meet at the creek, and the town would lie in both of them. Make sure of your jurisdiction.

Early plat or survey maps of very large holdings (manors, plantations, ranches, and federal government holdings surveyed under the Township and Range system) often are found in state or local archives or in the Bureau of Land Management offices. In some cases, they have been marked over by officials' scribblings so many times that they are hard to read. This is particularly true of township plats in public-domain states. The tract indices may be easier to read than the plats.

Surveyors kept field notes of the properties they were working on. Thus, survey field notes may be available in addition to a plat or instead of it. These notes usually are more complete than the final map, since, in addition to showing drawings of the houses and outbuildings, they also may contain comments about the terrain or about survey and land-title problems.

15
Reading the Survey

How much you need to learn about interpreting surveys may depend upon how recent are the deed descriptions you are working with and whether you already have found enough information from other sources. If you are lucky, you may find a complete surveyor's map of your property, so the work already is done for you. If the property description is straightforward and has remained unchanged for generations, you may not feel the necessity to consult early descriptions. However, survey descriptions usually can be helpful.

At the least, these descriptions can add a further dimension to a house history. At the most, they can provide a crucial clue as to when or where the house was built. If you are doing a very complete house history, a map drawn from a good survey description is a fine addition to the final report. Or, a description may enable you to draw a rough map, making it possible to better understand your total site and its development over the years. Thus, the need for understanding surveys or for drawing maps from them can vary. Certainly, if you are learning to do house histories as a business, you should have a working familiarity with the material in this chapter and its related appendices. They are designed to give you the means of learning to understand survey descriptions, to draw crude maps from them, and to "plot" them by making an exact map from compass bearings. How much use you make of the material will depend on your own specific situation.

Variations in Descriptions and Terms Used in a Survey

Some "surveys" simply are a crude description of the property boundaries, made by walking them. No compass bearings are given or even, in some cases, distances. The description may be as sparse as:

All that land situate on the road leading from Springfield to Riverton, bordered on the East by lands of Allen Johnson, on the south by lands of Bert Johnson, on the West by an unknown owner, being 38 acres more or less.

You will have no trouble understanding this description. On the other hand, it does not tell you much. In contrast, a complete survey of this same property could read:

All that piece or parcel of land lying in the Township of Riverton, State of Illinois beginning at a point on the east side of the highway leading from Springfield to Riverton and said point being 11,616 feet westerly from the intersection of said highway with the road leading to Sangamon. From said point of beginning the following courses and distances; South 80° East 1,520 feet along lands now or formerly of Allen Johnson to a rock at the corner of lands of said Allen Johnson and lands now or formerly of Bert Johnson; thence along lands of said Bert Johnson South 10° West 1,089 feet to a point; thence North 80° West 1,520 feet to a point on the south side of the aforementioned highway; thence North 10° East 1,089 feet along said highway to the point or place of beginning. And said parcel containing 38.00 acres more or less.

This description will be less easy for you to understand than the previous example only because of the compass *bearings* used to specify the *exact* direction in which each boundary runs. (These will be explained in the next section of this chapter.) Even without understanding these as yet, you can see that this description tells a great deal more about the location and shape of the property than did the previous example.

Besides compass bearings, the only other potentially confusing terms you may come across in a deed description are the old ones used to describe length or area. Long before "feet," "yards," and "inches," surveyors used other terms to describe distance. These appear in very early deeds and include "chain," "link," "mile," "rod," and "perch." These terms came into use because early surveyors literally dragged a chain up and down hill and dale, from point to point, to measure distance. As you can imagine, great accuracy was not achieved, but this way of measuring was better than merely eyeballing a potential land holding and estimating the acreage, as in the first example given. The following list explains the terms you may come across describing distance or acreage in earlier deeds:

Length

Chain = 100 links = 66 feet = 4 rods
Link = 7.92 inches

Mile = 80 chains
Rod = perch (British) = pole = 5.5 yards = 16.5 feet

Area

Acre = 100 square chains
Rood = 40 square rods = one-quarter acre

In survey descriptions, the terms rods, poles and perches, when used to describe *distance*, will follow after the compass bearings or directions, just as will chains and links. When used to describe *area*, they will appear after the word "Containing" as in the example given above.

As you can see from these various terms, you may come across several different words designating the same length. Do not be confused by this. For instance, in early deeds the distances often are listed in rods, or sometimes in perches or poles, instead of in chains or links. Perches and poles are derived from usage in various parts of Great Britain several centuries ago.

As explained in Chapter 14, deeds for sections, quarters and lots surveyed under the Township and Range system can be described by their location within their section within their township. For example, a lot may be described as SW 1/4 of SW 1/4, sec. 10, T3N, R5W, 2nd P.M. This means that the property is in the southwestern quarter of the southwestern quadrant of section ten in township three north of the base line and range five west of the second principal meridian. This is the legal description and constitutes a summary description of the more extensive surveyor's plat.

Compass Bearings (Boundary Directions)

All surveys are made, as in any other map, in accordance with the earth's north, south, east and west axes. When a survey specifies the compass bearings of a boundary—for example, South 20° West—it is telling you *exactly* in what direction the boundary lies. In this case, its basic direction is south, with a slight leaning westward, or, south southwest.

Surveyors established these exact directions or compass bearings by using a transit, or, more recently, a theodolite—a surveying instrument with a compass on its face. This compass is a circle, sometimes called a compass "rose." To understand a compass, imagine yourself standing in the center of a large, flat, circular plain. Face north, and south is behind you, east is on your right and west is on your left. These are the basic compass directions, and land all over the United States is surveyed with these as referent points. (Illustration 62.)

COMPASS

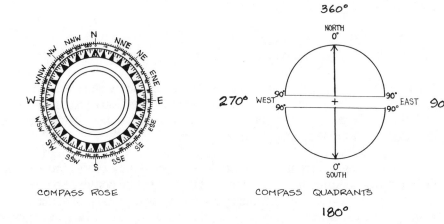

COMPASS ROSE   COMPASS QUADRANTS

With the exception of land surveyed under the Township and Range system, it is, of course, unusual to find property boundaries neatly aligned in direct north/south and east/west directions. Boundaries deviated, and still do, to allow for variations in terrain. Furthermore, surveys tend to follow already established routes, such as roads and rivers. Because of this, the compass circle or rose was, early on, divided into smaller sections to indicate the *degree* of variation from north, south, east or west.

Let us describe this in terms you may remember from high school geometry—the circle containing 360°. The compass circle starts at 0° (north) at its top. It then goes clockwise 90°, a right angle, to the east. It continues clockwise another 90° to 180°, south, and clockwise another 90° to 270°, west. It then goes the final 90° to a full 360° or, back to north. Within these 90° right-angles are further subdivisions, for example, north northeast, northeast, east northeast, etc. (Illustration 62.)

As you can see from the illustration, this is a very complex and crowded circle. To simplify working with all these subdivisions, 19th-century surveyors "cut it down to size" by working within each of the four 90° sections (quadrants) described above. Mid-top and -bottom both were 0°, while east and west were 90°. Survey descriptions were stated within each quadrant. For example, North 45° East was midway between north (top) and east (right). Or, South 60° West would be 60° up on the left arc from south (bottom). These latter examples demonstrate how much easier it was to work within a compact 90° than in a full circle—a right angle is easier to visualize and less cumbersome to work with than a 240° arc.

Whichever way the compass he used was divided, the surveyor then took an exact reading of the first compass bearing (direction) and then computed the other bearings based in this. The compass divisions provided the surveyor with a "language" in which to write down the exact bearings in a way which would be understood by others who also use this "language," usually with distances also specified for each—of every side of the property. Since a property can have three, four, five, six or more sides, depending upon natural landmarks and how it originally was divided, it is very important to be able to write such exact directions.

Converting Written Directions into Maps

The more detailed and exact the survey, the more detailed and exact the map that may be drawn from it, and such maps can be helpful to the house historian if there is no actual survey map. Even if the description is not very detailed, you may want to try to make some sense of it by converting it to a rough map. There are two ways of doing this. The easier way is to draw a map which roughly corresponds to any bearings (directions) and distances given in the description, and then pinpoint on it your buildings and the buildings of neighbors. The more complicated way is to actually "plot"—using a scale (ruler) and protractor—the compass points, and thus draw an exact map.

The remainder of this chapter gives examples of property descriptions (which vary in complexity) and helps you read your way through them. It provides a way to practice reading descriptions. It also shows you how to sketch in simple maps from these descriptions. If you wish to go further and actually "plot" an exact map, a practice guide, with step-by-step instructions, is given in Appendix B.

Rough Maps from Bounds Descriptions

Although it is an approximation and not very exact, a rough map is adequate when you need to locate general property shapes, structures and neighbors. If the description is vague, with only a few boundary markers, such as ". . . to a red oak tree . . ." and no degrees or distances given, as well as no acreage, a survey probably was not made. This is called a bounds description, and was common from the 17th to the early 19th century.

The following is a simple bounds description:

> All that certain farm of land situate, lying and being in the Town of
> Austerliz and bounded and described as follows; The said farm
> being situated on both sides of the Highway leading from the
> House of M. R. Beale to the House of William Baley and bounded
> Northerly on the farm, formerly owned by Stephen Davis

deceased. Easterly by lands of Allen M. Guildersleeve and lands
of Isaac Dean, on the South by lands of M.R. Beale and South
Westerly and Westerly by lands of M.R. Beale and William P.
Clark and computed to contain one hundred and ninety five acres
of land. more or less.

Your first question probably is, in what direction does the highway go?
Knowing that would help you find a reference point. Read further to partially
answer your question. You know a northerly boundary is the farm of Stephen
Davis and easterly are Allen M. Guildersleeve and Isaac Dean. If we assume
that the directions are being *listed in order and clockwise*, which was commonly
the case, then Isaac Dean is found south of Guildersleeve, south, southwesterly,
and westerly is M.R. Beale and westerly is William P. Clark. Now, since we see
that M.R. Beale is south on both sides of the road, William Baley must be north.
So, the road runs north and south. This road will be a reference point on a larger
map and help you to further orient the property.

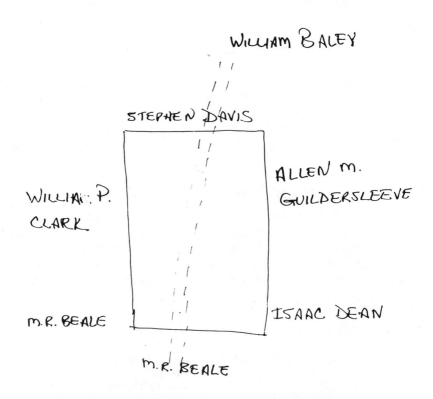

Rough Maps From Metes and Bounds Descriptions

Our second example of a property description contains, in addition to the bounds, a couple of measurements, making it a primitive metes and bounds description. It also is more descriptive than the last example:

> All that Certain piece parcel or Lot of Land Lying and Being in the Town of Hillsdale County of Columbia and State of New York Bounded as Follows Begining at the west Corner of said Lot Bounded on James Shepherds Land thence Northerly to a stake and stones about twenty five rods joining William White thence continuing North Along a piece of stone wall on said Whites Land thence continuing north to a Black Oak Tree marked thence Continuing north on said White to the Corner of Said Lot to a white oak Tree Marked thence runing North East to a stake and stones thence Southerly on Lands formerly owned by Mr. Coleman to a stake and stones a few rods south of an old Road thence Southerly to a Stake and stones to the Corner of James Shepherds Land thence West to the place of Beginining Containing Fifty two and a half Acres of Land be it the same more or less.

We are specifically told that the description begins on the west corner of the lot. Since we are instructed to proceed north from there, we know that James Shepherd's land is on the south and that William White and his stone wall, the black oak tree and the white oak tree are on the west boundary of the property as we keep going north. We are told, when we reach a corner, to change direction. So, the north boundary (going northeast) is from the white oak to the stake and stones. Another directional change tells us to go southerly. As we do this, we see that the east boundary goes from the stake and stones south through lands formerly owned by Mr. Coleman to another stake and stones south of an old road and ends at another stake and stones at the corner of James Shepherd's land. Again changing directions, we go west, along the southerly boundary, to the point of beginning. In this case, except for James Shepherd on the south, William White on the west and the land "formerly Mr. Coleman's" on the east, we do not know who the neighbors were. Therefore, we cannot, if we wish to, go to the deeds of adjacent neighbors. This is not uncommon, and simply means you go another route to find more information.

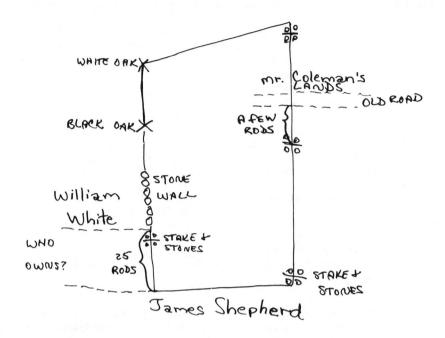

WHITE OAK X
mr. Coleman's LANDS
OLD ROAD
BLACK OAK X
A FEW RODS
STONE
William
WALL
White
WHO
OWNS?
STAKE &
STONES
25
RODS
STAKE &
STONES

James Shepherd

Rough Maps from Compass Bearings

As already noted, surveyors tend to work their way around a property, so that each side is described in order. If there are compass bearings with distances (metes) in the description, they will start at one point and continue around the property. Each general direction will be evident. For example, if the description starts at a point north and moves east, northeast, east, southeast, northeast, southeast, etc., you understand that you have started somewhere north on the property and are moving clockwise east and then south. Sometimes it is easier, in understanding a deed, to extract the compass points only—rather than making a map following the compass points—and place them on a blank piece of paper in the general directions of north (top), east (right), south (bottom) and west (left), much as you would read a map. You can do a more exact map later if you wish. The bearings summarized this way give you a quick view of the number of points in the boundary and its general directions.

A sample description, with compass bearings, reads:

All that certain, piece, parcel, tract and farm of land, situate lying and being In Hillsdale aforesaid Beginning on the hill on the West side of the Farm at a yellow pine trees, thence along Abraham Hainers land, South eighty five degrees forty-five minutes West two chains fifty links to Walnut staddle marked, south fifty seven degrees West, two chains seventy links, South thirty four degrees fifteen minutes East one chain seventeen links South eighty six degrees east four chains forty links, South seventy six degrees thirty minutes east, four chains fifty three links, South fifty three degrees twenty five minutes East six chains seventy links to Stake from which the South West corner of George Hainer's house bears North seventy three degrees East fourteen chains eighty links thence along the Road by Hainer's to Wiltsies, North forty six degrees forty five minutes East seven chains twenty links, North twenty four degrees forty five minutes West, nine chains to Walnut staddle, North twenty six degrees East seven chains twenty three links to a button Wood Stadle on the West bank of a Creek, North thirty three degrees East five chains ninety three links to a hard maple tree marked, North ten degrees west four chains fifty links to Stake to Thomas Wiltsie land, South thirty three degrees West twelve chains eighty four links, South fifteen degrees forty five minutes West four chains thirty links to poplar stadle marked, thence to the place of Beginning. Containing Eighteen Acres and ten perches of Land be the same more or less.

You are starting on the west side of the property and moving counter-clockwise southwest, southwest, southeast, southeast, southeast then northeast, northeast, northwest, northeast, northeast, northwest, southwest and southwest to the place of beginning. You may simplify it even more with the main directions: starting on the west draw a line southwest, then southeast, northeast, northwest, northeast, northwest and southwest to the beginning.

Now that you have summarized the general directions, you may want to draw a rough sketch of the property. Simplify this by drawing in the north/south, east/west axes. Then draw the map around the axes, using them as reference points.

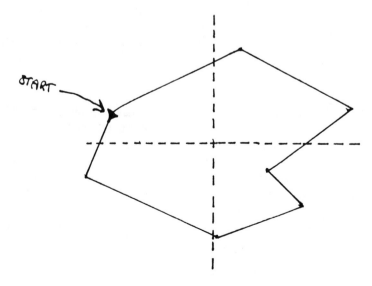

This map is not *exactly* what the property looks like. Rather it gives you an idea of what results when a complicated deed description is simplified for quicker comprehension (See Appendix B to learn how to plot a survey exactly from the written description.)

After you have made a basic seven-sided polygon, sketch in roughly the yellow pine trees, Abraham Hainer's land, the walnut staddle, the stake in relation to George Hainer's house, the road, the walnut staddle, the buttonwood staddle, the creek, the hard maple tree, the stake to Thomas Wiltsie's land and the poplar staddle.

When drawing a map, always sketch in the roads, buildings, streams, neighbors, etc. to give your map perspective. Houses, roads, trees and so on fill out a map so that it more accurately and completely reflects the general site orientation. This is why "walking the line" can be important during your on site inspection.   Although property boundaries do change over the years, it is surprising how often, especially in rural areas, the land in some parts of the survey description may not have changed that much in 100 years. You may recognize some of the bounds, such as creeks, or now-abandoned roadbeds. A stand of day lilies may mark the foundation of an old house, or apple trees still may stand in the dooryard. Thus, your map and on site inspection will complement each other.

Complete sketches or maps for all the deed or mortgage descriptions you find. This will help trace the development of the landholding. To most easily understand the changes over the years, start drawing your maps beginning with the earliest property description. Typically, some descriptions are repeated in several deeds. Draw each the first time it occurs. Thereafter, on subsequent deeds, write "Same as on Deed _____, p. _____ ." While drawing up descriptions, remember that neighbors typically are mentioned on more than one deed. Chances are that the property both grew and shrank in acreage over the years, so that at least one point in one of the deeds will be a building on a neighbor's property.

Modern Surveys

Modern surveys will not describe landmarks. Such referents have become "points" in 20th century surveys. Furthermore, the modern surveyor relies on instruments far more accurate than those used for these early surveys. Their electronic measuring devices can produce extremely accurate results, with only one error in 6,000,000 or even better.   These electronic angle-measuring instruments also give precise measurements. A modern surveyor measures land as if it were flat. If the property has any elevations, they are eliminated mathmatically, which means that hilly property actually contains more acreage than stated. (A straight line extended between two points, always will be shorter than a curved line.) This may partially explain discrepancies between an acreage listed on a 19th-century survey and again on one in the 20th. The later survey may list less acreage on paper, even though none of the property has been bought or sold since the 19th century. Surveys of any hilly acreage done years apart may exhibit this same result.

16

Other Kinds of Maps

Maps offer the house historian still another way of finding pieces of the puzzle. A map may locate a house by its owner's name and sometimes even delineate its shape at the time the map was made. It may show the shape of the property the house is on and any nearby bodies of water, roads and railroads. Or it may show the landscaping around the house.

Some "maps" use words, not pictures or measurements, to describe the exact physical location of people's houses or other structures. Such "maps" include road lists, tax lists, assessments, censuses, utility records and building permits. Each of these "maps" may provide particular, often unique, information, which helps corroborate other data already gathered for a house history.

Many different kinds of maps can be useful to a house historian. A county or town map targets the town or village where the property was or is located. Topographical maps show land contours and water sources which may explain why the site was chosen for the house. (For example, the terrain may have been too steep or the water source too distant to locate the house elsewhere on the property.) County and city maps of certain kinds also can be helpful. Aerial photographs can be used like a map, because they show hedgerows and other salient features of a property. Even architectural plans are a "map" of a specific building.

The following includes the major types of maps you will use most often besides the plats previously described. Many of these actually show geographic and topographic locations for houses.

County, Town and City Atlases

Although there were some isolated maps with earlier dates, by about 1850, commercial map-makers began producing wall-size county maps. These delineated towns, roads, major water sources and railroads. Throughout the

19th century, detailed village, town or city maps did the same with urban buildings. Within a few years these maps had become topographical, in that elevations above sea level were indicated. By the last quarter of the 19th century, the county atlas published in book form had replaced the wall map, and included blown-up versions of village and city maps showing the individual building shapes, as well as naming the occupants.

That these maps listed occupants—who were not necessarily the property owners—reflects the method used to compile the data for these maps. Generally, surveys were not used in the maps before circa 1860. Rather, salesmen, many of whom also had had some acquaintance with surveying or map-making, were sent out as representatives of the map companies. They would walk the roads, stopping at each house to solicit a subscription for the map that would be produced the following year. They created the map as they walked, writing down the names of the occupants along the way. Many of these occupants bought a subscription.

This early method of map-making could produce a variety of problems. First, the cartography was not always accurate since no official survey was used. There exist old maps on which entire roads or ponds with homes on or around them were inadvertently omitted. Second, the people whose names appeared on the map may have been the renters, not the owners, of the structures, which may have been a business structure, a house or both. Third, if an occupant was not at home when the reps came through, a neighbor volunteering information might have misspelled the occupant's name or given a wrong first name. Sometimes the occupant's house might have been omitted from the map, or his name and his neighbor's across the street might have been transposed. Finally, the information was a year old by the time it was published.

For all these reasons, be cautious in using these subscription maps to corroborate other information in your house history. Maps produced later in the 19th century, especially the Beer's maps and some others, are quite accurate and usually can be used as corroborating evidence in your house search. The blown-up, detailed village and city maps with the building shapes are especially helpful, because they identify businesses and homes, and also establish the shapes of buildings. If you can check several of these in sequence, it is possible that the development of a house can be traced via these pictures, which over the years will show added wings on the building shapes.

These 19th-century county wall maps often are found decorating real estate and insurance company offices. The atlases also can be found in local libraries or courthouses or on antique book-dealers' shelves. Reproductions of them have been a favorite fund-raiser for local historical societies. If a reproduction is not available, it may be possible to photocopy an original.

Insurance Maps

From the mid-19th century on, insurance companies produced maps containing a wealth of information from which the house historian can assemble an accurate depiction of the house at that date. These maps included street names and addresses, dimensions, number of stories and construction materials of homes and buildings and their placement on each lot. A fine example of these are the Sanborn fire insurance maps, which have been produced periodically since 1867. They detail the above-mentioned items and also show specific shapes of buildings. Since fire insurance was a requirement in urban areas before it was required in rural areas, the Sanborn maps are available for densely populated locations. The Sanborn maps were national in scope and set the standard for other insurance company maps to follow. Copies can be obtained from the Sanborn Map Company in New York City by sending them the street address or street boundaries of the target house; or, if there was no address, the town or city and state.

Sanborn maps from 1906 to the present are still under copyright. They usually are found at the tax or assessor's office. While it is sometimes possible to find the earlier maps in real estate offices, title insurance firms, city planning agencies or in the National Archives, where a catalog of all of the Sanborn map holdings is maintained, photocopies of these or later maps are not nearly as accurate as are those copies from the machines Sanborn uses to reproduce the originals. (Appendix A.)

Aerial Photos

One of the more glamorous ways of mapping a property would be a Cessna ride over it. Most small airports provide such services at reasonable hourly rates. From the air, stone walls and hedgerows marking property boundaries and variations in vegetation and creeks, can be photographed with a 35mm camera for later analysis. For instance, a low stone wall may outline a dooryard, especially if two large bushes or bushy trees can be seen at the edge of a shallow hole. Such landmarks help fix house locations.

It is possible to buy an orthophoto map, such as a United States Geological Survey (USGS) colorized topographic map that has been photographed from a plane. Some county real-property tax maps use the USGS maps with property delineations, numbers and coordinates superimposed on them. Such maps show buildings—when not concealed by trees—and provide the necessary coordinates to locate a building on its legal site for nomination to the National Register of Historic Places. USGS maps can be purchased from state geological survey offices or from the United States Department of the Interior. (See Appendix A.) County real-property tax maps can be ordered from the appropriate county tax office, for a fee.

Architectural Plans

Architectural plans and elevation drawings are another type of map—this time of the structure itself. These give a picture of the house, or of part of it, at a given time. While architects usually are associated with custom-made, more expensive buildings, they also designed the catalog houses, such as those sold by Montgomery Ward. (Plans were shipped along with the materials in order to provide a how-to guide, since many catalog house-buyers were inexperienced house-builders. They learned their first carpentry by reading the instructions on these plans.) Architectural plans also could have been copied from books.

If architectural plans are located for the building you are searching, carefully check their dimensions and details against those of the structure itself. Even when a house was custom-designed, it may have been changed during its construction. The owner may have modified the original design because of a change in ideas, or because of money available. Perhaps, through either error or deliberation, a builder may not have followed the plans exactly.

Our house, for example, ended up two feet longer than the architect planned, because the builder extended the foundation. He "forgot" to tell us, however, until he had put up all of the interior walls but the last, most important one, the plumbing wall. Since plumbing had to be run vertically through three floors, this wall could not be moved easily on the first floor without modifying the other two floors. We did not want to modify the two other floors, so the result was an inner hall the size of a nursery—wasted space that could have been better utilized elsewhere. No matter. This hall acquired two bookcases, a trestle table, a couple of chairs and is now called the telephone room.

This room is an example of a change in the original architect's plan, rather than a later interior change made after the house was built. This important distinction should be established when you have architect's plans in hand. The methods to use in deciding whether a change was original or was a later renovation are the same as those suggested in Section I.

Architectural plans often are found by accident in unexpected places if the previous owner did not pass them along to the new owner when he sold the house. Sometimes they have been turned over to a historical society or library, or they have been found in the possession of antique dealers and at flea markets. A few inquiries to the present owners, previous owners, the local historical society, antique and flea market dealers, et al are always suggested. But remember, it is exceedingly rare to find architectural plans.

Road Lists

There are other types of documents important to house histories, which can act as maps even though they are not pictorial. Perhaps the earliest of these were the road lists, many 18th-century samples of which can be found in town records. These can help *locate* a house. Once trails had been hacked wide enough to permit wagons to pass, and areas had been surveyed and settled, some form of local government assigned the duties and privileges of maintaining the roads to responsible individuals who lived along the right of way. Under most systems, each male head of household along a route was assigned a certain number of days to work annually—usually from one to six, depending on the amount of real estate owned or leased by him.

Certain men were assigned as "Captains" or "Overseers" or "Pathmasters" to coordinate the repairs, especially when roadbeds were changed or bridges were needed. Each of these men was assigned a "beat," which sometimes was described as, for example, "Jno Salsburys Path District from Richard Hold-ridges easterly to David Barrits. Taking ye Road to Jno Beebes." Or "John Pardy's Path District from David Barrits to Boston Line."

Along with these descriptions would be a roster of men, who presumably were listed in the order that they lived along the road. The neighbors surrounding the target name may be the same ones mentioned in a deed description. A bridge may be mentioned, or there may be other clues to pinpoint the location of a house you are researching. In some cases, as in the first quotation about "Jno Salsburys Path District," more than one road was included in the route. It usually is possible to identify the general location of the house and even the route of the "road list." The information may help to establish the likelihood that a house existed on the site you are researching, especially in the 18th century, when there were few, if any, maps, and surveys often were simple bounds descriptions only.

A word of caution: 20th-century roads may not follow the same beds as 18th- and 19th-century roads. Or old roads may have been discontinued by the 20th century. The house you are researching may have been on a road which no longer exists, or on a road behind or perpendicular to the one it is on now.

Also, district, town and county boundaries changed over the years. What now may be a county road, once may have been divided up among more than one town. As the districts and towns assumed responsibility for their own road maintenance, a road list would stop at the town line. Thus what may appear to be a logical route for a road list today, did not exist as such then. Or, sometimes road lists went around a large "block" covering perhaps eight miles, including four separate roads and a diagonal crossroad. Other times they seemed to zigzag on roads that are given different names today, rather than following what from our perspective, would seem a logical route. We can only speculate on what the reasons were for "oddities" in these road lists. But be careful about making assumptions from road lists without corroboration from another source.

Road lists can be found in district or town minutes at the local level or in the rent ledgers or land records (account books) of the large property owners. These latter papers may be found in state or local archives.

Special Tax Lists

There are still a few pre-Revolutionary tax lists in existence. They list the name, the acreage and the money value of real and personal property. Originally, tax lists arose from the need to raise revenues for the colony or crown. People were taxed in several different ways before the Revolution. The annual quitrent on real property has already been mentioned. (The quitrent system pretty much died out after the Revolution and was replaced by regular property-tax assessments.) Also, import duties were levied on several items, of which glass, painter's lead and lumber all pertained directly to houses.

In general, until the advent of the income tax law in the early 20th century, tax lists resulted from legislation passed to raise revenue to pay for wars: these were direct federal taxes. They were in addition to the regular property tax that became more commonplace as the 19th century progressed.

A few colonies had enacted colonial property taxes to help pay for the French and Indian War. By 1779 some state legislatures had enacted tax bills to help pay for the costs of the Revolution. This tax was based "land and personal" value—in other words, real and personal estate—with each person's property assigned a value in pounds.

In 1798 the federal government enacted a direct tax on real property and slaves because of the French War scare. The few tax lists that still survive from this are perhaps some of the more thorough listings of dwelling houses, their owners and tenants on record. Although incomplete, some records of this 1798 tax list do exist for Maine, New Hampshire, Massachusetts, Rhode Island, Connecticut, New York, Pennsylvania, Delaware, Maryland, District of Columbia, Tennessee and Georgia. There are also real property tax lists from 1812 and 1818.

In many cases the 18th-century tax list was divided geographically, and many of the same "captains" from the road list had a tax "beat." There were some differences, however. The tax beat had fewer captains, and each captain had at least ten times as many names to cover.

These tax beats or lists can be used in the same manner as road lists—that is, as a reference to house location. These, too, are unalphabetized names geographically bunched together. Even if the list was not specifically subdivided into beats, the names usually were arranged geographically. The route can be plotted from the names and neighbors on the tax lists and compared to the neighbors on the road lists to corroborate the house *location*.

In addition, the estate valuation in tax lists can be useful in giving a general idea of the *value* of the house at that time. Since the valuation was not broken down into acreage, land usage, waterways or buildings, only a limited amount can be learned. If the target house or property and its amenities (outbuildings, etc.) are known to have been in existence at that time—that is, are on the tax list—some tentative, very general comparisons can be made between it and other *similar* properties on the list. If you already know something of one of these (e.g., style, size, when built) you can draw some conclusions about the other's size at that time. Caution must be used, however, since these lists offer no detailed breakdown of the structures on the property, their construction material, function, etc.

Tax lists can be found in district or town minutes at the local level, as well as in state archives or large public or university libraries.

Assessments

More details than those given in the earlier tax lists can be gathered from early 19th-century data, when property taxes were determined by regular assessments and included more information. These assessments are scarce, but are very valuable. They offer corroborating data, filling in on deed and mortgage data. Various bits of this information can he helpful in solving part of your house puzzle or fleshing out your history. Assessment lists were organized differently from the earlier tax lists. The only way they were alphabetized was by the first letter of the surname. Otherwise, they were running lists (i.e., listed as the data came in and not alphabetized internally). Generally, these lists categorized property by the number of acres, real estate value, personal estate value, the aggregate (sum of the valuation), tax and, especially in sheep-farming areas, the dog tax.

In addition to these categories, following the individual's name were various personal descriptive designations, such as Wd. (widow), Dec. (deceased) or Estate. (The latter designation indicates that the deceased's property had not completed probate at the time.) Other designations were Minister Exempt $1500 (or some other amount) and N.R. (not a resident). This latter often referred to a person who had property straddling the border between two towns or who had inherited family property in an adjacent town.) Sometimes these personal descriptive abbreviations or terms were followed by descriptions of the property, especially if it was something other than a family farm. Some examples are: "Wood lot," "for Horton farm," "for Widow Read," "for Plaster Mill," "for Tavern Stand," "house and store," etc. While much of this information may not directly seem to apply to the existence of a house, it can provide clues to the uses of a house or outbuildings by designating an occupation or usage. The outbuilding along the creek may have been a mill or the front rooms of the house a store.

Unless they were for a large, urban center, assessment lists did not include addresses until the late 19th to early 20th century. Rather, these properties are identified by the owner's name. Be sure that you have correctly identified the property you are researching, because one owner may have several properties. Use the amount of acreage that you identified in your deed search to confirm that this is the same property on the assessment list.

On properties that were identified by street addresses, be advised that over time the house or building-numbering systems were changed on some streets, so that the same property may have different building numbers on separate assessments. Also, be aware that, particularly in urban settings, people did move next door. Be sure you are dealing with the same property.

Check at the assessment or tax-collector's office in your city for records showing when numbering systems may have been changed. If there is no separate record, you may be able to determine this information by comparing the fire insurance maps for the target house, such as the Sanborn maps, over a period of years. Since the maps detailed the building shapes, it may indicate where an ell or a wing was added on a building for a different residence or business, which necessitated giving it a separate number.

Using the Assessments

The data found in assessments—particularly property size and value—with a little application can be used to find out the size of the house at a given time. If you are able to locate this data for two, three, four or more different dates, changes in size or value may signal some kind of change in the property. You may be able to establish when additions were made on a house or, conversely, when the house was devalued, because of its run-down condition or, perhaps, because of a fire. The following are the four comparative methods used to complete this analysis. Compare:

- the development of the target house by acreage and value over several years on assessment rolls;

- the target property to other properties by category on the same aasessment;

- the target house with another house on the assessment for which information is already known;

- the assessment information with the same information found on deeds, mortgages and censuses of the year closest to the assessment.

The first method of analyzing a property is to compare its development over several years on the assessment rolls. A large jump in assessed value may indicate a property improvement, such as a barn or an addition on the house. A great decline in value may mean a devastating fire. Again, do not make superficial assumptions. A quick comparative study of several other properties should be made to see if there was an overall increase or decrease in the assessment roll values, or whether your target house stands out.

A second method of drawing conclusions via assessment lists is to compare properties falling within certain similar categories. For example, similar village houses on quarter-acre lots will have similar values. Widow's properties will be valued lower than men's. A man with a considerable personal estate usually will have a larger house even though he may not own much land. Does your house fit a category that you can readily identify? How does it compare to other similar properties on the list? Did it have a higher or lower value per acre? If a property appears to fit into a category, yet its value is extremely out-of-line with similar properties, you may want to do more digging to find the explanation. Insurance records, city or county directories or newspaper reports may pinpoint, for example, a lucrative business enterprise on the property.

A third method is to compare the target house to another property listed on the assessment which already has a significant amount known about it, because research had been completed previously on it by you or by someone else. There always is some house, often the "fancy" house in town, about which a great deal is known. If both houses have a comparable-style wing or ell, then, because you know the approximate date and cost of the "fancy" house's wing, you have an estimate of the time period in which to search assessment lists for your target house. You are looking for a similar change in value, which signals the addition of the wing.

Both appreciation and decline in assessment value were tied to the national economy. Throughout the 19th century there were inflationary periods followed by deflationary "panics." Some were national, some even international, and others affected only certain regions of the United States. One of the first "panics," as depressions were called then, was the Panic of 1837. It affected real estate prices, which declined severely below the 1820's levels. Before the century ended, there would be three more panics, affecting different parts of the county and the international market: these were in 1857, 1873-78 and 1893-97.

The fourth means of analyzing a property is a way of confirming your speculations about size and additions. Utilize the assessments to compare the assessed value with the deed and mortgage considerations and with the census's real estate or dwelling value on the year closest to the assessment. Generally, the values listed on assessments, censuses and deeds and mortgages will be the same value and will be the true value of the house and property, not the proportional value. If a house and property were assessed for $300, it sold for that amount (proportional evaluation is a 20th-century phenomenon).

If, after compiling these comparative statistics on the property values, you confirm a large increase or decrease in assessment, does it fit with your on site inspection analysis, genealogical information and deed and mortgage data to support your explanations? If everything meshes, you may draw tentative conclusions about the added wing or about the year the house was built.

Assessments can be hard to locate. Depending on state statute, two copies of assessments usually were made, the original for town records and a polished copy for state records. If not placed in the town hall, the town's copy often was found in the assessor's home. Because it was assumed, sometimes erroneously, that the state kept their duplicate copy for their archives, the town copy was destroyed or disbursed years later. In some states the assessments were not kept in archives, and were eventually destroyed. After all, people reasoned, why should anyone care what the taxes had been thirty years previously? For this reason extant copies are found in a variety of repositories: city or town records, state archives, or historical societies' holdings. You may have to dig for them.

Census

Although there were earlier local enumerations done in various locales, the first federal census was done in 1790 and has been compiled every ten years since. It is organized by jurisdiction (e.g., city, district or town). The census-taker usually started out at a boundary of the jurisdiction and worked along the roads, going from house to house. Thus the census is more like a "map" than are the assessment lists, since the latter are arranged alphabetically. In the census neighbors appeared on the listing near each other, which can help confirm the location of the house when compared with deed descriptions, road lists and tax lists. Each dwelling and each family were numbered and can be identified by these numbers. Since more than one family sometimes lived in the same house, each family had a different number, although their dwelling number was the same. Two-family and extended-family dwellings usually were larger than average dwellings.

Some censuses, such as that of 1850, include the value of real estate and whether it was rented or owned. Like the assessments, this was a true valuation and should be comparable to the circa 1850 assessments.

Within the census a wealth of information can be found in the manufacturer's or industry schedule (if it was used that year) and the agriculture schedule following each jurisdiction (e.g., town, village, ward, city, etc.). This extra information may include what goods were produced at the location, the occupation of the owner, the uses of the building, the value of machinery, the value of animals and crops, the number of bushels per acre, etc. Such facts may verify some assumptions you already have made about the house or its features.

State and County Censuses

Although the federal census can be useful to a house historian, the various state and county censuses, often compiled county-by-county in a variety of years, may be even more valuable. They may contain more information referring directly or indirectly to the house. However, the amount of information in these state schedules will vary, depending on the purpose of the census and where the information came from. Also, some state censuses were of registered voters only. In order to vote, a man had to be a property owner, so location of the property and its value are listed. In at least one state the state census listed the value of the dwelling and the material it was made of. In 1885 federal funds were used to conduct censuses in Colorado, Florida, New Mexico (which included Arizona), Nebraska, North Dakota and South Dakota. All states and the District of Columbia had some locally generated censuses, except Tennessee and West Virginia. In order to find out which of these census records still exist in your state, refer to the guide to state censuses found in the reference books, *The Source* and *U.S. and Special Census Catalog*. (See Bibliography.) In order to find out which state censuses contain information pertaining to houses, however, you would have to contact the individual state archives. (Appendix A.)

Inevitably, some people were not counted. Although all censuses (federal, state and local) are assumed to include all inhabitants, many families lived in remote areas and each area, whether rural or urban, had—and has—its pockets of reclusive and elusive individuals and groups. Furthermore, censuses were dependent on the federal mandate, which varied in the amount and kinds of information it required in different years. Listing of slaves, for example, was erratic and depended on the mandate of each specific census—some listed slaves as 3/5 of a person. Censuses also were dependent upon the perserverance and persuasiveness of the census-taker. Perhaps all these difficulties were best expressed by a frustrated census-taker in Texas who finished his report in 1850 with the words:

> I certify these to be sixty-four pages and a piece of the inhabitants
> and done as near in accordance with my oath as I could do it. The
> people was hard to get along with!

If they exist and are available, censuses are found at county courthouses, libraries, archives and historical societies. They are a mainstay of genealogists, so are fairly easy to find. Some historians have indexed local censuses, while published indices are available of some federal censuses, such as those of 1790 and 1850.

Directories

Directories were the forerunners of our modern telephone books. They are available for cities and counties. Persons living in towns were listed in the county directories. Directory entries will serve to locate an individual at a specific address, but will not necessarily tell you if he owned the house or business.

By the later 18th and 19th centuries, city and county directories were widely available. A few of the larger cities had directories even earlier. In 1665, in New York City, a grouping of residents by streets was compiled in the Records of the Dutch Magistrates. What is believed to be the first city directory-type listing was made in Baltimore and survives as a manuscript entitled "The Following List of Families, And Other Persons Residing in the Town of Baltimore, Was Taken in the Year 1752, by a Lady of Respectability." It is believed that Joseph Townsend printed this manuscript—which, apparently, was not a complete listing of the people living there—sometime in the 1830's. In 1782 and 1785 two directory lists of Charleston were published in the *South Carolina and Georgia Almanack*. In 1785 two directories were published in Philadelphia: John "MacPherson's Directory for the City and Suburbs of Philadelphia" and Francis White's "The Philadelphia Directory." David Franks compiled "The New-York Directory of 1786." These directories pertain primarily to large cities. Check in the archives of your local library to see if there is a manuscript (unpublished) listing of early residents of your town.

Although your local library or historical society may not have a complete set of city or county directories for each year that the directory was published in your area, it may provide them for some years. From these you can establish where a structure was located and who lived in it. Directories usually contain both a residential and a business section, listed alphabetically by surname, with the business or occupation listed afterward. If a person was a farmer, there may be a number after the word "farmer," which indicates the number of acres owned or leased. In some directories, lot and range numbers may follow a person's name, especially in those directories pertaining to areas settled from approximately 1820 on, where land was already surveyed under the Federal Township and Range system. These numbers then can be located on a survey map of the town, giving you the exact location of the house.

There also may be a section organized alphabetically by business and occupation, such as "Dentists, " "Dyer and Scourer," "Fancy Goods," "Hotels." If you know a person's occupation, it may explain variations in the structure or uses of different rooms. (Keep in mind that since the directories were paid for by businesses that advertised products or services, they often overlapped county boundaries.)

Directories generally did not appear with any consistency and did not list all area residents until the middle of the 19th century. Except in urban centers, specific street addresses were not listed in directories until late in the 19th century. (Even in cities, mail was not delivered to street addresses. People went to the post office to pick up their mail.) Despite these drawbacks, directories can provide useful information.

Urban "Maps:" Utilities, Permits, Assessments

In urban centers, early establishment of utilities was necessary to supply water and get rid of wastes. By the 1830's, piped-in water was available in large eastern cities, such as Richmond, Philadelphia, New York and Boston, but it was not until after the Civil War, in the 1870's, that most cities supplied water to all inhabitants.

The city's water bureau or department usually has records which indicate when service was begun to an address. Once piped-in water was established in cities, service to a structure began when a building needing water was built. Presumably the first date of service coincides with the date the house was completed.

In some cities—particularly cities in arid locations—the earliest water supplier was a private company. Usually their records then became part of the municipal government's files when the latter took over supplying water. In some cities, such as San Francisco, the municipal utility still maintains the original records of the private company. These kinds of records include the date of service, the number of rooms in the house, the number of people living there, the architect's or builder's signature and often a sketch of the structure. What a gold mine of information for the house historian!

Remember that address numbers did change, sometimes frequently. If you think this happened with a target property, check with the tax assessor's office in city hall. They should have the records of address-number changes and when they occurred.

Another utility, usually also private, is the gas and electric company. These usually can supply the date service was begun to an address. Commonly this would be a turn-of-the-century date, since the Columbian Exposition of 1893 (the Chicago World's Fair) effectively promoted electricity for home owners. Piped natural gas also became available at about this time.

Building permits, also kept in the urban tax assessor's office, can give the house historian a date when building was to begin. Dates of additions also can be pinpointed, because a building permit was needed before construction started. Of special interest to the house historian, the assessor's office can supply tax-account numbers and names of past owners, as well as his estimate of the structure's age. In some locales the tax number is used to locate the survey plat, which is housed in a separate office.

These utility records are particularly valuable in researching urban areas built after the Civil War. Rural areas, of course, relied on wells for water, and depending on the area, often did not get electric service until well into the 20th century. Gas was supplied in propane tanks sold by private companies.

Because urban lots are small, and houses are so close together that legislation is needed to maintain sanitary water and fire-safety conditions, urban houses may be easier to document than rural. There simply is more of a paper trace to follow, and in many cases, this paper trace is of more recent vintage— 1860's and later—than that pertaining to many rural structures. Even so, it is still a good idea to collect all possible data on any house, urban or rural, so that your conclusions are based on a variety of evidence.

Section IV
The Final Analysis

17

Getting It All Together

The research is completed. You have exhausted all possible sources which might provide data on your home. Or, if you have been working for a client, you have found as much as you could within a reasonable amount of time. (Unless your client gives you unlimited hours to work—a rare occurrence—you will feel constrained to work within the time and money limits you mutually have agreed upon.)

You have maintained a chronological time line listing the dates— including month and day if you have them—of events you have uncovered pertaining to the various home owners and the house. Data from birth and death records, wills and marriages, deeds and mortgages, road, tax and assessment lists, censuses—all are recorded on the time line, as are pertinent local dates (e.g., of incorporation of districts, towns and turnpikes). Now you are ready to start writing the narrative.

Style: Time Line or Narrative?

The style of the house history is chosen by your client. I give them the choice of either what I call a "glorified" time line (i.e., the chronological list of facts, but embellished with narrative explanations), or a straight narrative. In the glorified time line, the organization is exclusively chronological, beginning with the earliest date and ending with the current year. These dates are listed in a left-hand column with a narrative explanation opposite.The narrative begins with who, what, when, where and how much and continues with how and why. The advantage of a glorified time line is that sources or short explanations can be inserted easily when needed, thus avoiding footnotes. Another advantage of this method is built-in organization, by date and year.

The disadvantage is that the built-in organization by time sequence sometimes can be too narrow. Sometimes you have to list several facts in one column before you can devote a paragraph or two to explaining them in the other column. Their format dictates this. Because the dates are listed, there are no flashbacks or jumps forward. But, in the narrative style, you would have this flexibility.

Let us look at an example. A house *and property* is valued on an assessment at $850 for 40 acres in 1840. The 1850 census values them at $950. The 1854 assessment jumps to $1,250, yet the acreage remains the same. Finally, the 1855 state census, which lists only the house, now values the house alone at $900. You can explain this increase in house value by architectural changes in the house that you have noted. On a glorified time line you have to list, in the left-hand column, one below the other, the first four facts—the 1840 assessment, the 1850 census, the 1854 assessment and the 1855 census—before you can tie in, in the right-hand narrative, the excessive increase in value with the architectural changes. The glorified time line can leave the reader wondering about the "how and why" before enough data can be included to give the explanation. In other words, the format can be too restrictive.

A narrative better accommodates the time sequence, offering explanations in a natural, flowing style. The chronological order of the material can be manipulated to provide easy transition from topic to topic. In the time line you have no such control over the sequence of events. The client has to figure out the connections himself from the "bare-bones." These differences should be explained to the client to help him decide which style he would prefer.

Analysis

With research and analyses completed, the style of narrative is chosen. You start writing. But wait! Something is missing! You hadn't thought of that before! As you write down the combination of factual material and analysis, details noticed before, but not thoroughly analyzed, may take on more significance. The analysis is never complete until you actually start putting it all together on paper. Then you may see a connection you had not seen before. If an event seems more significant as you write, you must stop and recheck the data from the original source to make sure that now that you have a different perspective, you have included all of the necessary facts. Is there some additional fact in your data that you now realize clarifies something? (This is why photocopied material is so important to have at hand in your writing place.) *Analysis is an ongoing process that does not stop until you have typed the final copy.*

Historical Perspective

In getting it all together, some regional or national historical events should be included—broad historical facts that may have touched this house. For example, wars were fought on certain sites, and houses were destroyed, or were used as quarters. Turnpikes, canals and railroads changed the significance of older transportation routes, yet the homes on the older routes still exist. Houses were lived in even though their original function may have changed. Perhaps they no longer were used as inns, but as farmhouses. The house history must be set in this kind of historical context, not isolated.

The economy influenced real-estate values. In different areas of the country, values were lowered during the economic panics of 1819, 1837, 1857, 1873 and 1893. Also, little house building occurs during wars (e.g., 1861-65, 1914-18), while a few years after the wars there often is a housing boom. The California Gold Rush of 1849 also brought a housing boom to the West. There are other historical events which, along with technological advances, directly or indirectly influenced home owners and their houses, so that stylistic eras that we know of as Georgian, Federal, Greek Revival, etc. appeared.

Spelling Variants

Because I have chosen to use, in each house history, all items as they appear in the text cited, spelling variants do crop up. To explain such variations, I always use a footnote or explanation similar to the following:

Note that the spellings _____ and _____ vary. When quoting early sources—often handwritten—I faithfully reflect the spellings and punctuation—or lack of—in the manuscript or record. In many cases the same name is spelled several different ways. Rather than guess which version is the "correct" one, and to illustrate the casual attitude of our ancestors toward spelling and punctuation, I prefer to copy verbatim.

Other researchers choose the most common spelling, or the 20th-century one, and insert 20th-century punctuation conventions into their quotations. I prefer not to, because one then loses the authenticity of the quotations and, worse, because a mistake in interpretation may result from imposing 20th-century rules on 18th- or 19th-century punctuation and spelling.

Now let us look at two completed house histories illustrating the two most popular styles, the glorified time line and the narrative.

The Glorified Time Line

A list of sources consulted always follows the text of the time line. Because you are searching for data not contained neatly within limited resources in one archive, always include all sources consulted, as well as materials actually used. There are two reasons for this procedure: it shows the clients that few, if any, stones were left unturned, and that time was conscientiously spent and accounted for. Further, if the client decides to pursue application to a county, state or national historic register, this bibliography contains many of the sources needed for easy perusal by both client and reviewers. In addition, always supply the client with photocopies of as many of the sources as could be copied. These generally include maps, deeds, mortgages, wills, administration files and pages from local history books that pertain directly to the house and property. A few pages from a time line are shown below.

3/16/1753 First deed record of property bought by Daniel Morris of New
Haven in Salisbury, Connecticut. (Russell, II, p. 74)

1754 Daniel Morris born in Salisbury, son of Daniel and Elizbeth
Morris. (Russell, I, p. 20)

1756 Tax List, Salisbury: Daniel Morris paid £3.15.6. (Russell, II,
p. 123)

9/27/1756 Six Mile Tract Deed: Daniel Horse listed as a grantee. Written
in Sheffield, Hampshire County, Massachusetts. This deed records
the transaction between two Stockbridge Indians and 75 grantees
who bought what is now considered Austerlitz. (Hampden County
Deed Liber I, pp. 747-749) Sheffield preceded and included parts
of Great Barrington and Egremont. Lands west of Stockbridge and
Sheffield and east of Nobletown, New York, present-day North
Hillsdale, were considered Indian lands. These included parts
of present-day Alford, Egremont, West Stockbridge, Austerlitz,
Hillsdale and Canaan. (Berkshire Southern District Colonial Records
and Proprietary Plans, p. 715. Also Vital Records of Alford, unp.)
(Cf. Deeds Libers 1, p. 27; 2, pp. 245-6 and 254; 3, p. 189)
Daniel Horse may have been Daniel Morris, since the hand-written
deed is a copy, and Horse is not a common surname. Furthermore,
Morris and Morse are often interchanged.

9/14/1758 Last child born to Daniel and Elisabeth Morris recorded in
Salisbury. (Russell, I, p. 20) Note that the spellings of
Elisabeth here and in the 1754 birth record --Elizbeth-- vary.
When quoting early sources --often handwritten-- I faithfully
reflect the spellings and punctuation --or lack of-- in the
manuscript or record. In many cases the same name is spelled

several different **ways**. **Rather than** guess which version is
the "correct" one and to **illustrate** the casual attitude of our
ancestors toward spellings and punctuation, I prefer to copy
verbatim.

1760　　Tax List, Salisbury: Daniel Morris paid £ 84.17.0, a tax
significantly higher than the £ 3.15.6 paid in 1756 indicating
that he had bought and improved considerable property in four
years. (Russell, II, p. 124)

10/23/1761 Daniel Morris, a yeoman --a landowning farmer of some means--
of Salisbury purchased 269 acres of Eliathah Rew of Sheffield for
£ 418. It was part of the Shewanon Purchase from the Indians and
was located in present-day Alford, Massachusetts. (Berkshire
Southern District Deed Liber 1, p. 28)

12/29/1761 Daniel Morris married Prudence Curtiss in North Stratford,
Connecticut. (Bailey, Book 7, p.98) This was a second marriage.
Daniel would have been 44 years old. (Cf. 4/2/1806)

2/23/1762 Abigail Morris and Eliathah Rew announced their intentions of
marriage. (Vital Records of Great Barrington, p. 45) Abigail
was possibly a daughter of Daniel Morris or a considerably
younger sister. Neighborhoods played a large role in determining
familial relationships.

11/14/1762 Daniel Morris and his wife were admitted to the Great Barrington
Congregational Church. (Bostwick, p. 198)

1/29/1763 Daniel Morris of Barrington, Berkshire County, Massachusetts,
sold the last of his property in Salisbury, Connecticut.
(Russell, II, p. 116)

10/31/1765 Daniel Morris bought and sold property adjacent to his purchase in
to
1/20/1786 1761 in what is now Alford. (Deeds Libers 2, pp. 245, 246, 254,

464, 626; 3, p. 189; 5, p. 31; 8, p. 613) Part of this land
"is supposed to be in Albany County in the Province of New York."
(Deed L. 2, p. 254)

2/5/1776   Daniel Morris gave his son John Morris 60 acres of his property
in Alford "on which John Morris now lives." (Deed L. 6, p. 143)

8/27/1785 Daniel Morris sold his son Eleazer Morris 175 acres of his property
in Alford for £ 200. (Deed L. 9, p. 331)

12/26/1788 Daniel Morris partitioned the property that he had given Eleazer
leaving him with 1/3 use and benefit of the/dwelling house, horse
                                           lands,
house, barn and cider mill. This would amount to approximately 58
acres, the whole of which was Daniel's parcel with his own house.
Jeremiah Scripture (possibly a son-in-law?) received 2/3rds of
the above. (Deed L. 11, pp. 171 and 216)

5/4/1789   Daniel sold 4 acres to Daniel Griffis. This is the last deed
recorded for Daniel Morris in Massachusetts. (Deed L. 11, p. 76)

1790   Census: Daniel Morris: 1 male over 16, 5 males under 16, 4
females. This Daniel Morris, found in the vicinity of present day
Beale Road, lists only one male over 16 years --undoubtedly himself--
with 5 males under 16 and 4 females. In 1790 the Daniel
heretofore discussed would have been 73 years old. (Cf. 4/2/1806)
His son Daniel, except for his birth in Salisbury in 1754, is not
mentioned in any of the deed transactions in Massachusetts
including the deeding of acerage to his brothers John and Eleazer.
(Cf. 10/4/1806) In 1790 son Daniel would have been about 36.
(Cf. 9/7/1809) Other than the Massachusetts "Six Mile Tract"
deed mentioning Daniel Horse as one of the grantees, there are
no deeds or mortgages recorded in Columbia County with Daniel
Morris as either grantor or grantee. Columbia County was

formed 4/4/1786 from the southeastern section of Albany County. (Ellis, p. 35) If son Daniel had settled on his father's claim, there would have been no legal requirement for a deed recording.

On a ca. 1785 Road Beats list for King's District a Doct. Marse is mentioned and "ye Road by Morse" on a different beat. (King's District Record, unp.) On a 1795 deed to Matthew Beale, who lived at the northeast corner of present-day Route 203 and Beale Road, "Doct. Levi Morris's" is used as a bound for Matthew Beale's property: "begining...the Road leading from said Spencertown to Doct. Levi Morris's Running thence North 34 degrees West..." (Columbia County Deed Liber 126, p. 155) On an 1805 mortgage Levi Morris's almost 3 acres is southeast of Ebenezer Cadies', who lived on present-day County Route 9 in Chatham. (Mort. L. B, p. 671) Beale Road originally continued north and connected with County Route 9. (Cf. 1851 map) In 1807 Levi Morris owed $150 in debts and $8.50 in "damages, costs and charges." From a sheriff's sale deed Levi's location is further established, because the adjoining properties are Cady and Webster, the latter mentioned in the ca. 1785 Road Beat. (Deed L. C, p. 10)

What connection did Doct. Levi Morris have with Daniel Morris junior? The records show nothing leaving any association open to speculation. In fact other than the above mentioned citations, there is little else to be found on Levi. That Daniel junior was a doctor is the only concrete association other than the name. (Cf. 1807) That Levi lost his 3 acres in 1807, and Daniel Morris senior died in 1806 (Cf. 4/2/1806) not leaving a Levi Morris anything in his will may be circumstantial. (Cf. 10/4/1806)

On the other hand, that Levi and not Daniel Morris is mentioned
in the 1795 deed to Matthew Beale is odd. Daniel, not Levi, is on
the 1790 Census. There remains the remote possibility that Daniel
and Levi were the same person, although not likely, since no "L's"
or "Levi's" are found in the descendants of the Daniel Morris
family.

Jack Sobon, an architect/timber-framer, has found tapered
posts, often called gunstock posts, as late as the 1790's. The
gunstock posts found in the oldest section of the Morris house,
what is now the dining room, appear to be members of queen truss
oak framing, although this is difficult to see, because access
to the attic has been cut off. Wide board pine flooring in the
living room appears original. The boards up to 17" width suggest
early construction, while their position indicates that this
area was originally two rooms probably added to the dining room
during the Federal Period. The center entrance $1\frac{1}{2}$ story house
of 5 bay x 2 bay construction with cornice returns at the gable
ends and narrow cornices and corner pilasters was a typical
style employed during the Federal Period from 1790–1820.
(Andrews, p. xxii) During renovation sun-dried brick was found
in the oldest section between the dry wall stone foundation and
the sill and above the sill in the first floor wall. A 15' deep
cistern with laid-up stone walls was also discovered with some
water in it, an early method of water collection. Little else
readily visible remains of the earliest construction, because the
house has been extensively renovated. Since Daniel Morris was
there in 1790, his house most likely was constructed before that date.

The Narrative

The narrative style always begins with the geographic location. (As soon as the first spelling variant of the name appears, the footnote of explanation follows.) The narrative may flow more or less chronologically, with architectural descriptions interspersed as the house history develops. Or, you may separate the architectural descriptions into a section devoted exclusively to the changes that occurred in the house.

To make it easy to sort out dates from the text, I usually provide a one- or two-page abstract preceding the narrative. This abstract is a brief description of the text, outlining chronologically the steps in the development of the house. It is a quickly read overview of the house history and focuses on significant changes only. Following the narrative text are the footnotes, sources consulted, and a partial glossary of terms used in the text. A few pages from a narrative are shown below.

Contents

Abstract

The Parke-Jenkins House on School House Road near County Route 5 in Canaan, New York, was in existence at the turn of the 19th century. As little is known of the original owner, we can only speculate based on general knowledge of similar houses in the area.

Elijah Barrett probably lived in a two room house, one down with a half story loft up in what is now the saltbox section of the house, the second section from the west. In 1814 he sold the house, barn and other buildings to young Martin Parks, who operated a sawmill with his father and later his brother in Red Rock. He and his descendents added the three other sections of the house during the 19th century. The westernmost section probably was built second with the center two-and-one-half story section completed in 1822. The easterly section was built between 1860-66. The windows were changed and the porches added probably around 1882 when Ezra P. Jenkins, a grandson of Martin, assumed ownership of the house.

An accompanying family tree is a visual means to help sort out the sometimes confusing family relationships. It was designed to use as a reference while reading the text.

A Partial Smith Park Genealogy

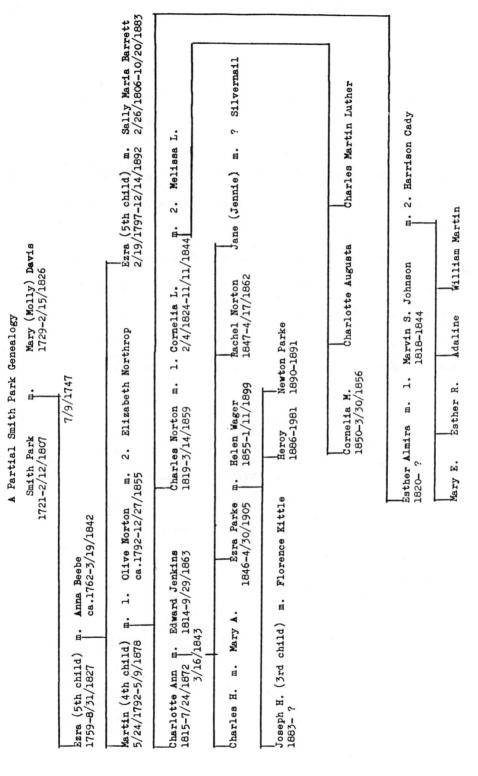

217

History

The Parke-Jenkins House on School House Road near County Route 5 in Canaan, New York, was in existence at the turn of the 19th century. In 1798 Elijah Berrit was listed on Captains John Darrow's and Celay [Jelah] Castles' road beat in Canaan.[1 & 2] In the settlement of early districts and towns, road maintenance was performed by property owners along the way. On the lists written in the town or district minutes "Captains" headed each crew, and the crew members were listed consecutively as they existed along the road beat. It is presumed that the men listed also lived where they were part of the crew. In 1798 Elijah Berrit would have been 24 years old and, perhaps, was newly married.[3]

In 1778 his father, David Barret, was the master carpenter for David Pratt's house in Spencertown. This meant that Barret cut the timber, hewed, scored (marked the places for the mortices and tenons used in the scribe rule construction method) and framed it.[4] Elijah would have been four years old in 1778.

David Barret was listed on the Land and Personal Tax List for the King's District in 1779 with his real and personal estate valued at 100 £.[5] The King's District was established in 1772 and was the forerunner of the Town of Canaan, which was established in 1788.[6 & 7] David had settled in the Mount Pleasant section near a ten acre trout pond that came to be known as present-day Barrett Pond near Beebe Hill in the Town of Austerlitz.[8]

Austerlitz was established as a town in 1818 and included part
of Canaan.[9]

When Elijah and Mary Barrett sold their property in 1814,
it totaled 60 acres in three parcels. Two parcels were divided
by School House Road. These and a wood lot located in present-day
Austerlitz were worth $1,645. The land on School House Road
included a dwelling house, barn and other buildings. Thomas
Barratt's garden, land, wood lot and barn are mentioned in the
deed as being located east of the property.[10]

Thomas Barratt was probably a brother of Elijah's father,
David, since he is listed as a contemporary of David on the Land
Tax List of the King's District in 1779 as having real estate
worth 60 £.[11] Thomas was also listed on the same road beats in
the 1780's/with David Barrit.[12] By comparing the 1792 and 1798
and '90's
road beat, Elijah Barrit replaces Thomas Barratt's name on the
list.[13] Perhaps it was a young man's turn to serve on the road
crew, since we know that Thomas still lived next door in 1814.

Elijah and Mary Barrett sold their house and property in
1814 to Martin Parks who was 22 at the time.[14 & 15] He was
married to Olive Norton who was the same age.[16] The house that
they moved into probably consisted of the section now located
second from the west. This original house on the site was the
one-and-a-half story section over a dugout cellar with one room
on each floor. The wainscoting on the first floor room with the
horizontal boards was common in the late 18th century.[17] The
westerly one story plus probably was added second over a crawl

18

Applying for Historic Registers

Historic registers are *lists* of structures and properties that are historically significant. Registers may be county, state or national. This chapter gives a general explanation of how a structure may become listed on such registers.

Implications of Historic Register Status

What does it mean to have a house listed on a historic register? At a county or town level, it may mean eligibility for a specially designed bronze plaque noting the construction date of the house. Only houses designated as historic by the local or county historical society may display these plaques. Furthermore, local zoning laws in most states respect the historic designation when variances are requested, because such structures, with few exceptions, are protected under state environmental-impact laws. Finally, the value of a house, especially a pre-1900 house, may appreciate faster if it is protected by a historic register listing or if it is located in a historic district.

If a structure is on the National Register, there are still other advantages. National listing recognizes the value of historic properties to the nation. The property may be eligible for federal tax incentives and other preservation assistance. Since 1976, the federal Internal Revenue code has contained incentives designed to encourage capital investments in historic commercial, industrial and, under specific conditions, residential buildings. These incentives include a twenty percent investment tax credit and favorable tax treatment for the certified rehabilitation of an income-producing building that is designated as a certified historic structure. Such buildings include: a train station whose interior space has been redesigned to serve as headquarters for a bank, a large warehouse carved into low-rent apartments, and a Victorian house turned into a bed and breakfast. After a structure has been placed on the National Register, the property owner must complete a historic preservation certification application and send it to the secretary of the interior, who issues a certified rehabilitation certificate.

Being listed on the National Register qualifies the property for certain federal and state grants for historic preservation and restoration — if funds are available. There are also private sources, such as foundations, which grant funds for historic structures.

Guidelines

What qualifies a structure for registry? The following guidelines are those listed for the National Register. (State and county historic registers generally follow these same basic guidelines but may amend some of the criteria to include locally significant homes or homes of famous people.)

In many areas the process of registering individual sites on the national level is backlogged several years. Several things are responsible for this backlog. One is the increased interest in history and historical places exhibited by the public since 1976, and their subsequent research into the description, origin and development of sites. Another is a reluctance on the part of government to allocate funds for additional personnel to handle the backlog of applications to be placed on registers.

The governmental solution in some areas has been to look more favorably on "windshield" survey applications. In these, an entire area or town has been surveyed for historic-district status, in somewhat less depth than for a specific site designation—by driving through the area and eyeballing structures to establish architectural eras and rough dating. Later research backs up this kind of survey. Such a survey in your area could provide you with another method of obtaining National Register status. The house you have researched may be included within a historic district, and thus can be placed on the National Register.

However, if you feel strongly that you must pursue an individual site-designation application, be aware that, because of the current glut of individual requests, criteria for individual registry are being applied more stringently. In general, the structure and/or property must be a historically significant representation for the locale, not just one more Greek Revival, Eastlake or Italianate structure.

If you are in the house histories business you may have a client interested in a house history as an avenue to achieving a historic listing. Other clients, however, may want historic register status *in addition* to having a house history done for personal interest. Always establish this clearly with the client at the time of the on site inspection. If the client's exclusive interest is historic register status, let him know *then* whether you think the house will qualify. If after completing the house history you believe that it does not qualify for national or state register, advise your client that you may be able to recommend its eligibility for the county register.

Criteria for National Register

Evaluations of your National Register application usually are made by comparing your structure with existing similar structures already on the National Register in your locale. If the new application represents a structure or property of *exceptional* importance, the following guidelines may be ignored or mitigated by the historic preservation officer.

First, the structure should be at least fifty years old and be located on its original site. Second, it should, according to the National Park Service, qualify under one or more of the following criteria:

- association with a significant historical event;

- association with a person significant historically (owner, builder, tenant, etc.);

- embodies "the distinctive characteristics of a type, period, or method of construction," or is the work of a master, or illustrates high artistic value, or as a whole represents "a significant and distinguishable entity," even though its "components may lack individual distinction;"

- yields important information "in prehistory or history."

In other words, does the structure/property have historical and architectural significance, or is it located near other historically important buildings? Is it associated with a well-known person or group of people involved with a social or political movement or historic event? Is the structure a unique example of an architectural style or period, or does it exhibit a unique construction method or building type? Is its siting, landscaping or relationship to other properties noteworthy? Within what labels would you place its significance?

Agriculture, archeology-prehistoric, archeology-historic, architecture, art, commerce, communications, community planning, conservation, economics, education, engineering, entertainment/recreation, ethnic heritage, exploration/settlement, health/medicine, industry, invention, landscape architecture, law, literature, maritime history, military, performing arts, philosophy, politics/government, religion, science, social history, transportation, other (specify)?

If, for example, the structure was the dwelling of a lawyer who was associated with one or more specific, well-known cases, who also was city mayor and helped design the local academy still-standing, and who had his own home designed and built by a master craftsman in a newly developed style unique to the city, this house *certainly* will qualify. Another qualifying structure could be one representing the only extant example of the earliest building style in a locale, such as a well-preserved two-story sod house or a primitive log house hidden within a larger, later home.

Structure Inventory Form

Consult with state field representatives from historic preservation offices. If they believe your structure might qualify for any historic register, a structure inventory form usually is filled out as the first step in the application process, whether it be for county, state or national. The same forms often are used for all three, and are available from the state historic preservation officer. (Appendix A.) Request also the inventory form instructions, which help facilitate an application. Most of the information already collected for the house history can be used in this form.

After submitting the structure inventory form to the proper agency—the county historical society, for example, or that state—there may be several months' wait for a historic preservation officer to make an appointment to view the structure. This inspection may be optional on a county level, but is mandatory for state and national register applications.

Usually it is simplest to get county designation as a historic structure. The county will respond within weeks of your applying. On the other hand, at the national level and possibly at the state, there are other papers besides the structure inventory form to be filled out. Also, national and state offices will take more time to respond.

After a successful inspection, a multipaged form titled "National Register of Historic Places Inventory-Nomination Form" must be filled out, accompanied by appropriate maps and photos. It is submitted to the state historic preservation office (HPO), which then submits it to the state historic preservation review board. This board makes a recommendation whether or not to approve the structure for the state and possibly for the national register.

While the state HPO is reviewing the nomination, the property owners—whether or not they initiated the application—and local officials are notified and given the opportunity to concur with or object to the nomination. If the majority of these concur, the state HPO submits the nomination to the National Park Service (NPS) to be considered for listing on the National Register. If it is approved by the NPS, the property is listed on the National Register.

Because of the amount of detail required in these forms, as well as the multitiered involvement of bureaucrats, application and approval for the National Register can take years. For these reasons it may be more expedient to apply at the county register level if your house is not in a historic district. Consult the field representative of the HPO in your district or state when you are considering applying for a historic register. His help can be invaluable, since he can give you some sense of whether your house might ultimately qualify for the National Register.

19
Short Cuts

As you gain more experience in doing house histories, you will find various short cuts that reduce the time it takes to do research. Since you probably charge by the hour, your clients will welcome any methods that cut down on time spent. Also, let them know that any information *they* can find for you translates to less time spent by you, and lower fees. Some common ways to cut time are explained in this chapter.

Similar Architecture

In any area there are houses exhibiting a similar period or style, or some-times, "trademarks" of the same builders or architect. As you become familiar with common local building styles, you will learn to spot such houses when you arrive to do your on site inspection. In these cases you already will have an-swered some of your usual questions about style and era, and you can whisk through these houses, paying special attention only to the distinctive features which any house always seems to have. For example, a Gothic Revival porch, with its gingerbread ornamentation, if attached to a front-gable Greek Revival facade with a wide-board frieze and Doric pilasters, will show marked contrast in styles. Or, the 2/2 double-hung sashes will be noticeable on a Georgian facade when 12/12 light sashes are more typical, especially if the windows at the rear of the house retain the original 12/12 style.

If you are going through a house fairly quickly because you have "recognized" it, do not appear abrupt. Houses, like one's name and family pets, are regarded "affectionately" by their owners even if you—or they—think them uninteresting. Keep this fact in mind, and if the owners are present, answer their questions carefully. Always find *something* complimentary to say about the house and voice it sincerely. This is not hard to do, because there is always something interesting about a house or its landscaping or siting. Even if you may not like a house, others do.

Acquire a Title Search

The more searching that is needed, the more time-consuming is your task. Use the client's title search or abstract to speed things along. If they do not have a copy, find out who did theirs before you start your paper chase at the courthouse. Either they or you may be able to obtain a copy of the title search, maybe for no charge.

It is impossible to tell before a search is commenced how long it will take. For this reason, if a title search is offered for a price, pay it—unless the price exceeds what you would spend doing it yourself at the courthouse. For a minimum-budget, less-complicated house history, eight hours at the court-house should be adequate time for a title search. It can take up to twenty hours to do a higher-budget search, especially if you run into a problem.

In states where title insurance firms are independent of real estate lawyers, your chances of purchasing or being given a title search may be greater than in states where the title insurance firm is affiliated with a law firm or is an integral part of a law firm. In the former states, many of the people you will rub elbows with at the courthouse are title searchers for independent title insurance firms. If you become friendly with them—or know the firm's owners—and the latter know that you are interested in the search exclusively for historical purposes, they are more likely to give you the search.

If your client's lawyer or title insurance firm is uncooperative, ask previous owners if they have a copy of an earlier title search. Sometimes, for personal or sentimental reasons, people keep records that technically should have been given to the new owner when the house was sold. These individuals may be willing to have the title search photocopied.

Short Cuts at the Courthouse

If an already completed title search does not materialize, there still are some short cuts. First, always photocopy all relevant documents that you are permitted to copy. It will save time in the long run. Although the likelihood of reusing the same information probably is remote, there is always is the off-chance that you may use it again on an adjacent house and property, or for a close relative of the owners. I have had the opportunity to do both. Furthermore, if a title search document exhibits unusual characteristics, such as a complete genealogy of a family or a discussion of tenants or how the house was divided among its occupants, you may even want to keep a photocopy for yourself. I often use such unusual examples to illustrate my talks. You may even use them to give a workshop.

Beside interviewing the home owner, talk to friendly old-timers, espeially to neighbors and the town historian or retired social studies teachers. They may, for example, give you clues to the names of previous owners or of changes made in the house. If any of these previous owners were individuals prominent in the local economy or in politics, such as town officials, follow up to see if their names figure in public records, such as in town or county histories or in newspapers. This will give you fill-in material for your social-history data.

Were any of these names found on the 19th-century maps or assessment rolls or censuses, or listed as town officials in newspaper accounts? If you can target any of them as probable previous owners, you may be able to shorten your title search, *if* your client is not interested in the 20th-century history. (By using one of these names to jump back into the late 1800's you ignore the 20th century, so check with clients first. You will be ignoring some recent owners by not chaining back from the current ones.)

If clients primarily want to know about the 19th century or earlier, and you have *some* names and dates that appear on 19th-century maps and records as noted above, start your search in the courthouse indices for the name or names at a time *prior* to this listing. Look in the grantee deed index first. If one of the names appears as owner, in the correct town and location, you may have found a short cut. Work backward and forward to make sure that you have located the right property.

Although this method can work, it is more risky and more open to chance than a full title search beginning in the 20th century and working back. It assumes that the property description has not changed since the 19th century. In other words, that no property was added or subtracted from the acreage listed in the 19th century and on the most recent deed description. Use this short cut with caution and only if you are *positive* that it is the same property you have been researching.

Home-Business Research Library

Because local documents often are scattered in many different locations, it is a real time-saver if you have collected major references in one location: your place of business. A home-business research library allows you to search your sources at home before—or instead of—going to the courthouse. Such a library should consist, at the least, of the most common sources you use repeatedly— photocopies of county, city or town histories, 19th-century maps, atlases or gazetteers, county or city directories and whatever else could be valuable in your work. My collection took almost five years to build up—transcribing takes time. It includes local histories of all types, United States histories, the World Almanac, 19th-century maps and atlases, assessments, tax lists, censuses, account books, local genealogies, town minutes, photographs of old local houses, monographs on architecture, dictionaries—whatever I discover that can be photocopied if it is out of print. However, if there are relevant sources still in print, buy them, because generally, they will be cheaper than making photocopies of them.

Experts

If you hit what appears to be a dead end in some phase of your research, consult an expert. A town or county historian, a professor at a local college, a genealogist, a title-searcher or abstracter, a librarian, a preservation expert, a restoration carpenter, a well-digger, any source who has an interest in local houses, usually is happy to share knowledge. For example, in hopes of learning the age of a specific dry-wall stone well from its method of construction, I consulted an experienced well-digger. If you are trying to establish the date an individual or family arrived at a house site, a genealogist may be able to find out where they lived before and the date of the last public record of them there. An abstracter may be able to explain an unusual legal phrase in a deed or mortgage. Ask around. You will be pleasantly surprised at the number of people knowledgeable of old houses from a variety of approaches, professions and skills. However, be sure to find several sources to corroborate whatever you glean.

Imagination and Intuition

In order to understand why houses were built and furnished the way they were in a given era, read reputable historical novels. Select ones that reflect the author's research to authenticate setting, time, characters, plot, ambience, etc. Try to identify with one of the characters in the historical novel. As you read more and do more research, you will be able to imagine yourself living in a previous century, and it will become easier and easier to put yourself in the place of someone who lived in another era. Then you will understand why many women spent much of their spare time spinning, weaving, knitting and sewing. You will comprehend how time-consuming it was to spend years and years clearing a few acres from a virgin forest of giant trees. You will respect the hand-done labor that went into even a modest home.

Experience

One day as we were driving past a newly constructed, Federal-style house, my twelve-year-old son asked, "Mom, in 200 years how could you tell that house was built in 1986 and not in 1786? It *looks* like a colonial house." Part of the answer, of course, is technology: the materials used, the tool marks—or lack of them—on the building materials, and the method of construction. But it also has to do with a "feeling" or an aura about a house. A house radiates "Georgian" or "Second Empire" or Spanish or German, but only after you have acquired enough expertise to feel that aura. My son recognized the general identification of a "colonial" house, yet his experience is not sophisticated enough to be able to analyze its individual parts and place the "colonial" house in a specific time period. Through knowledge of the details of a period, one develops such perceptiveness. You have internalized a collection of details as you observe different houses. With experience the details coalesce, to tell you that a specific house is a certain style from a certain era, a specific builder, or a specific ethnic group. Recognition is developed by repeated exposure to similar structures. In a word, you have become "experienced." It will become increasingly easier for you to identify houses, even when later changes cover up their origins.

Section V
Your Own Business

20

Setting Up Your Business

To set up a house histories business you first should gain some experience in researching houses and identifying how architectural periods were expressed in your area. You should know something about local history and where records are located, and have some experience in reading old documents. You should have developed enough contacts so that you feel confident and qualified to know where to look or who to ask for answers to a house history question. Then the time is ripe to start your own business.

Business Organization

There are three common ways to organize your business: sole proprietorship, partnership and corporation. In a small service business, such as house histories, which requires relatively little initial capital outlay, it is suggested that you register the business as a sole proprietorship. Then both responsibility and control are in the domain of one person, an arrangement considered by many as the most efficient way to conduct a small business. You alone have the responsibility for raising capital, running the business in a professional manner and making it a financial success.

A partnership is more complicated, because co-owners must be consulted. If the partners have invested equal amounts of capital in the business, they always must reach some consensus before making business decisions. Partners should be carefully chosen. Personality conflicts and differing life styles are common reasons for the dissolution of partnerships.

If, however, someone is willing to supply capital and trusts you and your abilities enough to become a silent partner, or a non-decision-making partner, you may be able to work without interference.

A corporation in which there may be only a few investors or several, has the advantage of absolving you from any personal financial loss if the business does not succeed. On the other hand, it involves setting up—at least on paper—a board of directors who could become decision-makers. You may not agree with their decisions. Also, scheduling meetings for this extra layer of administration may postpone decisions, hindering day-to-day operation.

Capital, Space and Equipment

You will need very little capital in order to begin a house histories business. You can start with only a desk or table and chair and a few cardboard files. Basic equipment will include a typewriter, a telephone, a few in-and-out paper files, bookends and a 35mm camera. Paper supplies will include bond paper— preferably 25% cotton fiber—legal-size envelopes, 10" x 13" heavy weight clasp envelopes, manila folders, yellow-lined note pads and a business telephone/address book. It is cheaper to buy the paper supplies by the box. If you answer some office-supply ads, you will get on their mailing lists and be notified of their sales.

It is important to have space to work in. The ideal office would be a separate room with a door to shut out extraneous noises and a doorknob to hang a "Quiet, Writing" sign on. The space should be large enough to house your furniture and equipment, the bookshelves should have one shelf for outsize books, and besides regular files, there should be one legal-size file. Also, a map file with pull-out drawers will hold, besides maps, the large, irregularly sized censuses and photostats.

Of course, if you can afford it, your ideal office would have a word processor and a photocopier. You may also want to hire a part-time assistant.

"Doing Business As—DBA"

You will need to decide on your business name and logo as you will need them for business cards, stationary and possibly a brochure. Before you finalize the design or printing of these, visit your county courthouse, or whatever jurisdiction in your state is the proper licensing bureau for small businesses. Check there to make sure that the business name you have chosen is unique and there is not another business with a similar name. You will want your business name to be easily recognizable and not readily confused with another business.

Once a unique business name is settled on, the next step, in most states, is the "DBA." If you do not use your own name as your business name, you will have to fill out a DBA form and register it at the proper jurisdiction. The DBA —Doing Business As—form can be purchased at a stationery or office-supply store. You will need at least two copies of this "Certificate of Conducting Business Under an Assumed Name" form. Fill them out and return to the clerk's office to date and sign them in front of the notary public there. The clerk or his designate will assign a number to your business, date the form, sign it and affix the jurisdiction's seal. After paying the recording fee, you are legally a business.

Your Logo

It is useful to have a logo, so that people associate a specific graphic image with your business. You may design your own or have it designed by a graphic artist. I designed mine using a stylized historic house as a model. The house is typical to our area—a late 18th-century center-chimney, three-bay, one-and-a-half story Connecticut house with a 19th-century wing added. You might want to consider a logo that reflects a type of structure common in *your* geographic location.

If you decide to design your own logo, it must be submitted to the printer "camera ready" since the photographs will show the flaws as well as the perfect copy. Execute your design with black pen on white paper. To ensure effective contrast in the reproduction, the black pen should be black—not grayish—and should color evenly. Its tip should produce clean, crisp lines. The design that you give the printer can be any reasonably small size. He will reduce it to harmonize with the appropriate type-size for a business card.

The name you choose should reflect what you do. I chose House Histories because it is exactly what I do. It always elicits questions, but any name you give this type of business probably will, because it is a new, uncommon business. There are other possibilities: "House Genealogies," "Historic Housework," "Home Histories," "House Memoirs," "House Research," "Home Research," "House Happenings," "House Tracing." Your imagination may supply other more romantic names. I chose "House Histories," because telephone books and other guides organized by subject would place it on or near the real estate listings —an advertising advantage—or under "houses."

Printed Supplies

Your business card should list your address and telephone number. I chose to list my name also because I personally dislike talking to a business name when I telephone. I prefer asking for a person. Because of the newness and obscurity of the business, I also decided to include on the card a four-line explanation of what House Histories does. In order to provide space for the explanation, a tent-style business card was used. This is a double size business card, 3 1/2" x 4", folded in the middle to form a tent. The logo, business name, my name, address and telephone number are on the front side. The explanation is on the inside.

When you choose the paper and print color, think ahead. One of the cheapest display ads is a reproduction of your business card. If the print is black and the paper white, newspaper or rubber-stamp makers can reproduce your logo and print style easily from your card. My business cards are slightly textured light buff with dark brown type, which has enough contrast for reproduction in newspaper advertising. Ask the printer's advice before you decide on colors.

If you do not want to spend money on letterhead, type your business name, address and telephone number on plain bond paper. A rubber stamp also can be used, for letterhead and other items, including return envelopes and file covers. If you do decide to have stationary and envelopes printed, remember, if you choose colors other than white, that they will become permanently associated with your business. Make a careful choice.

Your printer will advise you on numbers of business cards and stationery to print at first. The most expensive part of a printer's fee is the design and setup, not the printing. One thousand items cost approximately 40% more than 500 items, not 100% more. Usually a printer will not run less than 500 items and prefers at least 1,000. If you live in an urban area, 1,000 cards may not be sufficient, while those of us living in a rural area wonder how on earth we will ever use up 500. Always keep a few business cards in your wallet, and distribute them to related businesses, such as real estate and insurance agencies, and antique shops as you come across them.

You may decide to use a printed brochure, which can hold more than just the business card information. A brochure may be helpful in explaining what a house histories business is. When advertising through the mail, a brochure is preferable to a cover letter and a business card. The brochure explains what a house history is and how it is researched and includes excerpts from a completed house history. It also can be used as a handout when giving talks. A folded six-panel 8 1/2" x 11" brochure fits nicely into a business-size envelope. Five of the six panels contain copy, with visual relief provided by the logo and a picture. The sixth panel contains only the logo and business address, as the return address, to provide room for the mailing address and stamp.

Locating Customers

Names and addresses for a publicity mailing are limited only by your imagination. An obvious source is real estate agents since they sell houses, some of which are old. They may be interested in house histories either for themselves, to enhance their sales, or for their clients, who may be new to the area and curious about the house and previous owners. There is more than one source of lists of real estate agents. Approach your neighborhood real estate agent, explain your business and ask if his or her office could supply a photocopied list of real estate agents in the area. Another source of such mailing lists is the real estate board or multiple listing service. (You can, if you wish, join the real estate board as an associate or affiliate member.) Not all realtors will be members of the board. Consult the yellow pages for others.

Insurance agents, antique dealers, historical society members, museum curators and members, architectural preservationists and tradesmen who specialize in restoring or rehabilitating old houses are other promising groups of professionals to include on your mailing list.

Many local newspapers publish a weekly list of deed transfers—transactions that have occurred in the last week or so. These usually list the location, the seller, the buyer and how much the buyers paid in stamp tax. This may be $3, $4, or $5 per $1,000 of the purchase price. From this you can estimate the price paid. This purchase price—relative to price ranges in your area—suggests how affluent the buyers may be, and wealthier people are more likely to want a house history. Sometimes the published deed-transfer lists contain addresses, or try the courthouse where the deed transfers were filed. Before contacting a prospective client via this means, take a drive to see the property. It would be pointless to send out a brochure or cover letter and business card if the house is only a few years old.

As you become better known, you might want to expand your mailing lists to surrounding counties and states. When you cross a state border, however, be sure to research the business-licensing requirements in that state before you accept jobs there. You probably will have to register your DBA, and state tax laws may differ. A service, such as house histories, may not be taxed in your state, while it may be in an adjacent state. And, some states tax out-of-state workers at a higher rate than residents.

Advertising and Promotion

Other than direct mailings, how can you most effectively advertise your service? An excellent method is to give talks to organizations: real estate boards, historical societies, clubs, trade associations, church groups, Masons, the D.A.R., academies, libraries, and whatever else exists in you area. Organizations that need monthly or weekly speakers always are on the lookout for new topics or a new face. In this way, you are providing a free service while simultaneously promoting your business. It gives you a positive image and will turn up clients for you.

To date I have four prepared talks that I suggest to such groups:

• local genealogy gleaned through house histories;

• travel, transportation and entertainment through the eyes of adolescents—taken from 19th-century correspondence;

- 18th- and 19th-century social history discovered while searching houses;

- how to do house histories with a slide show or transparencies for visual support.

I usually ask beforehand if a group has a particular idea or emphasis that they want the talk to center around. Then I alter my "canned" talks to include information pertinent to the particular group or locale, so that the audience feels that I am relating directly to them. Always ask their time limit and respect it, leaving enough time for questions. Always include humorous anecdotes. Afterward, hand out brochures and business cards.

These talks give you exposure, future references for house histories and contacts. The people you meet may be well-known in a related field, such as preservation technology or genealogy or local history. Sometimes organizations will reimburse your mileage costs, provide you with a set, low honorarium, give you copies of their publications or pay for your meal.

The meeting and talk will be written up in the local paper. Ask for copies of this from the secretary or program chairperson for your publicity file.

Write Articles

Another effective advertising method is to write feature articles for the local newspaper in exchange for a display ad there. The articles may be mini-features on local historic houses or related local history, or on a historical or unique house currently for sale. To get material about the latter, approach real estate agents to suggest writing about a specific house listing. This gives them free advertising and gives you material. The agent provides you with the specs (construction details) and whatever else is known about the house. You fill in with the historical details gleaned from your own local library files. Either the agent or you provide the photos. The articles can be written on a regular basis with a specific newspaper, thus insuring regular exposure via the display ads for your business as payment. If this type of real estate advertising catches on and there are multiple mini-articles, you should ask for a percentage of the real estate ad fee to reimburse you for your time. The advantage of this means of advertising is double exposure: in your display ad and in your article. It also offers a chance to show off your researching and writing abilities for potential clients and maybe eventually realize income from them.

Historical Radio Minute

A third effective means for promoting your business is a "Historical Minute" about local history recorded by you and aired daily on a local radio station. Again, the obvious advantage is exposure and, hence, a chance for potential clients to judge your expertise. There could be one disadvantage: small-city radio stations may expect you to drum up your own sponsors to pay for the sixty-second spot. If it is aired daily during the week, that may mean locating five different sponsors, depending on the fee and the local interest. If you can coordinate your topics with your sponsors' business interests, and these are general enough, you may be able to sustain sponsor support for a longer period of time. The ideal spot would be prime time after the six o'clock news. Television spots are another possibility, as well as television and radio talk shows.

Display Ads

Paid display advertising comes last in the list of effective advertising, because it is effective only with repeated exposure and hence can become costly. Advertising only a few times, of course, can be effective if you are lucky enough to have a feature reporter see it and call you to do a piece on your unusual business. Feature editors and free-lance feature writers pursue display ads looking for something different to write about. I have been interviewed eight times —for five periodicals, a radio station and a television station—in three years. In most cases, the interviews resulted in more business, eventually extending to six counties in two states.

It is not recommended that you write self-promotion pieces thinly disguised as press releases. Although local newspaper may carry the piece because it fills up space and does not have to be paid for, larger, more completely staffed newspapers may be turned off enough to never write a feature about you. Self-promotional pieces also may turn off the reader no matter how good your services may be. An endorsement by an apparently disinterested third party, such as a reporter or a real estate board or an arts council, is much more effective.

Endorsement Lists

The last form of advertising is the endorsement listing. These are lists of individuals within a specific geographic area or subject range who are considered capable in their fields. Usually these people have attained at least local stature for being "good" at what they do. For example, local arts councils often compile lists of all types of artists, from performing artists to sculptors and writers. The lists include the type of product or mode of performance, as well as who will give talks, workshops, demonstrations, or readings. These lists usually are compiled at no cost to the "artist" and are a means of publicizing them. Although these lists do not usually mean an endorsement by the arts council, the public often perceives them as such. (I have been able to get such a listing as a house historian.)

Similar lists of services offered to home owners often are compiled by real estate boards. The advertiser pays a fee, perhaps $50, to be included on the roster. Again, this listing does not necessarily mean an endorsement, but there usually is a statement at the beginning of the booklet assuring buyers of the high quality or reliability of those advertising in it.

Obviously you will never know if ads work for you if you do not place them. To be able to accurately evaluate responses to different ads, be sure to key each ad in some way. Word the ad a little differently for different publications, or add a number or letter to your name or address. When a prospective client contacts you, always ask how they found out about your business. Drop the unproductive ads.

Credentials

As a brand-new business, you often may have to supply credentials to potential clients. These credentials will include any degrees you may have, any courses taken or talks given, as well as your experience. Perhaps one of the better ways to build your credentials is to join historical and genealogical societies or writers' guilds. If you cannot join all of those available, you can attend their meetings. You will pick up helpful information at their meetings or talks, and the exposure to people you meet there will help your business.

You may have the opportunity to publish local history articles. These will add to your credentials. Local weeklies often welcome historical articles about the area. My interest in houses, architecture and history was not "born overnight" by writing a couple of articles, however. I had loved a couple of history of architecture courses taken in college and had recently helped design our passive solar home. There probably are several things you have done during your life that were house-related. No matter what initiated your interest, there are many houses waiting for their histories to be discovered. By following the suggestions in these chapters, you can make this hobby into a business.

21

Dealing with Clients and Keeping Business Records

To prove to the Internal Revenue Service that you run a business, you must keep complete records of all daily business transactions. Hours spent, miles driven, purchases made — all must be logged. You also need a systematic setup for clients, so that you are dealing with each in the same way, on paper.

Pricing

How much will people pay for the luxury of history? I presently charge only twelve dollars per hour for research and writing the narrative. Most potential clients react with, "Oh, that's low!" Then I point out that expenses— mileage, long distance calls, photocopying, film and postage—also are charged.

Mileage can become a significant expense if a house historian needs to travel some distance to record repositories. (Our county courthouse is a forty-six-mile round-trip each time, and my charge is twenty cents a mile.) All trips to visit repositories, as well as to the target house, are included in house history costs. Photocopying is the next biggest expense, but the client does receive all of the photocopies.

My hourly charge is average. Is some areas similar researcher writers charge twenty to thirty dollars per hour, while in others five to eight dollars is the going rate. The researcher most often compared to a house historian is a genealogist, who charges five to twenty-five dollars an hour. I have chosen not to raise my fees, because $800-$1,000 per job is about what the market will bear in our locale. You will have to feel your way on this in your area, and determine what is appropriate and comfortable for you.

Time Required

How long does it take to do the average house history? I keep a running tally of the average number of hours it takes me to complete one. How long it will take *you* depends on the availability of records in your area and how long your area has been settled. Southerners tended to keep family papers and also kept good public records. In New England, fairly complete public records have been kept, while the Mid-Atlantic states were and still are more complicated in their record-keeping procedures and less stringent in their registration requirements. Because of the relative youth of the western states and the ready availability of records—they primarily were originated by the federal government so it may take less time to research these—a house history there may take only fifty hours.

I advise potential clients of the average time involved, so they will have a clear understanding of how many dollars the job may cost. If the potential client feels strongly that this is more than he or she wants to or can pay, I suggest setting a fixed limit, such as $500. Or, a client may have set a vague iimit of $500. In either case, when the job nears $350, I report my progress to them, thus leaving me a time-cushion for writing a brief time line if they want to stop there. If they do, I give them the report to date—the time line—and stop at the $500 limit. (Sometimes they may try to complete the house history for themselves. More often after they discover some of the difficulties that may be involved in researching old houses or when they weary of doing the legwork, they rehire me.) Still other people ask me to continue the research past $350 or $500, because their interest is piqued.

I never suggest an amount lower than $300, because a house historian will have very little to show in less than that amount of time. Three hundred dollars usually means two trips to the courthouse and one to the house itself, all the photocopying, and many hours of research and writing. Depending on where the house is located, you may spend thirty dollars on mileage and ten to fifteen dollars on photocopying. One hundred dollars means only a little over eight hours of writing, rewriting, typing time. That leaves just under thirteen hours for research and analysis. Although these times may sound generous, in reality they are not. It takes a great deal of time to do research properly.

Costs vary for each job and are hard to predict. Be cautious in your estimates. If a house was built in 1882 and had only five owners in the last 107 years, it would take less time to research than if it had had new owners every few years in the 20th century. A house built in the 1790's would take even more time than the 19th-century house, because there are ninety more years and several more owners to research and because, in many locales, records before about 1830 often are harder to trace.

Be Clear about Costs

Beware of clients who ask you to find the answers to off-the-wall questions, such as the reputation of the local in-ground swimming pool install-ers or which of the town representatives is sympathetic to historic rehabilita-tion. Make it clear beforehand that you will be happy to inquire, but that it is beyond the normal scope of a house history's contract. Otherwise, they may later object to the fee you charge—which included your time spent researching their inappropriate requests.

Always be sure to put in writing any verbal agreements you make with such clients. Write them a letter clarifying the verbal agreement and send it certified with a return receipt to make sure that they received it. (You also may want to send a completed house history in this manner for the same reason.)

Problems

Researching house histories is a relatively problem-free business. There are, of course, a few typical problems. Primary among these is time, a particular nemesis for the house historian. It takes much more time to unearth "history" than most people realize. People also tend to think that the history relating to their house is out there somewhere, a bunch of facts waiting for someone to re-trieve by pushing the right button on the computer. The truth is that history is thousands of facts and the house historian must select those which are pertinent to the house history. These facts, plus those collected from your on site inspec-tion, then must be analyzed and interwoven, to set your house in the broader historical context. There are a variety of historical interpretations that can be ap-plied. Once developed, this interpretation is unique to this house. It took time to do and time is money.

The misperception of the difficulties of such research can occasionally result in slow payment or non-payment by a client who views history as a free commodity. If you can spot these potential problem-clients at the outset, you may want to avoid undertaking their house history. These sorts of problems almost never arise, but their potential occurrence underscores the importance of keeping a running log, listing dates and what was done, as well as costs for each account.

Try to find out at the outset exactly what the clients want from your re-search. Beware of clients who ask for a house history, but who really are aiming to get their property listed on a historic register. Even though much of the re-quired initial work has been completed in the house history, listing a house on a register can take many additional hours. You must make it clear to your client that application to any register will include additional hours that will be billed separately. Depending on the age of the structure, its complexity and the volume of documents, it may take you an additional ten to fifty hours or more to fill out the forms, rewrite your narrative to follow the instructions, type the applications, photocopy all necessary documents and meet with the state historic preservation officer and possibly other officials, including the local ones.

Save all records on each house history. A few years down the line a former client may ask you to apply for a historic register. Or, they simply may need to know the phone number of a previous owner, because the septic system has failed and the plumber cannot locate the septic tank and leach beds.

In those states where the total house history costs tend to be cheaper because records are readily available, real estate brokers will hire you because the house has more value and is more saleable if its architectural style and/or past owners are verified.

I avoid doing house histories for clients who are buying a house, but do not yet own it. It is preferable to wait until after the closing. At the least, before you begin work confirm with the real estate agent that the buyers have put down a substantial binder, proving their sincere interest in it.

Contract

After clients request house history services, meet them at the house with a contract specifying what you will do for the fee. (On occasion I meet with a caretaker, but only after I have mailed a contract to the potential clients and have received a retainer.) After they sign the contract, begin your on site inspection.

The following is a copy of my contract:

HOUSE HISTORIES

Sarah (Sally) Light

P.O. Box 17, Harvey Mountain Road
Austerlitz, New York 12017

518/392-4270

Contract

We will search to determine names and dates of previous owners and data

pertaining to the _____

located at _____

currently owned by _____

name   telephone

    Various appropriate sources, such as interviews and documents,
will be employed to obtain information relevant to the history of the
above house. Pertinent documents will be photocopied when accessible.
Stories passed along by oral tradition will be included, if they can
be substantiated by two or more sources.

    The information will be compiled, typewritten in narrative form on
plain 8½" x 11" bond paper or a photocopy, whichever appears neater. A
variety of print formats and bindings are available as options, some of
which are noted below. The client will have the option of examining
the report in draft form prior to final typing or printing, if desired.

    Although the researcher takes all reasonable precautions in regard
to the accuracy of data reporting, since historical records themselves
occasionally contain errors, the researcher may not be held responsible
for these errors. The researcher, Sarah B. Light, retains the copyright
on each house history.

    If the search yields little historical information, the client
will be consulted concerning the depth of pursuit, and will decide the
point of termination. In such a case the client will be billed only
for the expenses and fees thus far incurred and will receive the data
obtained when the search is terminated. If the expenses and fees are
less than the retainer, the client will receive a refund.

The second page is the reimbursement or bill. At the on site inspection I always ask for a $100 retainer to insure sincerity of intent. The retainer is deducted from the final total upon completion of the house history. If, at any point during the beginning of research, the client decides not to complete the house history, I deduct the expenses and hours incurred to date and send any refund.

REIMBURSEMENT

Expenses   Fees

$_____ mileage $_____ _____ hours research

_____ telephone   _____ hours writing

_____ photo-copying/printing $_____ Total
         postage
$_____ Total $_____ Grand Total

                                  - 100. Retainer _____Date

                                  = _____ Total monthly payments
                                             made

                      Date _____ $_____ Balance due upon delivery

SPECIAL NOTES

Type of printing _____

Type of binding _____

Color of cover _____ Style of printing _____

Date desired _____

Upper limits _____

Other (photographs, etc.) _____

_____

_____

Signature of client   Date initiated

Signature of client   Date terminated

Signed: _____
         Sarah B. Light

246

Copyright

There is another reason for not pricing your business too high. I retain the copyright on each house history, because it is a potential money-maker. I am free to publish the house histories at some future time as, for instance, *Old Homes in Columbia County*, or to use excerpts from them. To date I have only used excerpts. If I were to use the completed manuscripts, I would, out of courtesy, ask the permission of the house owner, although legally I would not have to do so. If you decide to copyright your house histories, Form TX (for manuscripts) can be obtained from the Copyright Office. (Appendix A.) A ten dollar fee must be included with each application.

Monthly Invoice

Develop an invoice designed to be mailed monthly. This will help assure a steady income as you research, because you are billing clients as you complete work, rather than waiting for the finished product. Most people are used to paying bills monthly, and this also will stimulate you to keep moving ahead on the research. The invoice may be divided into two sections—a top and bottom —with the invoice number and amount indicated on both. Make up a system of invoice numbers any way you like. (I use the first three letters of the person's surname with a dash and a "1" the first time I bill them: LIG-1.) The top section includes the name and address of the account and the account number. The bottom section has the account number, your expenses itemized with hours spent and the total sum, along with a brief progress report. State the steps that still need to be done and, if possible, a guesstimate of how long it may take you. Err on the high side; it is better to overestimate hours than to underestimate them. If you honestly do not have the foggiest notion, do not attempt to estimate, because your client may try to force you to stick with your estimate.

Bank Account

After receiving your first $100 or so, open a bank account in your business name with your name as the owner and your social security number as your tax number. Keep your business and family or personal accounts separate for income tax purposes and maintain complete records of all transactions. Your accountant can be only as effective as your daily records are complete and accurate.

Record Keeping

The more complete records are those maintained daily. I have trained myself to head for the ledger as soon as I walk into the house, to record where I went, how many miles, tolls and parking fees there were and how much I spent on photocopying, office supplies, etc. Always ask for receipts.

I record daily all expenses and income in a general business ledger, because I do more than write house histories for income. I also write newspaper articles and ad copy related to historical houses for sale. Also, I am continually collecting archival material—the kind that surfaces periodically in someone's attic or barn and belongs to a family, rather than being available as a public document—so that I have it in my file to be used at some future date. Photocopying the material before returning it to its owners generates expenses which must be recorded.

An easy means of recording all these items is to maintain running lists of income and expenses itemized separately on ledgers under the accepted Internal Revenue Service categories for income and deductions. Thus I write all office expenses in one column, all car and truck expenses in another, all advertising expenses in a third, and so on. Income is listed on a separate ledger.

When I am working on a specific house history, I keep two 8 1/2" x 11" yellow-lined note pads in the house history folder. One note pad is used for notes on the content of the house history. The other is used as an account log. Each day that I work on the house history, I log the date, the times started and ended (the hours spent) and whether the hours were for research or writing; any money spent and for what (usually photocopying); telephone calls made, including time, name and number; miles driven, tolls, parking fees. This method insures that I have records for each house history account, as well as one general business ledger. After two or three days of working on a house history, I add up the expenses and fees to date to make sure I am keeping within the limits set by the client.

Business Expenses

There are several expenses recognized by the Internal Revenue Service as legitimate business expenses incurred by small profit-making businesses, which can be deducted from your income. Check with your accountant annually —the easiest time is at the end of the year when you are in touch with him to submit the year's accounts for tax purposes—to ascertain that the deducted expenses remain the same for the following year. Otherwise you may be keeping records that are obsolete for that year, or missing new deductions.

The following is a brief description of deductible expenses that you may incur as a house historian. These deductions are taken from Part II of Schedule C "Profit or (Loss) From Business or Profession (Sole Proprietorship)" of Form 1040.

Advertising would included all display ads, business cards, brochures and any other product that you use for promoting your business, such as pens with your business name engraved on them.

Bank service charges, of course, can be deducted on your business account.

Car and truck expenses will include all mileage, tolls and parking fees, as well as repairs, if you used the vehicle exclusively for business. If you use it also for pleasure, figure what percentage of miles were used for business and use that percentage to figure the amount of repairs applicable for business purposes.

You may have *depreciation* to deduct on office equipment and machines. Keep receipts of purchase prices and dates bought and check with your accountant to determine which depreciation method to use.

Dues and publications pertaining to business and professional organizations , (historical societies, architectural historians' associations, etc.) you belong to or materials you buy exclusively for business purposes, such as periodicals.

You may have *insurance* on your office furniture. These premiums are deductible, as are premiums for "library" insurance. (Once you have collected a few thousand dollars worth of photocopied references and books in your business library, you may want to have insurance on "valuable papers." Generally, this insurance has a minimum premium of $500 with a $250 deductible. In order to make a claim, you have to have proof of the existence of these "valuable papers." A written inventory of them should be kept in a safe deposit box, and all books and photocopy receipts should be kept for each year.)

Interest deductions would include *mortage interest* if your business is housed in a building mortgaged separately from your residence; and *other interest,* such as interest on a business loan.

Legal and professional services include your accountant's annual fee for the business reporting of your income tax and any other services which he provides, and a lawyer's fee for writing up, for example, a house histories contract, or any other legal services you require.

Office expenses include office supplies, postage, film, photocopying, etc. (Remember to keep track of photocopying expenses for your library collection.)

If you *rent* an office, this rent can be deducted.

Repairs needed for office equipment, such as typewriters, computers or photocopiers are deductible.

Taxes would be applicable if your business is housed in a separate building on which you pay property taxes.

Travel and entertainment would include any business trips or business entertaining that were necessary functions of your job. For example, if you attend a conference to give a paper or talk related to house histories, your travel, room and board expenses would be deductible.

Utilities and telephone expenses constitute another business deduction. If you work out of a room in your house that is used exclusively for your business, you can figure the square footage and deduct it from the total square footage of the house. Then find the percent that your office space represents of the whole and multiply your utility bills by that percent to figure that deduction. Of course, if your business is housed separately, all utilities will be deductible. Even if you do not have a business phone separate from your house phone, you can deduct all long-distance phone calls made for business purposes. You must keep a log, and a tally of the numbers called to be able to prove such a deduction.

The last typical deduction for a house historian is *wages* paid to someone else. If you decide that you need part-time office help, the easiest way is to hire someone in a subcontractor relationship. An example is the services of a person who runs their own electrical business. In this way, you avoid being responsible for benefits, such as health insurance, unemployment insurance, social security, etc. If the subcontractor earns more than $600 in one year, you must supply the IRS with a form 1099 for this person. Consult with your accountant before hiring.

This concludes the usual list of deductions allowed by the IRS. Your state may apply these deductions in their tax schedule or include others or disqualify some of the above. Unless you have part-time help, your greatest deduction probably will be your car, followed by your office expenses. When you are starting up your business, advertising may be the third most costly item until you learn which advertising is the most effective. As you accumulate your library, dues and publications will probably be the fourth most costly item. As your business grows, wages paid to a jobber will become a more significant part of your expenses.

In addition to paying taxes on your profits, you must pay the social security self-employment tax if your net or profit exceeds $400. The form to use is Schedule SE of Form 1040. Since the percent, as well as the maximum salary limits, change yearly, your accountant should figure this tax.

All other record-keeping will depend on how your state, county and city taxes are figured. Again, check with your accountant before finalizing your record-keeping categories.

Until you make substantial profits, you will have to file only by the usual April 15th date. If you net $2,000 or more quarterly, at the least you would have to send quarterly payments of estimated social security self-employment taxes. Again, check with your accountant.

It usually takes at least two years for a business to become profitable. The IRS expects a business to show a profit twice every five years to be declared a business and not a hobby. This is only a guideline, however, and not a rule. If the IRS suspects that the intention of the business is not to show a profit, or, in other words, is for self-recognition, they can throw out all previous declarations and impose heavy penalties by declaring the business an expensive hobby. An example: if excessive losses of $5,000 are incurred for three of the five years and minimal profits of $200 are registered for two years, the IRS may declare the business an expensive hobby. They want you to watch costs and adjust prices upward to insure a profit. They do not want to foster an expensive hobby in which expenses—as deductibles—are allowed to be subtracted from slim profits in order to show a loss.

Hired Help

College students, especially those majoring in languages, literature, history or fine arts/architecture are a particularly good resource for helping out on a part-time basis with house histories. They may have had experience working with old materials, such as archives and records, and have a general enough academic background to be open to learning your methods.

Students may be available during the January term, which in many colleges is a month-long term designed for internships. During internships the student works on a project for a grade or for experience. The employer's responsibilities are to train and evaluate, but not to pay. As a small business, you may be expected to room and board them also. After training them, you may want to offer them a part-time job immediately, or ask them to work for you during the following summer.

Writing house histories is a rewarding business. In few others are you rewarded financially for uncovering facts that interest you. Clients usually are pleasant, enthusiastic and eager to know whatever you can find out about their house. The work is stimulating and fun. You are your own boss, set your own schedule and make your own rules. What better framework for working?

Section VI

Appendices

A

Resources/Where to Write

National Park Service

For information on the National Register of Historic Places, Historic American Buildings Survey, Historic American Engineering Record, Preservation Assistance Division, Archaeological Assistance Division, contact:

Associate Director, Cultural Resources,
Keeper, National Register of Historic Places
National Park Service
P.O. Box 37127
Washington, D.C. 20013-7127
202-343-4747

Or, your regional office of the National Park Service:

Alaska Regional Office
National Park Service
2525 Gambell Street, Room 107
Anchorage, Alaska 99503
907-257-2690; FTS 257-2690

Mid-Atlantic Regional Office
National Park Service
143 South Third Street
Philadelphia, Pennsylvania 19106
215-597-7013; FTS 597-7013

Midwest Regional Office
National Park Service
1709 Jackson Street
Omaha, Nebraska 68102
402-221-3431; FTS 864-3431

National Capital Regional Office
National Park Service
1100 Ohio Drive, SW
Washington, D.C. 20242
202-426-6612; FTS 426-6612 and FTS 426-5720

North Atlantic Regional Office
National Park Service
15 State Street
Boston, Massachusetts 02109
617-565-8800; FTS 835-8800

Pacific Northwest Regional Office
National Park Service
83 South King Street, Suite 212
Seattle, Washington 98104
206-442-5565; FTS 339-5565

Rocky Mountain Regional Office
National Park Service
12795 West Alameda Parkway
P.O. Box 25287
Denver, Colorado 80225
303-969-2000; FTS 327-2500

Southeast Regional Office
National Park Service
75 Spring Street, SW
Atlanta, Georgia 30303
404-331-5185; FTS 242-5185

Southwest Regional Office
National Park Service
1100 Old Santa Fe Trail
Santa Fe, New Mexico 87501
505-988-6388; FTS 476-6388

Western Regional Office
National Park Service
450 Golden Gate Avenue
P.O. Box 36063
San Francisco, California 94102
415-556-4196; FTS 556-4196

Other Useful Addresses

Register of Copyrights
Library of Congress
Washington, D.C. 20559

Sanborn Map Co.
629 5th Avenue
Pelham, New York 10803

United States Department of the Interior
Western Distribution Branch
U.S. Geological Survey
Denver Federal Center
P.O. Box 25425
Denver, Colorado 80225

National Archives and Records Centers

Reference Services Branch
7th and Pennsylvania Avenue NW
Washington, D.C. 20408
292-523-3220 8:45 a.m.-9:45 p.m. Mon.-Fri.; 9 a.m.-5 p.m. Sat.

Washington National Records Center
4205 Suitland Road
Suitland, Maryland 20409
(Serves the District of Columbia, Maryland, Virginia and West Virginia.)

For the following branches address inquiries to:

Director, National Archives (name of city) Branch

Atlanta
1557 St. Joseph Avenue
East Point, Georgia 30344
404-763-7477 8:00 a.m.-5:00 p.m. Mon.-Fri.
(Serves Alabama, Florida, Georgia, Kentucky, Mississippi, North Carolina, South Carolina and Tennessee.)

Boston
380 Trapelo Road
Waltham, Massachusetts 02154
617-647-8100 8:00 a.m.-4:30 p.m. Mon.-Fri.
(Serves Connecticut, Maine, Massachusetts, New Hampshire, Rhode Island and Vermont.)

Chicago
7358 South Pulaski Road
Chicago, Illinois 60629
312-581-7816 8:00 a.m.-4:30 p.m. Mon.-Fri.
(Serves Illinois, Minnesota and Wisconsin. Also Indiana, Michigan and Ohio for U.S. Court records.)

Dayton
3150 Springboro Road
Dayton, Ohio 45439
513-225-2852 7:30 a.m.-4:00 p.m. Mon.-Fri
(Serves Indiana, Michigan and Ohio except U.S. Court records, which are found at the Chicago branch.)

Denver
Building 48
Denver Federal Center
Denver, Colorado 80225
303-236-0818 8:00 a.m.-3:30 p.m. Mon.-Fri.
(Serves Colorado, Montana, North Dakota, South Dakota, Utah and Wyoming.)

Fort Worth
501 West Felix Street
P.O. Box 6216
Fort Worth, Texas 76115
817-334-5525 8:00 a.m.-4:00 p.m. Mon.-Fri.
(Serves Arkansas, Louisiana, New Mexico, Oklahoma and Texas.)

Kansas City
2312 East Bannister Road
Kansas City, Missouri 64131
816-926-7271 8:00 a.m.-4:30 p.m. Mon.-Fri.
(Serves Iowa, Kansas, Missouri and Nebraska.)

Los Angeles.
24000 Avila Road
1st Floor
P.O. Box 6719
Laguna Niguel, California 92677-6719
714-643-4220 8:00 a.m.-4:30 p.m.
(Serves Arizona; the southern California counties: Imperial, Inyo, Kern, Los Angeles,
Orange, Riverside, San Bernardino, San Diego, San Luis Obispo, Santa Barbara and Ventura;
and Clark County, Nevada.)

New York
Building 22
Military Ocean Terminal
Bayonne, New Jersey 07002-5388
201-823-7252 8:00 a.m.-4:30 p.m.
(Serves New Jersey, New York, Puerto Rico and the Virgin Islands.)

Philadelphia
9th & Market Streets
Room 1350
Philadelphia, Pennsylvania 19107
215-597-3000 7:30 a.m.-4:00 p.m. Mon.-Fri.
(Serves Delaware and Pennsylvania.)

San Francisco
1000 Commodore Drive
San Bruno, California 94066-2350
415-876-9009 7:45 a.m.-4:15 p.m. Mon.-Fri.
(Serves California except the southern counties, Hawaii, Nevada except Clark County and the
Pacific Ocean area.)

Seattle
6125 Sand Point Way NE
Seattle, Washington 98115
206-526-6507 7:45 a.m.-4:15 p.m. Mon.-Fri.
(Serves Alaska, Idaho, Oregon and Washington.)

State Historical Archives

Alabama Department of Archives and
History
624 Washington Avenue
Montgomery, Alabama 36130
205-261-4361

Alaska Historical Library
P.O. Box G
Division of State Libraries
Juneau, Alaska 99801-0571
907-465-2925

Arizona State Department of Library,
Archives, and Public Records
1700 West Washington Street, Suite 200
Phoenix, Arizona 85007
602-542-4035

Arkansas History Commission
1 Capitol Mall
Little Rock, Arkansas 72201
501-682-6900

California State Archives
1020 O Street
Sacramento, California 95814
916-445-4293

Colorado Division of State Archives and
Public Records
1313 Sherman Street
Denver, Colorado 80203
303-866-2055

Connecticut State Library
231 Capitol Avenue
Hartford, Connecticut 06106
203-566-4777

Delaware Division of Historical and Cultural
Affairs
Hall of Records
Dover, Delaware 19901
302-736-5314

Florida Division of Archives, History, and
Records Management
R.A. Gray Building
500 South Bronough Street
Tallahassee, Florida 32399-0250
904-488-1480

Georgia Department of Archives and
History
330 Capitol Avenue
Atlanta, Georgia 30334
404-656-2393

Hawaii State Archives
Iolani Palace Grounds
Honolulu, Hawaii 96813
808-548-2355

Idaho State Historical Society
610 North Julia Davis Drive
Boise, Idaho 83702
208-334-3890

Illinois State Archives
Archives Building
Springfield, Illinois 62756
217-782-4682

Indiana State Library
140 North Senate Avenue
Indianapolis, Indiana 46204
317-232-3675

Iowa State Historical Society
600 East Locust
Des Moines, Iowa 50319
515-281-3007

Kansas State Historical Society
120 West 10th Street
Topeka, Kansas 66612
913-296-3251

Kentucky Department of Libraries and
Archives
300 Coffee Tree Road
Frankfort, Kentucky 40601
502-875-7000

Louisiana State Museum
751 Chartres Street
P.O. Box 2448
New Orleans, Louisiana 70116-2448
504-568-6968

Maine State Archives
State House Station 84
Augusta, Maine 04333
207-289-5790

Maryland State Archives
300 Rowe Avenue
Annapolis, Maryland 21401
301-974-3867

State Library of Massachusetts
341 State House
Boston, Massachusetts 02133
617-727-2590

Michigan History Division
Michigan Department of State
717 West Allegan Street
Lansing, Michigan 48918
517-373-0510

Minnesota Historical Society Division of
Archives and Manuscripts
1500 Mississippi Street
St. Paul, Minnesota 55101
612-296-6980

Mississippi Department of Archives and
History
100 South State Street
Jackson, Mississippi 39201
601-354-6218

Missouri State Archives
Secretary of State
Records Management and Archives
Division
P.O. Box 778
Jefferson City, Missouri 65102
314-751-3280

Montana Historical Society and Archives
Board of Education
225 North Roberts Street
Helena, Montana 59620
406-444-2694

Nebraska Historical Society and Archives
1500 R Street
Lincoln, Nebraska 68508
402-471-4771

Nevada State, County, and Municipal
Archives
101 South Fall Street
Carson City, Nevada 89710
702-885-5000

New Hampshire State Division of Historical
Resources
71 South Fruit Street
Concord, New Hampshire 03301
603-271-2236

New Jersey Bureau of Archives
New Jersey State Library
185 West State Street
Trenton, New Jersey 08625
609-984-3297

New Mexico State Records Center and
Archives
404 Montezuma
Santa Fe, New Mexico 87503
505-827-8860

New York State Archives
Cultural Education Center
Empire State Plaza
Albany, New York 12230
518-474-1195

North Carolina Division of Archives and
History
109 East Jones Street
Raleigh, North Carolina 27611
919-733-7305

State Historical Society of North Dakota
North Dakota Heritage Center
Bismarck, North Dakota 58505
701-224-2666

Ohio Historical Society Division of
Archives and Manuscripts
1985 Velma Avenue
Columbus, Ohio 43211
614-297-2510

Oklahoma Department of Libraries
200 North East 18th Street
Oklahoma City, Oklahoma 73105
405-521-2502

Oregon Division of Archives
Office of Secretary of State
1005 Broadway, NE
Salem, Oregon 97310
503-378-4241

Pennsylvania State Archives
State Museum of Pennsylvania
3rd and Forster Streets
P.O. Box 1026
Harrisburg, Pennsylvania 17108-1026
717-787-3023

Rhode Island State Archives
State House, Room 43
Smith Street
Providence, Rhode Island 02903-1119
401-277-2353

South Carolina Department of Archives and
    History
1430 Senate Street
P.O. Box 11669
Columbia, South Carolina 29211
803-734-8577

South Dakota State Archives
E. Highway Bypass
Pierre, South Dakota 57501
605-774-3408

Tennessee State Library and Archives
403 7th Avenue North
Nashville, Tennessee 37219
615-741-2764

Texas Library
1201 Brazos
P.O. Box 12927
Austin, Texas 78711
512-463-5455

Utah State Archives
Archives Building
State Capitol
Salt Lake City, Utah 84114
801-538-3012

Vermont Division of Public Records
State Administration Building
Montpelier, Vermont 05602
802-828-3288

Virginia State Library
11th Street and Capitol Square
Richmond, Virginia 23219
804-786-2331

Secretary of State
Division of Archives and Records
    Management
P.O. Box 9000
Olympia, Washington 98504-9000
206-753-5485

West Virginia Department of Archives and
    History
Capitol Complex
Science and Culture Center
Charleston, West Virginia 25305
304-348-0230

Wisconsin Historical Society
Division of Archives
816 State Street
Madison, Wisconsin 53706
608-262-3338

Wyoming State Archives and Historical
    Department
Barrett Building
Cheyenne, Wyoming 82002

State Historic Preservation Officers

State Historic Preservation Officer
Alabama Historical Commission
725 Monroe Street
Montgomery, Alabama 36130
205-261-3184

Chief, Office of History and Archeology
Division of Parks
Pouch 7001
Anchorage, Alaska 99510
907-762-2626

Chief, Office of Historic Preservation
Arizona State Parks
800 West Washington, Suite 415
Phoenix, Arizona 85007
602-255-4174

Director, Arkansas Historic Preservation
  Program
The Heritage Center, Suite 300
225 East Markham
Little Rock, Arkansas 72201
501-371-2763

State Historic Preservation Officer
Office of Historic Preservation
Department of Parks and Recreation
P.O. Box 942896
Sacramento, California 94296-0001
916-445-8006

State Historic Preservation Officer
Colorado Heritage Center
1300 Broadway
Denver, Colorado 80203
303-866-3392

Director, Connecticut Historical
  Commission
59 South Prospect Street
Hartford, Connecticut 06106
203-566-3005

Director, Division of Historical and Cultural
  Affairs
Hall of Records
P.O. Box 1401
Dover, Delaware 19901
302-736-5313

Director, Department of Consumer and
  Regulatory Affairs
614-H Street, NW, Suite 321
Washington, D.C. 20002
202-727-6053

Director, Division of Archives, History, and
  Records Management
Department of State
The Capitol
Tallahassee, Florida 32301-8020
904-487-2333

Commissioner, Department of Natural
  Resources
1252 Floyd Towers East
205 Butler Street, SE
Atlanta, Georgia 30334
404-656-3500

State Historic Preservation Officer
Department of Land and Natural Resources
P.O. Box 621
Honolulu, Hawaii 96809
808-548-6550

Historic Preservation Coordinator
Idaho Historic Society
610 North Julia Davis Drive
Boise, Idaho 83702
208-334-3356

Director, Illinois Historic Preservation
  Agency
Old State Capitol
Springfield, Illinois 62701
217-782-4512

Director, Department of Natural Resources
608 State Office Building
Indianapolis, Indiana 46204
317-232-4020

Director, Iowa State Historical Department
Office of Historic Preservation
Capitol Complex
East 12th Street and Grand Avenue
Des Moines, Iowa 50319
515-281-6825

Executive Director, Kansas State Historical
    Society
120 West 10th Street
Topeka, Kansas 66612
913-296-3251

State Historic Preservation Officer and
Director, Kentucky Heritage Council
Capitol Plaza Tower, 12th Floor
Frankfort, Kentucky 40601
502-564-7005

Assistant Secretary, Office of Cultural
    Development
P.O. Box 44247
Baton Rouge, Louisiana 70804
504-925-3884

Director, Maine Historic Preservation
    Commission
55 Capitol, Station 65
Augusta, Maine 04333
207-289-2132

State Historic Preservation Officer
The Maryland Historic Trust
45 Calvert Street
Annapolis, Maryland 21401
301-757-9000

Executive Director, Massachusetts
    Historical Commission
80 Boylston Street, Suite 310
Boston, Massachusetts 02116
617-727-8470

Director, History Division
Department of State
208 North Capitol Avenue
Lansing, Michigan 48918
517-373-6362

Director, Minnesota Historical Society
690 Cedar Street
St. Paul, Minnesota 55101
612-296-2747

Director, State Of Mississippi Department of
    Archives and History
P.O. Box 571
Jackson, Mississippi 39205
601-359-1424

Director, State Department of Natural
    Resources
P.O. Box 176
Jefferson City, Missouri 65102
314-751-2479

State Historic Preservation Officer
Montana Historical Society
Veterans Memorial Building
225 North Roberts Street
Helena, Montana 59620
406-444-7715

Director, The Nebraska State Historical
    Society
1500 R Street
P.O. Box 82554
Lincoln, Nebraska 68501
402-471-4767; FTS 541-3270

Director, Department of Conservation and
    Natural Resources
Nye Building, Room 213
201 South Fall Street
Carson City, Nevada 89710
702-885-4360

Commissioner, Department of Libraries,
    Arts, and Historical Resources
P.O. Box 2043
Concord, New Hampshire 03302-2043
603-271-3483 or 3558

Commissioner, Department of
    Environmental Protection
CN 402
Trenton, New Jersey 08625
609-292-2885

State Historic Preservation Officer
Historic Preservation Division
Office of Cultural Affairs
Villa Rivera, Room 101
228 East Palace Avenue
Santa Fe, New Mexico 87503
505-827-8320

Commissioner, Office of Parks, Recreation,
    and Historic Preservation
Agency Building #1
Empire State Plaza
Albany, New York 12238
518-474-0443

Director, Division of Archives and History
Department of Cultural Resources
109 East Jones Street
Raleigh, North Carolina 27611
919-733-7305

Superintendent, State Historical Society of
  North Dakota
North Dakota Heritage Center
Bismarck, North Dakota 58505
701-224-2667

State Historic Preservation Officer
Ohio Historic Preservation Office
Ohio Historic Center
1985 Velma Avenue
Columbus, Ohio 43211
614-297-9600

State Historic Preservation Officer
Oklahoma Historical Society
Wyley Post Historical Building
2100 North Lincoln
Oklahoma City, Oklahoma 73105
405-521-2491

State Parks Superintendent
525 Trade Street, SE
Salem, Oregon 97310
503-378-5019

State Historic Preservation Officer
Pennsylvania Historical and Museum
  Commission
P.O. Box 1026
Harrisburg, Pennsylvania 17108-1026
717-787-2891

State Historic Preservation Officer
Historical Preservation Commission
Old State House
150 Benefit Street
Providence, Rhode Island 02903
401-277-2678

Director, Department of Archives and
  History
P.O. Box 11669 Capitol Station
Columbia, South Carolina 29211
803-734-8577

State Historical Preservation Officer
Historic Preservation Center
P.O. Box 417
Vermillion, South Dakota 57069
605-773-3458

State Historic Preservation Officer
Department of Conservation
701 Broadway
Nashville, Tennessee 37203
615-742-6758

Executive Director, Texas State Historical
  Commission
P.O. Box 12276 Capitol Station
Austin, Texas 78711
512-463-6100

State Historic Preservation Officer
Utah State Historical Society
300 Rio Grande
Salt Lake City, Utah 84101
801-533-5755

Director, Historic Preservation and State
  Historic Preservation Officer
5858 East State Street
Montpelier, Vermont 05602
802-828-3211

State Historic Preservation Officer
Division of Historic Landmarks, Department
  of Conservation and Historic Resources
221 Governor Street
Richmond, Virginia 23219
804-786-3143

State Historic Preservation Officer
Office of Archeology and Historic
  Preservation
111 West 21st Avenue
KL-11
Olympia, Washington 98504
206-753-4011

Commissioner, Department of Culture and
  History
State Capitol Complex
Charleston, West Virginia 25305
304-348-0220

State Historic Preservation Officer
State Historical Society of Wisconsin
816 State Street
Madison, Wisconsin 53706
608-262-0746

Director, Wyoming State Archives,
    Museums, and Historical Department
Barrett Building
2301 Central Avenue
Cheyenne, Wyoming 82002
307-777-7013

National Organizations for Historic Preservation

Advisory Council of Historic Preservation
Old Post Office Building
1100 Pennsylvania Avenue, NW, Suite 809
Washington, D.C. 20004
202-786-0503 or 0505

National Alliance of Historic Preservation Commissions
Hall of the States
444 North Capitol Street, NW, Suite 332
Washington, D.C. 20001
202-624-5465

Chairman, National Association of Statewide Preservation Organizations
17 Commerce Street
Baltimore, Maryland 21202
301-685-2886

National Conference of State Historic Preservation Officers
Hall of the States
444 North Capitol Street, NW, Suite 332
Washington, D.C. 20001
202-624-5465

National Trust for Historic Preservation
1785 Massachusetts Avenue, NW
Washington, D.C. 20036
202-673-4000

Preservation Action
1350 Connecticut Avenue, NW, Suite 400-A
Washington, D.C. 20036
202-659-0915

Historical Societies

Alabama Historical Association
205 20th Street North
Birmingham, Alabama 35203
205-324-2000
The Alabama Review

Alaska Historical Society
P.O. Box 100299
Anchorage, Alaska 99511-0299
907-276-1596
Alaska History News

Arizona Historical Society
949 East 2nd Street
Tucson, Arizona 85719
602-628-5774
The Journal of Arizona History

Arkansas Historical Association
History Department
Ozark Hall, Room 12
University of Arkansas
Fayetteville, Arkansas 72701
501-575-3001
Arkansas Historical Quarterly

California Historical Society
2090 Jackson Street
San Francisco, California 94109
415-567-1848
California History

Colorado Historical Society
1300 Broadway
Denver, Colorado 80203
Colorado Heritage News

The Connecticut Historical Society
1 Elizabeth Street
Hartford, Connecticut 06105
203-236-5621
Bulletin

The Historical Society of Delaware
505 Market Street Mall
Wilmington, Delaware 19801
302-655-7161
Delaware History

Florida Historical Society
University of South Florida Library
Room 511

Tampa, Florida 33620
813-974-3815
Florida Historical Quarterly

Georgia Historical Society
501 Whitaker Street
Savannah, Georgia 31499
912-651-2128
Georgia Historical Quarterly

Hawaiian Historical Society
560 Kawaiahao Street
Honolulu, Hawaii 96813
808-537-6271
The Hawaiian Journal of History

Idaho State Historical Society
610 North Julia Davis Drive
Boise, Idaho 83702
208-334-3890
Idaho Yesterdays

Illinois State Historical Society
Old State Capitol
Springfield, Illinois 62706
217-782-4836
*Journal of the Illinois State Historical
Society*

Indiana Historical Society
315 West Ohio Street
Indianapolis, Indiana 46202
317-232-1882

State Historical Society of Iowa
Capitol Complex
Des Moines, Iowa 50319
515-281-5111

OR

State Historical Society of Iowa
402 Iowa Avenue
Iowa City, Iowa 52240
319-335-3916
The Palimpsest; Annals of Iowa

Kansas State Historical Society
120 West 10th Street
Topeka, Kansas 66612
913-296-3251
Kansas Historical Quarterly

Kentucky Historical Society
Old Capitol Annex
300 West Broadway
P.O. Box 8
Frankfort, Kentucky 40602
502-564-3016
Register; Kentucky Ancestors; Kentucky Heritage

Louisiana Historical Society
10 Trianon Plaza
New Orleans, Louisiana 70125

Maine Historical Society
485 Congress Street
Portland, Maine 04101
207-774-1822
Maine Historical Society Quarterly

Maryland Historical Society
201 West Monument Street
Baltimore, Maryland 21201
301-685-3750
Maryland Historical Magazine

Massachusetts Historical Society
1154 Boylston Street
Boston, Massachusetts 02215
617-536-1608
Proceedings; Collections

Historical Society of Michigan
2117 Washtenaw Avenue
Ann Arbor, Michigan 48104
313-769-1828
Chronicle

Minnesota Historical Society
690 Cedar Street
St. Paul, Minnesota 55101
612-296-6126
Minnesota History

Mississippi Historical Society
100 South State Street
Jackson, Mississippi 39205
601-354-6218
Journal of Mississippi History

State Historical Society of Missouri
1020 Lowry Street
Columbia, Missouri 65201
314-882-7083
Missouri Historical Review

Montana Historical Society
225 North Roberts
Helena, Montana 59601
406-444-2694
Montana, the Magazine of Western History

Nebraska State Historical Society
1500 R Street
Lincoln, Nebraska 68508
402-471-3270
Nebraska History

Nevada Historical Society
1650 North Virginia Street
Reno, Nevada 89503
702-789-0190
Nevada Historical Society Quarterly

New Hampshire Historical Society
30 Park Street
Concord, New Hampshire 03301
603-225-3381
Historical New Hampshire

The New Jersey Historical Society
230 Broadway
Newark, New Jersey 07104
201-483-3939
New Jersey History

Historical Society of New Mexico
P.O. Box 5819
Santa Fe, New Mexico 87404
La Cronica

New York State Historical Association
Lake Road, Route 80
P.O. Box 800
Cooperstown, New York 13326
607-547-2533
New York History and Heritage Magazine

North Carolina Division of Archives and History
109 East Jones Street
Raleigh, North Carolina 27611
919-733-7305
North Carolina Historical Review

State Historical Society of North Dakota
North Dakota Heritage Center
Bismarck, North Dakota 58505
701-224-2666
*North Dakota History; Journal of the
Northern Plains*

Ohio Historical Society
1985 Velma Avenue.
Columbus, Ohio 43211
614-297-2300
Ohio History

Oklahoma Historical Society
Wiley Post Historical Building
2100 North Lincoln Boulevard
Oklahoma City, Oklahoma 73105
405-521-2491
The Chronicles of Oklahoma

Oregon Historical Society
1230 S.W. Park Avenue
Portland, Oregon 97205
503-222-1741
OHS Quarterly

Historical Society of Pennsylvania
1300 Locust Street
Philadelphia, Pennsylvania 19107-5699
215-732-6200
*The Pennsylvania Magazine of History and
Biography*

Rhode Island Historical Society
110 Benevolent Street
Providence, Rhode Island 02906
401-331-8575
Rhode Island History

South Carolina Historical Society
100 Meeting Street
Charleston, South Carolina 29401
803-723-3225
South Carolina Historical Magazine

South Dakota State Historical Society
900 Governor's
Pierre, South Dakota 57501
605-773-3458
South Dakota History

Tennessee Historical Society
War Memorial Building
Nashville, Tennessee 37219
615-242-1796
Tennessee Historical Quarterly

Texas State Historical Association
Richardson Hall 2-306
University Station
Austin, Texas 78712
512-471-1525
Southwestern Historical Quarterly

Utah State Historical Society
300 Rio Grande
Salt Lake City, Utah 84101
801-533-5755
Utah Historical Quarterly

Vermont Historical Society
State Street
Montpelier, Vermont 05602
802-828-2291
Vermont History

Virginia Historical Society
428 North Boulevard
P.O. Box 7311
Richmond, Virginia 23221
804-358-4901
Virginia Magazine of History and Biography

Washington State Historical Society
315 North Stadium Way
Tacoma, Washington 98403
206-593-2830
Columbia Magazine

West Virginia Historical Society
P.O. Box 5220
Charleston, West Virginia 25361-0220

State Historical Society of Wisconsin
816 State Street
Madison, Wisconsin 53706
608-262-3266
Wisconsin Magazine of History

Wyoming State Archives and Historical
    Department
Barrett Building
Chèyenne, Wyoming 82002
307-777-7518
Annals of Wyoming

B
Additional Information

Independent Urban Areas

The general rule of thumb in searching for information is to go first to your county courthouse. In the following cases, however, information is most likely to be found in municipal or city/county records. Try these first. Primarily these are urban jurisdiction or cities that are independent. That is, they are not subject or partially subject to county authority and are categorized by the Census Bureau according to their style of government.

The first are independent cities, not subject to county authority:

Baltimore City, Maryland; St. Louis, Missouri; Carson City, Nevada; several burgs in Virginia: Alexandria, Bedford, Bristol, Buena Vista, Charlottesville, Chesapeake, Clifton Forge, Colonial Heights, Covington, Danville, Emporia, Fairfax, Falls Church, Franklin, Fredericksburg, Galax, Hampton, Harrisonburg, Hopewell, Lexington, Lynchburg, Martinsville, Newport News, Norfolk, Norton, Petersburg, Portsmouth, Radford, Richmond, Roanoke, Salem, South Boston, Staunton, Suffolk, Virginia Beach, Waynesboro, Williamsburg and Winchester; and Washington, D.C.

The second category are cities operating as such, but subject to some county jurisdiction:

Jacksonville, Florida; Indianapolis, Indiana; Baton Rouge, Louisiana; New Orleans, Louisiana; Nantucket, Massachusetts; New York City: Bronx, Kings (Brooklyn), New York (Manhattan), Queens and Richmond; and Philadelphia, Pennsylvania.

The third category are areas labeled as city-county:

San Francisco, California; Denver, Colorado; and Honolulu, Hawaii.

The fourth grouping includes areas listed as metropolitan:

Davidson County and Nashville, Tennessee.

The fifth listing includes unorganized areas that function as counties:

Fairfield, Hartford, Litchfield, Middlesex, New Haven, New London, Tolland and Windham, Connecticut; and Bristol, Kent, Newport, Providence and Washington, Rhode Island.

The sixth category is unorganized areas affiliated with other counties for governmental purposes:

Shannon, Todd and Washington, South Dakota.

A final category includes national parks, parts of Alaska, etc.

Plotting the Indiscriminate Survey

To plot a survey description, you will need a 6" protractor of 180°, graph paper with 10 squares to the inch, a scale, and a calculator, if available. You can buy a ruler (scale) graduated into tenths. It is easiest to use 10 squares to the inch, because each inch can be said to equal 100', making it easy to count, divide or convert from the decimals that you are going to be using. An alternative, since most rulers are divided into 8ths or 16ths, is to tape a piece of graph paper along the ruler so that the dimensions of the graph and the ruler agree.

With practice you can "rough out" the survey on plain paper—as noted in Chapter 15—to predetermine its approximate dimensions and shape. This will help guide you in selecting your starting point on the graph paper.

The following simple, four-sided survey description is designed to illustrate how to plot a survey. Use this example to practice on until you feel confident. Then try some more examples from your own research.

Sample Survey Description

> 1. Beginning at the east corner of said lot near the southwest corner of the barn. 2. Thence north 85° west 3 chains 48 links to a stake and stones (N 85° W 3 ch 48 1). 3. Thence north 21° west 2 chains 73 links to a black oak tree marked (N 21° W 2 ch 73 1). 4. Thence north 82° east 4 chains 85 links to a stake and stones (N 82° E 4 ch 85 1). 5. Thence south 5° west 3 chains 79 links to place of beginning (S 5° W 3 ch 79 1). (Illustration 1.)

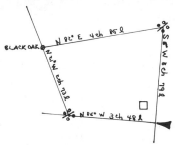

Jot down the compass points and lengths for each of the four lines, consecutively, on a piece of paper. Convert the chains and links to feet and then to the number of inches and squares to be plotted on the graph paper. For this example a scale of 1" = 100' will be used.

1. N 85° W 3 ch 48 becomes N 85° W. 3 ch 48 1 = 3.48 ch x 66' per chain = 229.68'. 229.68' divided by 100' per inch = 2.2968" = 2.3 on the graph paper.

Since there are 10 graph squares per inch, 2.3" = 2" + 3 squares. Thus we will be plotting N 85° W 2" +3 squares for the first line. To be even more accurate, you can use the scale rather than counting the squares.

2. N 21° W 2 ch 73 1 becomes N 21° W. 2 ch 73 1 = 2.73 ch x 66' per chain = 180.18'. 180 = 18' divided by 100' per inch = 1.8018" = 1.8" on the graph paper. 1.8" = 1" + 8 squares on the graph paper. Thus the second line will be N 21° W 1" + 8 squares long.

3. N 82° E 4 ch 85 1 = N 82° E 4.85 ch. 4.85 ch x 66' = 320.1' divided by 100' = 3.201" =3.2 or 3" 2 squares long. Thus the third line will be N 82° E 3" + 2 squares long.

4. S 5° W 3 ch 79 1 = S 5° W 3.79 ch. 3.79 ch x 66' = 250.14' divided by 100' = 2.5014" = 2.5" or 2" + 5 squares. Thus line four will be S 5° W 2" + 5 squares long.

Now we are ready to plot the degrees on the graph paper. First write in north (top), south (bottom), east (right) and west (left) in their proper places on the edges of the graph paper.

Since we are starting on the east, place a point on the second vertical 1" from the right line below the middle of the paper. Place the protractor with the straight edge to the right, lined up north-south with the center of the protractor on the point. Count to the west (left) down from the north (top) 85° and place a point on the outside of the protractor (N 85° W). Draw a line connecting the two points. Next starting at the right hand point measure out 2" + 3 squares and place a point. Erase the first point placed outside the protractor or the line will be too long. (Illustration 2.)

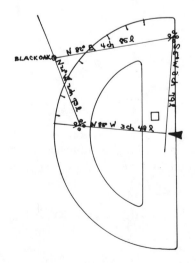
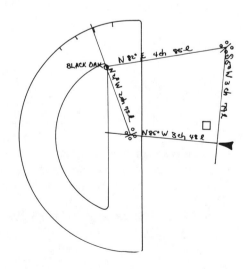

Now you are ready to plot the second compass bearing (N 21° W). Since it is an angle northwest of the first line, again line up the protractor with the straight edge to the right and the center of the protractor on the second point. Make sure the straight edge is lined up parallel to the north-south line. Count from the north (top) 21° to the west (left) and place a point on the outside of the protractor at 21°. Connect the second and third points. Now measure 1" + 8 squares from the second point along the line toward the third point and place a point. (Erase the remaining line to the latter point, because it will extend beyond the points and look messy.) (Illustration 3.)

Now plot the third angle (N 82° E). Since the third line will be drawn east (to the right) of the third point, place the protractor with the straight edge on the left aligned north and south, with the center of the protractor on the third point. From the north (top) measure 82° to the east (right) and place a point outside the protractor edge. Draw a line connecting points three and four. Next measure 3" + 2 squares to find the correct length. Place a point and—this time—you may have to add to the line if you have a protractor 6" or less, because it is longer than the sighting point. (Illustration 4.)

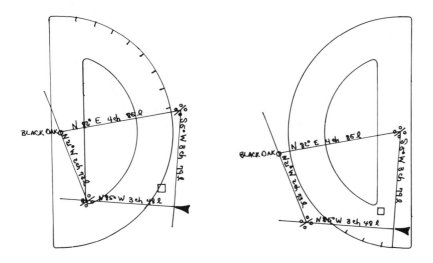

You are now ready for the last line. This compass bearing is S 5° W, so that you will have to place the protractor with the straight edge to the right aligned north and south and the center of the protractor on the fourth point. This time measure from the south (bottom) 5° to the west (left) and place a point on the outside of the protractor. Next draw the last line connecting the points. If you have placed your points accurately, this last line should run directly through the first point, thus closing the survey. Check this last line to make sure that it is 2" + 5 squares. Voila! You have completed plotting your first survey. (Ilustration 5.)

One word of caution: when converting chains and links, remember to convert the numbers starting from the right. You are dealing with a specific number of links out of 100 links, so you need a two-place number after the decimal (e.g., 3 ch 12 1 = 3.12 ch). In other words, when working with links less than 100, you must add a "0" before the number to indicate its placement out of 100 (e.g., 3 ch 8 1 = 3.08 ch).

When you are plotting a survey description, there may be several lines to be drawn or only a few. Generally, the larger the tract the more complicated the shape of the plat will be.

If your lines fail to meet by more than a few tenths of an inch, carefully check the deed description against your drawing on the graph paper. Redo it. Check the handwriting if it is hard to read. "North" and "south," "east" and "west," "easterly" and "westerly," etc. can be easily interchanged. If there is a direction that you can not decipher and have arbitrarily assigned one to it, try using its opposite (e.g., north instead of south, west instead of east) to see if that resolves the problem. If the error is extravagant—a big one—*and* you have checked for *your* possible math errors, suspect an error in copying by a clerk. Remember that you are reading a *copy* of the original deed, and that mistakes did happen in copying. In that case, check with other deeds to see if their compass points agree with the one you are using. You may find the correct compass point in an earlier deed or, perhaps, a correction in a later deed after a new survey was completed.

After you have plotted the property boundary, draw in descriptive symbols for the bounds, such as the stakes and stones, black oak tree, etc. Even sketch in the approximate locations of buildings for clarity.

Major Architectural Eras

Because of regional variations in the application of different architectural styles, it is difficult to establish their exact beginning and end dates. Thus, the dates used here reflect the popular use of these styles. Even the experts disagree. The following list uses the traditional perimeters with the extensions in parentheses following the major categories.

Colonial 1630-1790 (1630-1820)
> English, Dutch, French, German, Spanish 1630-1790
> Georgian 1735-1790 (1700-1820)

Federal (Adamsesque) 1790-1820 (1776-1830)
Greek Revival 1820-1850 (1820-1860)
Early Victorian 1840-1860
> Gothic Revival 1845-1860
> Italian villa 1840-1860
> Octagon 1860's
> Exotic Revival 1840-1860

Victorian 1860-1900
> Italianate 1860-1900
> Second Empire (1840-1900)
> Gothic (sometimes called folk Victorian) 1860-1885
> Queen Anne 1880-1900
> Stick/Eastlake 1860-1880
> Shingle 1880-1900
> Richardsonian Romanesque 1870-1900
> Renaissance 1860-1900

Late 19th and Early 20th Century 1895-1920
> Beaux Arts 1875-1915
> Revivals: Colonial, Classical, Mission/Spanish, Tudor 1890-1920's
> Bungalow/Craftsman 1895-1915
> Prairie 1895-1920

20th Century 1920-1960
> Art Deco 1925-1940
> International Style 1925-1955

Looking at a House

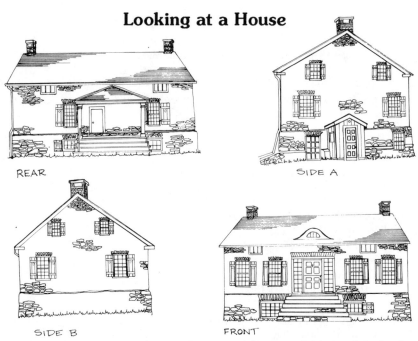

REAR

SIDE A

SIDE B

FRONT

This analysis assumes that you have read the text of this book beforehand and thus will be familiar with the concepts and terms used here.

A perceptive analysis of any house requires, first of all, that you pay attention to details. A dependable, simple, and necessary technique is that you quietly sit and stare at the house. Systematically shift your gaze along its facades and silhouette. Do not even think, but just keep looking. You will find that your eyes begin to return certain details. (Your subconscious, having internalized all the visible material, is beginning to sort out what is different or unintegrated with the rest.) Ask yourself why your eyes keep returning to certain things. What is it that seems slightly awry, different, even, wrong? It is by this process that we begin to analyze the house we are looking at so methodically.

Now let us practice on the illustrations of a "simple" house. There are several items on each facade of this that draw our attention. The first and last illustrations show its rear and front brownish-gray, coursed, cut fieldstone exterior. The second and third show the sides of this 5-bay x 2-bay house, with its gable roof and two interior end chimneys. There is a belt line around the basement, which is more than just a course line, and the basement actually is a few inches wider than the upper walls. The stones in this cellar are considerably larger than those of the upper stories, with noticeably small stones near the roof edge. When there are shutters on the windows, they are batten shutters with four holes drilled to suggest a diamond.

Let us look at each facade to analyze the changes made in the house over the years. In the rear facade there are four different window styles. The earliest style is found in the two first-floor windows (12/12 double-hung). The 8-light, single sash on the cellar level to the left of the porch is the next oldest, while the 6-light, single-hung cellar window to the right of the porch came next. The two 3-light eyebrow windows under the roof eaves are the latest. Although hard to discern, the lintels over the cellar windows are of cut stone, while the first floor lintels are of red brick.

The off-center porch is a later addition to the original, probably from the Colonial Revival period. It is designed to fit between the first floor windows. Because of this, the interior shutters of both windows must fold out against the porch. The door is placed off-center and is modern (20th century), as is the gutter system.

Side A is the fullest elevation, showing three stories. Here the cellar can be walked into with a full height door. There is a wide ledge about 26" down from the top edge of the cellar. The roof line shows the cornice returns typical of Federal period houses. The earliest windows are the two 12/12 double-hung sashes on the first floor and the 8/8 double-hung sash to the right of the door. The two second floor 6/6 double-hung windows are later with the large 6/6 double window to the left of the cellar door the most recent. The board entrance passage is a modern addition. The door is a copy of the original Dutch door and similar to the front door. Other details also noted on the rear elevation are evident here, such as gutters and the diminishing stone size.

Side B is the opposite end of the house. It is built into the hill, so does not have as much of the cellar wall exposed. Because of the lack of as many details as Side A, the graduated fieldstone sizing is more noticeable.

The front elevation shows the full five bays. The center entrance is the dominant focal point. It consists of an 8-panel, wide Dutch door with full height double-row sidelights typical of the Federal period. The four 12/12 double-hung first floor windows are the oldest. The 8-light cellar window to the right of the steps matches the window found opposite it on the rear facade. The 10/10 cellar window to the left of the steps, the 3-light eyebrow windows and the eyebrow dormer all are later. The rest of the front elevation details have been noted previously.

How do these observations translate into usable facts about this house? Some details can be interpreted by looking behind them inside the house, while others can be explained by the exterior analysis. The decreasing stone size, for example, can be explained by the use of readily available, on site fieldstone. The largest stones were used in the cellar foundation, the medium-sized stones for the first floor. With the depletion of these stones, the smallest ones were used nearest the roof line.

The small, cut stone lintels were used over the cellar windows. By the time the first floor was completed, there was a brickyard available in the area, so bricks were used as lintels on this and the second floor. The cellar was raised out of the ground, because the house was built into a gently sloping hill and was designed so that the cellar could be entered at ground level, a Germanic custom.

Some of the other unique details can be explained upon entering the house. Begin at the side entrance. The larger-paned, more modern windows in the cellar to the left of this entrance, to the right of the rear steps and to the left of the front steps are windows to the kitchen and dining room. The smaller-paned 8/8 is the only original window in the cellar.

The cellar was the original living quarters for the family. It probably remained so for a few years, because the size of the fireplace suggests pre-Revolutionary times, while the upper stories exhibit characteristics of a house built after 1790. The 12/12 first floor windows, the sidelights on the front entrance, the lintels with a keystone and the cornice returns all signal the Federal period. The shutters and doors may exhibit ethnicity, rather than architectural period. The batten shutters are more primitive than the paneled Dutch doors. The diamond-shaped pattern in the shutters is typically Germanic.

The 6/6 second floor windows are typically late Federal, while the eyebrow windows are Greek Revival, although the lights and the frame around the latter are both large enough to suggest a 20th century addition. The eyebrow dormer definitely is: it is the window for a bathroom made out of the end of the second floor hall.

The rear door is off-center because it is placed on one side of the center hall and shares the hall space with the stairs to the right as viewed in the rear elevation.

This house is a relatively easy-to-read example of a structure built over a period of several years. Either the owner or the builder was of Germanic ethnicity. The house was built to the first floor and used as living quarters as the stone walls were raised over the occupants. The basic structure outline and first floor exterior details were built during the Federal period with the second floor exterior details finished during the late Federal period and, perhaps, the 20th century. Over the years some windows were changed and a porch and a covered side entrance were added. Uniquely, what did not change was the kitchen and dining room placement in the cellar. They still exist as such in the late 20th century. There are many more interior details to illustrate and confirm this analysis. Another house may not have such obvious changes, but much can be determined with quiet observation. Learn to pay attention to whatever your eyes return to notice. It may be significant.

Indexing

Deeds

Different courthouses have different ways of indexing their deeds. Some may have used several systems over the years, depending on which was in fashion at a given time. These can be easily explained by the clerk or through instructions given at the beginning of the volume. Printed, cumulative deed indices usually are in alphabetical or alpha order.

Most deed ledgers are organized by date. Thus the indices for these ledgers are chronological indices. Because they are continuously being added to as people transfer property, there is never a chance to stop the accumulation of names in the books, so the surnames never are completely alphabetized. (This may sound complicated, but as soon as you pick up a deed index you will see what is meant here.) As a result, various methods of indexing were developed.

In one common method, all surnames were organized by first letter only (initial order), so all A's were lumped together unalphabetized, all B's together, etc. However, as towns and counties became more populated, more flexible and specific indexing systems were needed. Several commercial companies then developed partial alphabetization methods. One of the more common of these systems used the first letter and vowel, so that, for example, all surnames beginning with Ce- would occur on the same page. Another common system involved the first three letters of a surname. All surnames beginning with Caa-, Cab-, Cac-, and Cad-, for example, would be found on the same page. Illustration 1.)

C	A	B	C	D	E	F	G	H	I	J	K	L	M	N	O	P	Q
A	294	294	294	294	295	295	295	296	297	297	297	298	303	309	312	312	312
E F	340	340	340	340	340	340	340	340	340	340	340	340	340	340	340	340	340
H	341	341	341	341	350	350	350	350	352	352	352	354	354	354	354	354	354
I	358	358	358	358	358	358	358	358	358	358	358	358	358	358	358	358	358
K L M N	359	359	359	350	371	371	371	371	374	374	374	374	374	374	376	376	376
O	379	380	381	383	383	384	386	387	389	389	389	390	401	403	418	426	426
R S	447	447	447	447	453	453	453	453	455	455	455	455	455	455	456	456	456
U V	465	465	465	465	465	465	465	465	465	465	465	466	465	470	470	470	470
W Y Z	481	481	481	481	481	481	481	481	481	481	481	481	481	481	481	481	481

Always scan the list of first names rather than the surnames when looking in those deed (or mortgage) indices in which the first name is listed first by alphabet groups (e.g., A-E, F-J, L-O, P-T, U-Z) with the different surnames following. Because these first names are categorized in alphabet groups rather than on consecutive lines, they are spaced farther apart and are easier to scan. This method is especially valuable when the surname is a common one, such as Johnson, Smith, Miller, etc. (Illustration 2.)

Index of Mortgages, Warren County, N. Y.
COMMENCING 1813.

AB CDE	FGH IJ	KL MNO	PQR ST	UVW XYZ	MORTGAGOR.	MORTGAGEE.	Dis.	Liber.	Page	
		Eaton			Eastwood	Ebenezer Schofield		A.	241	
Bingham Charles					Eaton	Robert Gilchrist	Dis	A.	467	
			Rice		Eaton	James Ware		C.	20	
					Eaton	John Thurman		C.	26	
				Jadrek	Eaton	William Brown	Dis	C.	201	
	Martin				Eastwood	Caleb Dean	Dis	D.	115	
	Martin				Eastwood	William H. Pearce			262	
					Eastwood		Dis	J.		
					Eaton	Amos R. Wells	Dis		55	
					Eastwood	Adam Cotterell	Dis	J.	165	1896
	Martin				Eastwood	Wallie Gur	Dis		227	
			Thomas		Eaton		K.		38	
						McDonald	Dis		352	1897
					Eastwood	Robert McElroy	Dis		162	1899
					Eastwood		Dis		351	1897
	Martin				Eastwood	Amos R. Wells	L.		86	
	Martin				Eastwood	George Clendon	M.		47	1852
John S.					Eastwood	Martin Eastwood	Dis		467	1853
					Eastwood				505	1855
	Martin				Eastwood	Rachel			405	
					Eaton	James L.	Dis		423	
	Marvin				Eastwood	Martin Eastwood	O.		241	1856
					Eaton		Dis	P.	8	1857
					Eaton		Dis		76	
	Martin J.				Eastwood	Martin Eastwood			712	1858
	Martin				Eastwood	Amy Lapham	L.		309	1860
					Eaton	Charles A. Mott			714	
	Marvin				Eastwood	Charles Rice			547	
	Marvin				Eastwood	Martin Eastwood	R.		135	1861
	Marvin				Eastwood	Martin Eastwood			136	
	Martin M.				Eaton	Julia Ann Poor	Dis		459	1862
	Martin				Eastwood	John H. Smith			548	
	Martin J.				Eastwood	Martin Eastwood	S.		24	
					Eastwood	Abel Scripter			98	
					Eastwood	Simon Barber	Dis	Y.	93	1865
	Julius C.				Eastwood	Phebe Barber	Dis	Y.	271	1868
	Julius C.				Eastwood	Albert Vermillia	Dis		67	1870
					Eastwood	Alexander St.		3.	51	1872
Jane					Eaton	Charles H. Baxter	Dis	8	476	1876

281

Another, the consonant system, often called the l, m, n, r, t system, uses these consonants as the key letters following the first letter of a surname. For example Bailey, Bloch and Bylo all would occur on the same page. Still another system uses the initials of the surname followed by those of the given name. In this, Ann Downing, Alexander DeSantis and Arthur Drinkwine all would occur on the same page.

Mortgages probably will be indexed in the same way as deeds in the same archives. They usually are located in separate ledgers, however, so they have their own indices. Sometimes the early mortgages will be center-filed in the deeds. If you cannot find the mortgage indices, ask someone working in the room—title searcher, abstracter or government clerk—to point you in the right direction. When you locate them, look up the grantee's name in the proper year under mortgagor. On occasion the older mortgage volumes may have an indexing system different from the deed index. For example, in one courthouse the 19th century mortgages that had been satisfied were arranged alphabetically in the mortgage index, while the foreclosed mortgages were arranged in unindexed volumes entitled "Sale." These latter were arranged chronologically. However the information is recorded, someone in the courthouse will know how and where to direct you.

Wills

Once you have located the court library or archive in which the will records are kept, locate the indices These usually are arranged alphabetically by the surname of the testator—the person who left the will—and are running indices, (i.e., arranged chronologically). This means that all of the surnames beginning with "M" will be listed by the date the will was recorded. A volume letter or number and a page number also will be listed. Sometimes the file box number will follow the volume and page number. The volume and page will contain only a copy of the will. The file box will contain all of the scraps of paper and legal records pertaining to the will, such as appraisals of inventory, requests for guardians of minor children, denials of the wife's requests to be appointed the legal guardian, etc.

The following is a sample of what you may find under "M:"

Name	Year	Book	Page	File Box
Miller, Johannes	1796	B	29	32
MacLean, James	1796	B	130	87
Moore, Care	1798	C	101	129
Mabey, William	1799	E	5	176

In some courts, although the indices are chronological, no recording date appears after the name. In these cases, jot down all of the people listed with an identical name and match the name in the volume with the date and location you are searching to establish which is the correct person.

In some probate courts you will find a reverse index, that is an index which lists the beneficiaries of the will rather the maker of the will. If such an index exists in your jurisdiction it can be very useful. Instead of having to guess (see page 126) that Alice F. Tryon is Caleb Forbes' daughter, you would look up Alice F. Tryon as a devisee (receiver of real property). Caleb Forbes would be listed as the devisor (testator or, more specifically, the giver of real property), along with the date, book number and page. North Carolina, for example, is one of the few states that maintains reverse indices.

Letters of Administration

In some courts, the letters of administration are indexed separately from wills. In that case the letters will be indexed in the manner described for wills. In other courts, all probate records are indexed in the same books. In this latter situation it is not unusual to find master probate indices in which all documents filed for each probate case are listed. There you can choose the documents from the index to the inheritance of real property or to the house, such as an inventory of goods and chattel. This system is less time consuming for you than having to thumb through the unindexed file box hoping to find an inventory.

These indexing systems can vary even more. In some court libraries the early books contained all of the probate records, interfiled, even though the index gives no indication of this. In one court library the older system separated wills and letters of administration in different volumes, but the volumes were interfiled together under one set of numbers. Thus, for example, Book A would be wills, while Books B and C might be letters, Book D wills, etc. Ask the clerks to explain any quirks in the indexing of the particular court library before you begin

Glossary

A

Adamsesque — Refers to the Adams brothers whose delicate sculptured ornaments characterized decoration during the Federal period.

adobe — "Unburned brick." A mixture of earth, sand, clay and straw or other binder and water in wooden molds about 1 1/2' long, then left to sun dry.

adz — a tool used for dressing wood, with an arched blade set at right angles to the handle.

alpha order — Names in alphabetical order.

appurtenance — Something added to a more important thing, such as an accessory, right or privilege (e.g., right of way). Also, a minor property, such as houses, outbuildings, gardens or fences incident to the principal property for passage of title.

arcade — A series of arches supported by columns or piers.

architrave — The part of the entablature that rests on the capital of the column and supports the frieze. Also door or window trim.

ashlar — Cut square or rectangular stone.

assignment — A change in mortgage ownership when a mortgagee can no longer act as such, because of death or other reason.

B

balloon framing — A framing method popularized after 1860 in which standard sizes of sawed lumber were used to create a wooden house frame characterized by two-story studs supported on the second floor by a 1" x 4" ribbon strip let into the studs. Wire nails were used extensively to hold the frame together.

baluster — A small column or other upright in a series to support a handrail, as in a balustrade.

balustrade — A handrail on balusters.

bargeboard — A decorative face board with cutouts placed vertically under the roof eaves.

batten — A narrow strip of wood covering a joint between two or more boards.

batten door — Two, three or four boards joined vertically on the outside face by two or three battens placed apart and horizontally on the inside face.

bay — That section or space in a house wall contained between the columns or piers within the walls, that is, between the upright posts supporting the structure. Originally in England a bay was the space between the principal rafters (trusses). This space varies from ten to sixteen feet.

beam — A large horizontal timber designed to transfer the weight of the house to the posts that support it.

beehive oven — An oven characterized by a rounded, usually brick, ceiling similar to a beehive.

beneficiary — The recipient of items in a will.

board — A flat piece of wood 1" or less thick and 4" or more wide.

board and batten — A siding or fabric in which wide boards (10"-12") are placed adjacent to each other with small boards 2" wide placed over the joint where the boards abut.

boast — To surface a stone with a broad chisel (a boasting chisel) and mallet.

bounds — The directions a boundary line takes including landmarks, such as a surveyor's pipe, heap of stones, a staddle, a white oak tree.

brackets — Wooden supports — often decorative — which support the roof eaves.

brad — A small finish nail sometimes having a slight side projection instead of a head.

brick bond — The pattern made in laying brick by alternating stretchers and headers with mortar in between, so that the joints overlap.

broadax — An ax with a wide flat head and comparatively short handle.

bush-hammer — A tool made of steel plates bolted together with channels between the cutting edges and used by a stone mason for facing stone.

C

cantilever — A projecting beam supported by a downward force behind the fulcrum.

capital — The top member on a column, often highly decorative and supporting the entablature.

"central" — The telephone operator who placed calls for people before direct dialing.

chancery court — An equity court in which "reasonable justice" or "common good" is decided, because following the letter of the law would be unjust.

chattel — Movable property, such as removable fixtures, household goods, slaves, personal property.

cistern — A reservoir for holding water, the source for which is not necessarily from underground, but may be from rain water.

clapboard — A board that is thin on one edge and thicker on the other for ease in overlapping horizontally to form a weatherproof fabric.

collar beam/tie — A horizontal board between opposite rafters to stiffen the roof frame.

consideration — Money exchanged in a deed or mortgage.

consort — Wife.

corbel — A type of bracket usually formed by extending successive courses of masonry or wood beyond a wall.

cornice — The projecting member at the top of a column or wall or the upper member of the entablature.

coursed masonry — A stone or brick wall with continuous horizontal layers.

court docket — A bound book of court agendas.

court of common pleas — A court having general jurisdiction, originally a court in England to hear civil cases between commoners.

crown colony — A colony established by the English king.

cupola — A roofed structure, square to round in plan, rising above a main roof.

cut nails — A type of nail whose shank was formed by pushing an iron plate into a shear blade suspended from above.

D

dado — A skirting above the baseboard of an interior wall, often extending from it to the chair rail. It sometimes mimicked a porch railing and balusters.

decedent — Term referring to a deceased person of a will.

defendant — A party against whom a suit is being brought. In a public auction it may be the mortgagor(s).

devisor — One who gives or transmits real property in a will.

dogtrot — A log house in which two pens were separated by a path, which commonly was enclosed as a center passage and ultimately as a center hall.

Doric — The oldest of the three orders of classic Greek architecture, characterized by fluted columns with plain saucer shaped capitals and a bold, simple cornice.

dormer — A roofed projection with a window on its front vertical face, built out from the main roof.

double door — A two-leaf door.

double-hung — A window divided horizontally in which the top and bottom sections slide past each other vertically. In original double-hung windows, the top section was fixed and did not slide.

dower right — The privilege of a widow to inherit one-third of all real property held in fee simple.

drapery — A typical Adamsesque sculptured ornament mimicking loose folds of cloth tied by a brooch.

drawshave — A knife-like tool used to shave shingles into a wedge shape.

drove — A mason's blunt or broad-edged chisel for facing stone.

dry wall — An unmortared stone wall.

dugout — A primitive home that was dug into the top or side of a hill (half dugout). Stones or logs were used to make the exposed walls and a framework of poles and brush held up the sod roof.

E

eaves — (Plural in form). The projecting overhang at the lower edges of the roof.

ell — An addition placed at a right angle to the main section and usually representing the shorter horizontal stroke of an "L."

ellipse — A single-hung sash with a series of lights in the shape of a flattened circle, separated by leaden or wooden muntins (dividers).

English bond — In brickwork, alternating courses of headers and stretchers in a variety of pattern rows, so that the joints are staggered.

English garden wall — A brick bond characterized by three rows of stretchers alternating with a row of headers.

entablature — The horizontal group of members above the column capitals (or over a door, etc.) divided into three parts: architrave, frieze and cornice.

eyebrow window — Sometimes called a "lie on your stomach" window, it is placed on the second-story directly under the eaves of a 1 1/2 story house.

F

fabric — Siding, or the material that covers the outside of the walls of a house. It may be clapboards, shingles, veneer brickwork, metal or vinyl siding among other materials.

facade — Face or exterior side of a building.

fanlight — A shingle-hung sash with a series of lights radiating in the shape of a fan (or half an ellipse) and separated by leaden or wooden muntins (dividers).

fee simple — A deed in which property is transferred free from any and all types of conditions and encumbrances; the title is clear.

fence wall brick — "Great bricks" or bricks 12" x 6" x 3".

festoon — In wallpaper, a border with garlands of leaves, flowers and ribbons.

fieldstone — Uncut and untreated stone naturally found in fields.

firebox — The space in a fireplace or stove or furnace where the fire actually is laid.

fireplace surround — The decorative wood or stone face placed above and on both sides of a fireplace.

Flemish bond — In brickwork, alternating headers and stretchers in each course, so that the joints are staggered.

Flemish common variation — A brick bond characterized by five rows of stretchers alternating with one row of the stretcher-header-stretcher pattern.

Flemish double stretcher — A brick bond characterized by the placement of two stretchers before a header.

Flemish diagonal — A brick bond characterized by alternating rows of stretcher-header-stretcher and all stretchers.

Flemish garden wall — A brick bond characterized by rows in which three stretcher-a header-three stretchers occur.

fluted — Decorated with regularly spaced, vertical grooves as on a column or pilaster.

folk myth — Stories believed as true, but which contain only a core of truth.

foreclosure — The act of depriving a mortgagor of the right to redeem mortgaged property because he has failed to pay his premiums.

foundation — Traditionally the stone or brick or a combination thereof underlying and being the underground support for the structure built above ground over it.

frame — The skeletal structure of a building.

freehold estate — A situation in which the tenant under a lease had the privileges of ownership, such as voting, but did not own the land.

frieze — Wide boards flush against a wall under a roof edge.

froe — A wedge-shaped blade set perpendicular to its handle.

fulcrum — The support or point on which a lever turns.

G

gable — A style of roof characterized by a ridge with two sides pitched away from it.

galerie — A French style of porch that often extended around at least three sides of the house and often was raised off the ground to the second-story level. It was supported by the house's roof which extended beyond the house walls thus making the galerie intrinsic to the original house construction.

gambrel — A style of roof characterized by a change in pitch between the ridge and the eaves.

garland — A typical Adamsesque sculptured ornament, usually in relief, in the form of a swag or festoon of flowers and fruits.

garden wall cross — A brick bond characterized by a row of three stretchers-a-header-three stretchers alternating with a row of stretchers.

Germanic post and girt — A style of construction in which each post was placed 4' apart, was comparatively small (e.g., 4" x 4") and had a comparable girt connecting paired posts.

"gingerbread" — Decorative cutouts on the exterior of a house made by using a jigsaw.

girt — Beam placed at the top of the first floor posts and on the second floor posts at the gable end.

glasshouse — A factory where glass was manufactured.

grantee — Receiver (often the buyer) in a deed.

grantor — Giver (often the seller) in a deed.

gudgeon — The stationary flat section (leaf) of a hinge.

H

half-timbered house — A framework of heavy timbers mortised and tenoned together and infilled with a variety of materials, often brick or plaster.

header — The short end of the brick.

hereditament — Any kind of property that can be inherited.

hewn wood — Wood squared by a broadax and an adz along its faces.

HL hinge — A hinge in which the vertical parts of the "H" and the "L" are stationary leaves and are attached to the face of the jamb, rather than to the edges.

hip — A style of roof characterized by four planes in which, at the intersection of two of the planes, the eave lines are not parallel.

hood mold — An upside down"U" over a window or door.

"horse" — A supporting frame with four legs used to clamp shingles in order to shape them.

I

improvements — Any buildings on real property.

infill — The nogging in a half-timbered house.

initial order — Names alphabetized by the first initial of the surname, often further indexed in running order.

intestate — Having no valid will.

inventory — A list of real and personal property.

Ionic — The second oldest of the three orders of classic Greek architecture, characterized by a capital with two opposed volutes.

iron, corrugated — Stamped iron used as metal ceilings.

J

jamb — The side of a window, door or fireplace. In a window or door opening, the side against which the sash or door abuts.

judgment — A judicial decision.

jurisdiction — The territorial range of authority or control, which often is arbitrary and forms political subdivisions, thus enabling more efficient government management.

K

king post truss — A truss in which one post was placed from the collar beam to the gable peak, often in connection with a ridgepole, on each gable end. On occasion two additional diagonal struts were placed adjacent to the foot of the king post and reached to the middle of each side of the gable.

L

L-head — A type of wrought finish nail, also called a brad.

label mold — A hood mold which extends across the head of a window or door and down the sides for a few inches.

lampblack — A black pigment or soot that accumulates on the glass lamp chimney when carbonaceous materials are burned.

latilla — Split cedar or aspen saplings which were placed perpendicular to the *vigas* to form a mat on which mud or tamped earth was placed to make a flat roof.

lease — An agreement which creates a landlord-tenant relationship. It transfers an aspect of real property. The title transferred is less than fee simple and is subject to certain conditions, such as annual rent and the duration of the lease.

lessee — A person who leases land.

letter of administration — When a person dies intestate, this letter gives authority to someone to act as the executor to settle the estate.

liber — A book or volume or ledger.

lien — The right to take and hold as security or sell the property of a debtor in payment for a debt.

life estate — An estate for the duration of a life. If a married couple had a life estate, it often was for two lifetimes, the husband's and wife's.

light — A glass pane in a window.

lintel — A beam with its two ends resting on two posts, often over a wall opening, such as a window or door.

louvers — Movable horizontal slats that can be tilted to close our the sun, rain and snow, but still permit the passage of air.

M

mansard — A style of roof characterized by two slopes on all four sides, the lower of which is almost vertical and the upper almost horizontal.

manteltree — A massive hewn timber used as a lintel over the fireplace and placed in the stone fireplace surround.

massed plan — A house design in which the room organization is two rooms deep.

maul — A wooden club with a variety of uses. One was to hit a froe in making shingles. Another was to hit wooden pegs into holes to hold the tenon in the mortise.

mete — The length in chains or feet of a boundary.

mortar — A mixture used to bond mineral substances, such as adobe, brick or stone together.

mortgage bond — A promise to pay principal and interest on a loan secured by a lien or title conveyance on a specifically named property.

mortgagee — A giver of the money of a mortgage.

mortgagor — The receiver of the money of a mortgage.

mortise — A cutout piece of wood in one member creating a "hole" or socket designed to receive the tenon of another member to which it is to be joined.

muizetanden — The mousetooth edging of a gable end wall in which bricks at the edge of the gable are set at right angles to the slope. It is also called Dutch cross bond, diapering (in England) and tumbling (in Virginia).

mullion — The vertical division member between windows or doors of a close series.

muntin — A bar divider supporting lights and separating these panes of glass in a window or door.

N

newel post — The post at the bottom, top or landing of a stairway where the handrail terminates.

nogging — A filler in a half-timbered house, usually of clay and straw, but sometimes of brick or boards.

novelty siding — The horizontal board siding in which the upper and lower boards are connected by means of various simple joints, such as a rabbet or shiplap.

O

ogee, double — Opposite double-pointed arches formed with a double curve, like an elongated "S", slightly convex at the top and bottom. Also called an inflected arch.

orthophoto map — A colorized, topographical map photographed from an airplane, showing geographic and botanical details by means of shadings.

P

palisade log house — A house built of logs placed vertically into the ground.

Palladian window — A tripartite window with a large, arched center window flanked by two narrower rectangular windows.

pane — A glass light in a window.

panel — A sheet of wood held in a frame.

parapet — A low, solid, protective wall along the edge of a roof and often associated with a lower flat roof.

patent holder — An individual appointed by the crown (the English king) to hold a patent or paper granting land ownership of a colony or part of it.

patronymic — The father's first name plus a suffix to mean "son of" or "daughter of" used as the second name of his children.

pediment — A triangular face of a roof gable, or a door or window header molding.

peen-hammer — The end of a hammer head opposite the flat striking surface, often wedge-shaped and used to chip a parallel design into stone.

pen — A one room log house.

pent — A relatively narrow roof of a single sloping plane often over the first floor.

personal property — Personal items, household goods or removeable fixtures.

pier — A vertical supporting structure which may be isolated or part of a wall.

pigment — A granular substance used to color paint.

pilaster — A shallow pier of wide face boards on the facade of a house, usually abutting at the corners or framing the front door.

pintle — An upright pin or bolt used as a pivot for a gudgeon or fixed leaf of a hinge.

pit saw — A long two-man saw which was used vertically with one man in the pit under the saw and another man above guiding it. The log was placed horizontally.

pitch — The angle of the roof line.

plaintiff — The party instituting a court suit. In public auctions often the mortgagee(s).

plane — A carpenter's tool with an adjustable blade for smoothing, leveling and shaping wood.

plank — A thick board usually between 1 1/2" and 3 1/2" thick and over 6" wide.

plank frame — An early style of house frame in which 1 1/4"-2" thick oak planks 12"-15" wide were placed flat-sided about 2" apart into a rabbet on the exterior of the sill and plate. These plank studs extended two stories and were attached to the sill, girt and plate with oak pins. Exterior siding was attached to these planks.

plat — A surveyor's map.

plate — A beam capping the exterior posts or studs to support the rafters.

platform framing — A wood framing method in which a house is built a floor at a time, with the floor extending to the outside walls. Wall units are nailed together while they are lying flat on the floor (platform) and then tilted into place and secured by nailing.

porch — A roofed space outside the main walls of a home and at an entrance.

portico — An entrance porch, often with a pedimented roof supported by classical columns.

post and girt — A framing system consisting of large squared timbers. The posts are vertical while the girt are horizontal. The frame supports the floors and roof.

poteaux en terre — "Posts in the earth." A house made palisade fashion with logs placed vertically 3' into the ground about 5"-6" apart. Long, floor-to-ceiling diagonal corner braces stabilized the vertical logs.

poteaux sur solle — "Posts on a sill." A palisade method of log-house construction in which the vertical logs were seated into a log sill placed on a rock foundation and itself in a trench. Otherwise the same as poteaux en terre.

premise — In a deed this means a house is located on the property.

primogeniture — The right of the eldest son to inherit the bulk of the family property.

probate — To legally present a will as the last will and testament of the decedent. Also a noun used to encompass all of the matters over which a court of probate has jurisdiction.

probate court — A court in which wills, letters of administration and such probate records are kept in some states.

public auction — Á property is put up for sale at a public auction if the taxes have not been paid for a specific period of time, if there was a default on the mortgage or if a lien was made on the property for non-payment of improvements, such as building repairs.

puddling — A mud-wall construction method in which plank forms were placed on either side of the wall, filled with clay, mud and straw and tamped to remove air bubbles and allowed to dry. After the layer was dry, the forms were moved up the walls and the process repeated.

purlins — Boards connected horizontally to the rafters to strengthen them.

Q

queen post truss — A truss in which two posts were placed between the roof and the outside edges of the collar beam. Another beam capped the posts to stiffen this truss.

quitrent — An annual tax, usually under early leases, a token payment by the tenant of a freehold estate to the landlord.

quoin — A large, rectangular, cut stone corner block placed alternately so that the mortar joints do not coincide vertically.

R

rabbet — A right angle wooden strip cut out from a timber designed as a seat for a plank or board.

racking — The twisting of some material, such as lumber, out of its original plane.

rafter — A roof support found immediately under the roof boards.

rainspout — A pipe projecting through an upper wall and designed to lead water off the roof of an adobe house. Also used with a gutter system in frame houses.

real property — Land with all of its inherent natural resources and any man-made improvements of a more or less permanent nature.

referee — The person presiding over a public auction who acts as grantor in the sale.

relict — Widow.

renovation — The act of improving by repairing or remodeling, often to restore to an earlier condition.

restoration — Rebuilding to attempt to put a structure back into its prior or original condition.

reverse index — One that lists the beneficiary in a will or a devisee, rather than the devisor.

ribbon strip — A 1" x 4" board in balloon farming which was set on edge and let into the two-story studs on the second floor.

ribbon window — Three or more contiguous windows.

ridgepole — The top horizontal member of a sloping roof against which the upper ends of the rafters are set.

rose head — A type of wrought common nail with a head that resembled a flower after the head was pounded on.

row window — A ribbon window.

rubble — Undressed or uncut stone.

running index — One that is organized in chronological order.

S

saddlebay — A style of two-pen log house in which the chimney became central to the two pens.

saltbox — A house style in which a half room was added to the first story rear of a 2 1/2 story house.

sash — A frame in which glass is set.

sash saw — A vertical saw blade clamped into a rectangular frame called a sash and powered by water.

satisfaction — Of a mortgage, occurs when the mortgage bond has been paid completely.

sawed wood — Wood characterized by teeth marks which may be parallel and straight, or crescent-shaped.

seized or "died seized" — Died in possession of.

shake — A hand-split shingle.

shard — A fragment of a brittle substance, such as glass or pottery.

"shave" — Shingles made by hand (i.e., shaved with a froe and maul while held in a horse).

sheathe — To place planks or boards next to each other to cover a structural frame.

shed — A roof having only one sloping plane.

shingle — A wedge-shaped piece of wood or other material placed in overlapping courses to cover a roof or exterior wall.

shiplap — A beveled joining of two boards to form a weather-resistant exterior wall siding.

sidelight — Two, often single-hung, frames containing a series of lights placed vertically on both sides of a door. The muntins may be leaden or wooden.

sill — A large hewn beam that rests on the foundation and supports the wooden house frame.

single-hung — A window sash that does not open.

slaked lime — Calcium hydroxide, a soft white powder used in making mortar, cement and paint, among other mixtures.

sod house — A temporary home in which sod building blocks were cut by a special plow and stacked like bricks to form walls. Poles, sticks and brush supported the sod roof. A milled, stock door and one or two windows completed the house.

split wood — Cut by a froe and maul along its grain.

sprig — A small brad without a head.

staddle — Either a stump or a platform upon which hay or straw is stacked.

stepped gable — A gable roof whose end wall is raised above the roof plane in steps. Also called crow-stepped or corbie-stepped.

stoop — A broad platform step at the entrance to a house and outside of it.

strap hinge — A hinge in which one leaf is a flat decorative strap and both leaves are attached to the face of the jamb and of the door rather than to the edges.

stretcher — The long side of a brick.

strut — A brace under compression used to strengthen a framework.

stucco — Exterior plaster composed of water, lime and stone dust or oyster shell.

stud — A small post. When used instead of a post, it is positioned closer together than posts usually are, the distance apart depending on the size of the studs.

survey — A legal description of the outline of a property.

survey field notes — The working notes that a surveyor makes in the field; usually more complete than the final plat.

T

T-head — A type of wrought common nail whose head and shank resemble a "T" after the head was pounded on.

tenement — Anything held by tenure; often applied only to houses and other buildings.

tenon— A projection — a "tongue" — on the end of a wooden member designed to fit snugly into the socket or mortise in another, thus forming a joint.

tenure — Occupancy or tenancy or possession.

terneplate — A seamed metal roof made of thin sheets of iron or steel coated with zinc.

testament — A written document providing for the disposition of personal property.

testator — The person who leaves a will.

thatched roof — A roof covering of rushes, straw or similar plant material fastened together to shed water.

thumb latch — A door fastener opened by pressing the thumb on a lever.

timber — Large, squared wooden members used as the frame in a post and girt — or timber frame — house.

timber frame — post and girt frame.

title — What one receives upon complete conveyance of a property.

topographical map — One that shows land contours. In the 19th century this usually was done by means of curved lines.

transcription — The act of writing out or transferring information from one copy to another.

transom — In the late 18th century, a single-hung window of a series of lights separated by muntins capping a door. (In the late 19th to 20th centuries an awning style window with a single light.)

tread — The horizontal part of the stair that is walked on.

treenails — Wooden pins or pegs, similar to iron nails, used early to pin together wooden members.

trompe l'oeil — A style of painting designed to create an illusion of reality by accurately representing details, scenes, etc.

truss — A framework of wood beams or metal bars, placed in rigid triangles to stiffen a roof.

two-leaf door — An entrance characterized by two, 2'-wide symmetrically-opposed doors which latch into each other, thus having their opening hardware in the center of the entrance.

U

U-shaped arches — Round arches.

ux. — Uxor or wife.

uxor — (Latin) wife.

V

veneer — A thin layer of selected wood for gluing to another less desirable wood. Also, a layer of special material, such as brick, to cover a wall.

veranda — A long, gallery-like porch off the first floor, sometimes two-storied.

vergeboard — See bargeboard.

vernacular — Architecture characteristic of a locality, often constructed of local materials by individuals with home-learned skills.

vigas — Poles placed horizontally across the width of the house under the roof line of a parapet roof.

vital statistics — Birth, death and marriage dates.

volute — A spiral, scroll-like ornament, such as that used on Ionic capitals.

vx. — Uxor or wife.

W

wainscoting — A wood lining on interior walls, usually less than the height of the room.

wall anchor — A wrought iron bolt which tied the brick facade to the wooden gable end girt. It had a decorative design in the part that was seen on the exterior (e.g., the date the house was built, crosses, trefoils, etc.).

wallpaper — A paper or cloth with a decorative design printed on it and used to cover a wall.

wattle and daub — Woven sticks and clay used as infill material.

weatherboard — A type of horizontal siding in which wide boards are placed with the lower edge overlapping the next board below.

Western platform framing — Platform framing.

will — A legal declaration of how a person wishes his property to be disposed of after his death.

wing — An addition added to the side of the main section and often smaller than the main section.

wire nail — A nail usually made out of steel and the predominant nail in the 20th century.

witness — The person who witnesses the signature of the signer of a legal document.

wrought nail — Type of nail made from a nail rod, a strip of iron the diameter of a specific nail size. This was cut and heated and the tapered shank shaped and cooled. Then the top of the shank was heated and wedged into a heading tool and the separate head was pounded on.

Z

zeitgheist — Spirit (gheist) of the time (zeit).

zinc — A metallic element often galvanized with iron to prevent rust.

Bibliography

"Adobe." *Funk & Wagnalls New Encyclopedia*. 1979 ed.

"Ambidexderity." *Funk & Wagnalls New Encyclopedia*. 1979 ed.

Andrews, Wayne. *Architecture, Ambition and Americans. A Social History of Americans and Architecture*. New York: The Free Press, 1964.

"Arsenic." *Funk & Wagnalls New Encyclopedia*. 1979 ed.

"Austerlitz Assessment Rool [sic] July 15th-1836." Austerlitz, N.Y.

Bailey, Christopher M. Telephone interviews. 3 Nov. 1987 and 15 Jan. 1989.

Bailey, Dorothy J. Telephone interviews. 19 Aug. 1987 and 22 Sept. 1987.

Bakst, Aaron. *Mathematics. Its Magic and Mastery*. Princeton: D. Van Nostrand, 1967.

"Banks and Banking." *Funk & Wagnalls New Encyclopedia*. 1979 ed.

"Barberry." *Funk & Wagnalls New Encyclopedia*. 1979 ed.

"Bartlett, Ted. "Foundation Plantings: Concerns and Cautions." *House Notes*, No. 6 (1986).

Beers, D. G. and Co. *Atlas of Columbia County, New York*. Philadelphia: D.G. Beers, 1873.

Benjamin, Asher. *The American Builder's Companion*. 1806; rpt. New York: Dover Publications, 1969.

Berkeley, Edmund C. *A Guide to Mathematics for the Intelligent Nonmathematician*. New York: Simon and Schuster, 1966.

Better Homes and Gardens. "Restorers Need to Sleuth House's History." *Democrat and Chronicle*, 7 Nov. 1987, Sec. E, 41.

Blackburn, Roderic H. Telephone interviews. Fall 1987 to 27 Jan. 1988.

Blackburn, Roderic H. and Ruth Piwonka. *Remembrance of Patria, Dutch Arts and Culture in Colonial America 1609-1776*. Albany, N.Y.: Albany Institute of History and Art, 1988.

Blumenson, John J. *Identifying American Architecture: A Pictorial Guide to Styles and Terms, 1600-1945*. Rev. ed. New York: Norton, 1981.

"Brass." *Funk & Wagnalls New Encyclopedia*. 1979 ed.

"Brick." *Funk & Wagnalls New Encyclopedia*. 1979 ed.

Brown, Kathi Ann. "How Old Is Your House?" *Early American Life*, Oct 1985, 44-49, 87.

Brown, Norman. "Your House's Roots." *Early American Life*, April 1986, 14-16.

Brown, William H., ed. *History of Warren County*. Glens Falls, N.Y.: Board of Supervisors of Warren County, 1963.

Browning, Joe C. Letter to author 28 April 1988. Telephone interviews. April 1988.

Buechner, Thomas S. "History of Glass — United States." *The New Encyclopaedia Britannica*. 1982 ed.

Buel, Joy Day and Richard Buel, Jr. *The Way of Duty*. New York: Norton, 1984.

The Builder's Dictionary: Or Gentleman and Architect's Companion. Vols. I & II. 1734; rpt. Washington, D.C.: The Association for Preservation Technology, 1981.

"Building By the Book." *Colonial Homes*, May-June 1980, 80-83.

Burr, David. *Map of Albany County*. [New York State]: Surveyor General of New York State, 1829.

Candee, Richard M. "The Rediscovery of Milk-based House Paints and the Myth of 'Brickdust and Buttermilk' Paints." *Old-Time New England*, Winter 1968, 79-81.

Capone, Lisa. "Mapping the Mountains." *The Christian Science Monitor*, 31 May 1988, 19-20.

Carnahan, Frances. "Early American Life: Keeping Room." *Early American Life*, Oct. 1987, 2-3.

Cassill, Kay. *The Complete Handbook for Freelance Writers*. Cincinnati: Writer's Digest Books, 1981.

"Chain." *Funk & Wagnalls New Encyclopedia*. 1979 ed.

Chase, A.W. *Dr. Chase's Recipes; or, Information for Everybody: An Invaluable Collection of About Eight Hundred Practical Recipes*. Ann Arbor: A. W. Chase, 1866.

Cheeseman, Bruce. Telephone interviews. Aug. 1987.

Cherubini, Jay. Telephone interview. 30 Sept. 1988.

Child, Hamilton, ed. *Gazetteer and Business Directory of Columbia County, New York for 1871-1872*. Syracuse, N.Y.: The Journal Office, 1871.

Clark, Edie. "Having a Roof of Stone." *At Home in New England*. Dublin, N.H.: Yankee Publishing, 1986, 2-3.

"Clay." *Funk & Wagnalls New Encyclopedia*. 1979 ed.

"Clocks and Watches." *Funk & Wagnalls New Encyclopedia*. 1979 ed.

"Coal." *Funk & Wagnalls New Encyclopedia*. 1979 ed.

Cockburn, William, Fred Hausen and William Cockburn, Jr. *Map of the Several Farms and Unappropriated Lands in the Town of Claverack and Corporation of Hudson, A. D. 1799*.

Columbia County Board of Realtors. *At Your Service*. Kinderhook, N.Y.: Stuyvesant Press, 1986.

Columbia County Clerk's Office. Personal Interview. 5 Nov. 1987.

Columbia County Clerk's Office. *Deed Liber A*. Hudson, N.Y.: 27 Jan. 1802, 356.

Columbia County Clerk's Office. *Deed Liber B-1*. Hudson, N.Y.: 6 April 1784, 56.

Columbia County Clerk's Office. *Deed Liber B-1*. Hudson, N.Y.: 16 Oct. 1802, 25.

Columbia County Clerk's Office. *Deed Liber B-1*. Hudson, N.Y.: 8 March 1803, 82.

Columbia County Clerk's Office. *Deed Liber LL*. Hudson, N.Y.: 22 May 1845, 104-106.

Columbia County Clerk's Office. *Deed Liber 1*. Hudson, N.Y.: 27 July 1854, 41-44.

Columbia County Clerk's Office. *Deed Liber 95*. Hudson, N.Y.: 27 Dec. 1796, 2-3.

Columbia County Clerk's Office. *Mortgage Liber B*. Hudson, N.Y.: 7 May 1804, 476.

Columbia County Clerk's Office. *Mortgage Liber B*. Hudson, N.Y.: 4 April 1805, 671-672.

Columbia County Clerk's Office. *Mortgage Liber II*. Hudson, N.Y.: 30 March 1858, 531-532.

Columbia County Clerk's Office. *Mortgage Liber 39*. Hudson, N.Y.: 23 June 1875, 413-414.

Columbia County Surrogate Court Library. *Will Liber C*. Hudson, N.Y.: 12 Feb. 1807, 151.

Columbia County Surrogate Court Library. *Will Liber D*. Hudson, N.Y.: 9 June 1811, 164-166.

Columbia County Surrogate Court Library. *Will Liber D*. Hudson, N.Y.: 25 Feb. 1812, 132-140.

Columbia County Surrogate Court Library. *Will Liber D*. Hudson, N.Y.: 1 Feb. 1817, 419.

Columbia County Surrogate Court Library. *Will Liber E*. Hudson, N.Y.: 31 Aug. 1820, 2.

Cooper, Linda Gilbert, ed. *A Walker's Guide to the Old Croton Aquaduct*. New York State Office of Parks, Recreation & Historic Preservation, Taconic Region: n.p., n.d.

Corsaro, James. Personal interview. 8 Aug. 1984.

Cousin, Pierre-Henri. *Collins Pocket French Dictionary: French-English, English-French*. London: William Collins Sons, 1985.

Cummings, Abbot Lowell. *The Framed Houses of Massachusetts Bay, 1625-1725*. Cambridge, Mass.: The Belknap Press of Harvard University Press, 1979.

"Currency." *Funk & Wagnalls New Encyclopedia*. 1979 ed.

"Currency and Banking." *Funk & Wagnalls New Encyclopedia*. 1979 ed.

"Day Book of Hamlin, Pilling and Co., Austerlitz, Columbia County, New York. Sept 9 1865." 163.

Deimling, Paula. *1986 Writer's Market*. Cincinnati: Writer's Digest Books, 1985.

DeLameter, Glenn. Telephone interview. 17 May 1988.

Derry, Anne, et al. "Guidelines For Local Surveys: A Basic For Preservation Planning." *National Register Bulletin, No. 24* Rev. 1985 by Patricia L. Parkey. Washington, D.C.: National Park Service, 1985.

"Dictionary." *Funk & Wagnalls New Encyclopedia*. 1979 ed.

Doddridge, Joseph. "Housebuilding on the Frontier—c. 1750."*The Chronicle of the Early American Industries Association*, 41, No. 2 (1988) 31.

"Dollar." *Funk & Wagnalls New Encyclopedia*. 1979 ed.

Dorsey, John. "Furniture Finders Guide to Grain." *The Knickerbocker News*, 21 Nov. 1985, Sec. B, 6,8, cols. 1-2.

Downing, Andrew Jackson. *Victorian Cottage Residences*. 1873;

rpt. New York: Dover Publications, 1981.

Drake, Greg. Personal interview. 14 July 1987.

Drew, Bernard A. and Donna M. Drew. *Mapping the Berkshires*. Great Barrington, Mass.: Attic Revivals Press, 1986.

Dunbar, Michael. "Old House Myths." *Early American Life*, April 1988, 28-31.

Dunton, Anna Mary. *Reflections, Canaan, New York, Bicentennial 1976*. Canaan, N.Y.: Canaan Historical Society, 1976.

Eakle, Arlene and Johni Cerney. *The Source: A Guidebook of American Genealogy*. Salt Lake City, Utah: Ancestry Publishing, 1984.

"Edmund Gunter." *Funk & Wagnalls New Encyclopedia*. 1979 ed.

Emerson, George Barrell. *A Report of the Trees and Shrubs Growing Naturally in the Forests of Massachusetts*. Boston: Dutton and Wentworth, State Printers, 1846.

"Farmer's Paint — House or Fence Paint." Austerlitz, N.Y.

"Finance." *Funk & Wagnalls New Encyclopedia*. 1979 ed.

Finberg, Joscelyne. *Exploring Villages*. Gloucester, Eng.: Alan Sutton Publishing, 1987.

"Fire Department." *Funk & Wagnalls New Encyclopedia*. 1979 ed.

"Fire Engine." *Funk & Wagnalls New Encyclopedia*. 1979 ed.

"Fire Fighting." *Funk & Wagnalls New Encyclopedia*. 1979 ed.

"Fire Insurance." *Funk & Wagnalls New Encyclopedia*. 1979 ed.

Fire Insurance Maps in the Library of Congress; Plans of North American Cities and Towns. Produced by the Sanborn Map Company. Washington, D.C.: Library of Congress, 1981.

Fitch, Asa. *Their Own Voices: Oral Accounts of Early Settlers in Washington County, New York*. Ed. Winston Adler. Interlaken, N.Y.: Heart of the Lakes Publishing, 1983.

Fitchen, John. *The New World Dutch Barn*. Syracuse, N.Y.: Syracuse University Press, 1968.

Flaherty, Carolyn. "A Glance Back At Tin Ceiling." *The Old-House Journal*, March 1979. 29-30.

Foley, Mary Mix. *The American House*. New York: Harper & Row, 1980.

Franzwa, Gregory M. *The Story of Old Ste. Genevieve*. Gerald, Mo. : Patrice Press , 1973.

"Freemasonry." *Funk & Wagnalls New Encyclopedia*. 1979 ed.

Gebhards, Elizabeth L. *The Parsonage Between Two Manors, Annals of Clover-Reach*. Hudson, N.Y.: Bryan Printing, 1909.

Gillon, Edmund V., Jr. and Clay Lancaster. *Victorian Houses: A Treasury of Lesser-Known Examples*. New York: Dover Publications, 1973.

Glassie, Henry. "The Variation of Concepts Within Tradition: Barn Building in Otsego County, New York." *Geoscience and Man*, 5. 10 June 1974, 177-235.

Goerlich, Shirley Boyce. *Genealogy, A Practical Research Guide*. Sidney, N.Y.: RSG Publishing, 1984.

Grant, Jerry. Telephone Interviews. Jan. 1988.

Greenwood, Val D. *The Researcher's Guide to American Genealogy*. Baltimore: Genealogical Publishing, 1983.

Gustafson, William A. Telephone interviews. 17 Aug. 1987-1 Mar.1989.

"Gypsum." *Funk & Wagnalls New Encyclopedia*. 1979 ed.

Hale, Richard W., Jr. "Methods of Research for the Amateur Historian." *History News*, 24, No. 7 (1979).

Hallock, Terry. Telephone interviews. 1986-1988.

Hallock, Terry and Beverly. "Finding a House to Call Home." *Yankee*, June 1981, 64-69.

Hamlin, Talbot. *Greek Revival Architecture in America*. New York: Dover Publications, 1964.

Hampden County Clerk's Office. *Deed Book I*. Springfield, Mass.: 27 Sept. 1756, 747-749.

Handler, Mimi. "The 18th Century House, c. 1970." *Early American Life*, Feb. 1988, 26, 35.

Harrison, Henry S. *Houses*. New York: Charles Scribner's Sons 1980.

Hartschuh, Gordon. Personal interview. 2 June 1988.

Hayes, Robert. Personal interview. 3 June 1988.

Hendrick, Ulysses Prentiss. *A History of Agriculture of the State of New York*. New York: Hill and Wang, 1933.

Herron, Robert. Telephone interviews. 7 Sept. 1987 and 10 Sept. 1987.

"Historic American Building Survey." *Early American Life*, April 1986, 96.

History of Columbia County New York. Philadelphia: Everts &

Ensign, 1878.

Hoadley, R. Bruce. *Understanding Wood*. Newtown, Conn.: The Taunton Press, 1980.

Hoadly, Charles J. *The Public Records of the State of Connecticut, from October, 1776, to February, 1778, inclusive*. Hartford: Press of the Case, Lockwood & Brainard, Co. 1894. Vol. I.

Hoadly, Charles J. *The Public Records of the State of Connecticut, from May, 1778, to April, 1780, inclusive*. Hartford: Press of the Case, Lockwood & Brainard, Co. 1895. Vol. II.

Horgan, Edward R. *The Shaker Holy Land, A Community Portrait*. Harvard, Mass.: The Harvard Common Press, 1982.

Howe, Barbara J., et al. *Houses and Homes, Exploring Their History*. Nashville: The American Association for State and Local History, 1987.

Howe, Randall. "At Home With the Past." *Berkshire Week*, 31 July 1988, 5-6, 22-23.

Hudson, Patricia L. "In Mr. Jefferson's Garden." *Americana*, Jan./ Feb. 1987, 50-55.

Hunt, James C. Telephone interview. 1 Jan. 1989.

Irving, Washington. *Diedrick Knickerbocker's A History of New-York*. 1854; rpt. Tarrytown, N.Y.: Sleepy Hollow Press, 1981.

Irwin, Robin J. "Wisconsin's Rural Detective." *Historic Preservation*, 40, No. 1 (1988), 24-26, 95.

Isham, Norman and Albert F. Brown. *Early Connecticut Houses, An Historical and Architectural Study*. New York: Dover Publications, 1965.

Janijewski, Jeff P. Telephone interview. 15 July 1987.

Janson, H.W. and Dora Jane Janson. *History of Art*. Englewood Cliffs, N.J.: Prentice-Hall, 1966.

Joedicke, Jürgen. *A History of Modern Architecture*. Trans. James C. Palmes. New York: Frederick A. Praeger Publisher, 1963.

Johnson, Jim. Telephone interview. 29 June 1988.

Johnson, Sabeeha H. "Interiors." *Upstate Magazine*, 27 Nov. 1988, 9.

Jones, Henry Z. "Palatine-Livingston Connections." New York Chapter Palatines to America. Germantown, N.Y. 7 May 1988.

Jordan, Terry G. *American Log Buildings: An Old World Heritage*. Chapel Hill: The University of North Carolina Press, 1985.

Kalm, Peter. *Travels Into North America*. Trans. John Reinhold Forster. Barre, Mass.: The Imprint Society, 1972.

Keller, Alan. *Life Along the Hudson*. Tarrytown, N.Y.: Sleepy Hollow Press, 1976.

Kelly, Arthur C.M. *Baptismal Record of Reformed Church, Claverack, New York, 1727-1899*. Rhinebeck, N.Y.: Arthur C. M. Kelly, 1970.

Kelly, J. Frederick. *Early Domestic Architecture of Connecticut*. New York: Dover Publications, 1963.

Kempster, Michael. "Restoring Old Plaster." *Early American Life*, Oct. 1981, 40-42, 60.

Kern, Marion L. *Cemeteries in the Town of Austerlitz, Names Identified on Tombstones from 1754-1984*. Rhinebeck, N.Y.: Wambach Communications Group, 1985.

Kern, Marion L. Personal interviews. 17 Aug. 1987 and 16 Sept. 1987.

Kim, Sung Bok. *Landlord and Tenant in Colonial New York: Manorial Society, 1664-1775*. Chapel Hill: The University of North Carolina Press, 1978.

Kings District. "Records of Kings [sic] District. Canaan, N.Y. 1772-1788.

Kings District. "A Tax List of Kings [sic] District." Canaan, N.Y. 23 Oct. 1779.

Kirkham, E. Kay. *The Handwriting of American Records for a Period of 300 Years*. Logan, Utah: The Everton Publishers, 1973.

Kirkham, E. Kay. *How To Read The Handwriting and Records of Early America*. 2nd ed. Salt Lake City: Deseret Book, 1964.

Kirkpatrick, Konstance. "On the Crest of Put's Hill at the Gateway to New England." *Daughters of the American Revolution Magazine*, Jan. 1976, 23-24.

Kohan, Carol Eve. "'Paysage a Chasse' Convservators Restore 19th Century French Hunting Scene at Lindenwald." *The Chatham Courier*, 9 Jan. 1986. Sec B, p. 3, cols 1-5.

Konikow, Robert B. *Discover Historic America*. Chicago: Rand McNally, 1976.

La Fert, Kathy. Telephone interview. 29 July 1987.

Langdon, William Chauncey. *Everyday Things in American Life*

1607-1776. New York: Charles Scribner's Sons, 1937.

Lank, Edith. *Modern Real Estate Practice in New York for Salespersons and Brokers.* Chicago: Real Estate Education, 1983.

Larkin, David, June Sprigg and James Johnson. *Colonial Design in the New World.* New York: Stewart, Tabori & Chang, 1988.

Leccese, Michael. "Digging Up Your House's Past." *Country Home,* Aug. 1986, 14.

"Lien." *Funk & Wagnalls New Encyclopedia.* 1979 ed.

Light, Sarah B. "Names for the Court of Probate: Statistical Analysis." Austerlitz, N.Y.: 1987.

Lindberg, Marcia Wiswall. *Genealogist's Handbook for New England Research.* 2nd ed. Boston: NEHGS, 1985.

Little, William. *The Oxford Universal Dictionary on Historical Principles.* Rev. ed. C. T. Onions. London: Oxford University Press, 1955.

Lord, Philip L., Jr. *Mills on the Tsatsawassa, A Guide for Local Historians.* Albany, N.Y.: The State Education Department, 1983.

Lord, Philip L., Jr. Telephone interview. 28 Feb. 1989.

Lynn, Catherine. *Wallpaper in America from the Seventeenth Century to World War I.* New York: Norton, 1980.

Lyons, Chuck. "Home Is a Rock Pile." *Upstate Magazine,* 27 Nov. 1988 4-7.

Mackie, B. Allan. *Notches of All Kinds.* Prince George, B.C.: Log Home Publishing Company, 1983.

Maffabmy, Judy. Telephone interview. 27 July 1987.

Mahnke, Susan. "Painted Decorations for the 'Period' Look." *At Home in New England.* Dublin, N.H.: Yankee Publishing, 1986, 56-58.

Mahnke, Susan. "Reproduction Wallpaper." *At Home in New England.* Dublin, N.H.: Yankee Publishing, 1986, 50-56.

Maney, Susan. "Appropriate Landscaping for Your Old Home." *Gardener's Journal,* Rochester, N.Y.: Landmark Society of Western New York, 1986.

Martin, Michael and Leonard Gelber. *Dictionary of American History.* Student Ed. A. W. Littlefield. Ames, Iowa: Littlefield, Adams & Co., 1956.

McAlester, Virginia and Lee McAlster. *A Field Guide to American Houses.* New York: Alfred A Knopf, 1986.

McGinty, Brian. "Roy Underhill, Williamsburg's Woodwright." *Early American Life,* Feb. 1988, 36-39, 76.

McKee, Harley J. "Amateur's Guide to Terms Commonly Used in Describing Historic Buildings." Rochester, N.Y.: The Landmark Society of Western New York, 1967.

McKee, Harley J. *Introdution to Early American Masonry, Stone, Brick, Mortar and Plaster.* Washington, D.C.: National Trust for Historic Preservation and Columbia University, 1973.

McMullin, Phillip. *New York in 1800. Index to the Federal Census Schedules of the State of New York. With Other Aids to Research.* Provo, Utah: Gendex, 1971.

Monahan, Robert. Telephone Interview. 15 Oct. 1987.

"The Monetary System of the United States." *Funk & Wagnalls New Encyclopedia.* 1979 ed.

"Money." *Funk & Wagnalls New Encyclopedia.* 1979 ed.

Morris, William. *The American Heritage Dictionary of the American Language.* New York: American Heritage Publishing, 1976.

"Mortgage." *Funk & Wagnalls New Encyclopedia.* 1979 ed.

Moss, Roger. *Century of Color, Exterior Decoration for American Bulding 1820-1920.* Watkins Glen, N.Y.: American Life Foundation, 1981.

Mulholland, James A. *A Histry of Metals in Colonial America.* University, Ala.: The University of Alabama Press, 1981.

Mullins, Lisa C., ed. *Colonial Architecture of the Mid-Atlantic.* Harrisburg, Pa.: National Historical Society Publications, 1987.

Mullins, Lisa C., ed. *Early American Community Structures.* Harrisburg, Pa.: National Historical Society Publications, 1987.

Mullins, Lisa C., ed. *Early Architecture of Rhode Island.* Harrisburg, Pa.: National Historical Society Publications, 1987.

Mullins, Lisa C., ed. *Early Architecture of the South.* Harrisburg, Pa.: National Historical Society Publications, 1987.

Mullins, Lisa C., ed. *The Evolution of Colonial Architecture.* Harrisburg, Pa.: National Historical Society Publications, 1987.

Mullins, Lisa C., ed. *Homes of New York and Connecticut.* Harrisburg, Pa.: National Historical Society Publications, 1987.

Mullins, Lisa C., ed. *New England by the Sea.* Harrisburg, Pa.: National Historical Society Publications, 1987.

Mullins, Lisa C., ed. *Survey of Early American Design.* Harrisburg, Pa.: National Historical Society Publications. 1987.

Mullins, Lisa C., ed. *Village Architecture of Early New England.* Harrisburg, Pa.: National Historical Society Publications, 1987.

Natale, Philip. Telephone interview. 2 March 1989.

"National Grange." *Funk & Wagnalls New Encyclopedia.* 1979 ed.

National Park Service. *The National Register of Historic Places.* Washington, D.C.: U.S. Government Printing Office, 1983.

National Park Service. "National Register of Historic Places Inventory-Nomination Form." Washington, D.C.: U.S. Government Printing Office, 1981.

Nelson, Lee H. "Nail Chronology As An Aid to Dating Old Buildings." *History News,* 24, No. 11 (1968).

Nelson, Peter and Clifton Nelson, Sr. Personal interviews. 1 Feb., 1988 and March 1988.

Nesmith, Achsah. "A Long, Arduous March Toward Standardization." *Smithsonian,* March 1985, 176-178, 180, 182, 184-186, 188, 190-192, 194.

New York State Legislative Commission on State-Local Relations. "History of Firefighting and Fire Protection." *New York's Fire Protection System, Services in Transition, An Interim Report of the New York State Legislative Commission on State-Local Relations.* 1988.

Newcomb, Rexford. *The Colonial and Federal House: How to Build An Authentic Colonial House.* Philadelphia: J. B. Lippincott, 1933.

Nylander, Richard C. Telephone interview. 20 April 1988.

Nylander, Richard C., Elizabeth Redmond and Penny J. Sander. *Wallpaper in England.* Boston: SPNEA, 1986.

Olmsted, Elizabeth W. *Selections from the Correspondance [sic] and Diaries of John Olmsted 1826-1838.* n.p. Copy Cat, 1968, 129-130.

O'Malley, Leslie C. "Researching Local History." *RCHA Technical Information,* No. 73, June 1984.

Orcutt, Georgia. "The Truth About Wood Floors." *At Home In New England.* Dublin, N.H.: Yankee Publishing, 1986, 27-30.

Osmond, Edward. *Houses.* New York: MacMillan, 1956.

"Palladia, Andrea." *Funk & Wagnalls New Encyclopedia.* 1979 ed.

Palmer, Arlene. "Glass Manufacture." *Funk & Wagnalls New Encyclopedia.* 1979 ed.

Palmer, Arlene. "History of Glass." *Funk & Wagnalls New Encyclopedia.* 1979 ed.

Palmer, Arlene. "Types of Glass." *Funk & Wagnalls New Encyclopedia.* 1979 ed.

"Paris Green." *Funk & Wagnalls New Encyclopedia.* 1979 ed.

Parker, Patricia L. "Guidelines for Local Surveys: A Basis for Preservation Planning." Rev. *National Register Bulletin,* No. 24. Washington , D.C.: National Park Service, 1985.

Phleps, Hermann. *The Craft of Log Building.* Trans. Roger MacGregor. Ottawa: Lee Valley Tools, 1982.

Pilling, Arnold R. "Dating Early Photographs by Card Mounte and Other External evidence: Tentative Suggestions." *Image,* March 1974, 11-16.

Piwonka, Ruth and Roderic H. Blackburn. *A Visible Heritage: Columbia County, New York. A History in Art and Architecture.* Kinderhook, N.Y., : The Columbia County Historical Society, 1977.

Poppeliers, John C., S. Allen Chambers, Jr. and Nancy B. Schwartz. *What Style Is It?* Washington, D.C.: The Preservation Press, 1983.

"Portland Cement." *Funk & Wagnalls New Encyclopedia.* 1979 ed.

"Public Lands." *Funk & Wagnalls New Encyclopedia.* 1979 ed.

"Railroad Sparked Creation of Chatham Fire Department." *The Chatham Courier,* 9 July 1987, Sec T, 15.

Rand McNally Road Atlas: United States-Canada-Mexico. Chicago: Rand McNally, 1982.

Raub, Deborah Fineblum. "Rediscovering Patterns in Pigment." *Rochester Museum & Science Center Focus,* 2, No. 1 (1985) 4-9.

Rawson, Marion Nicholl. *The Old House Picture Book.* New York: E. P. Dutton, 1941.

Reilly, James M.. *Care and Identification of 19th-Century Photographic Prints.* Rochester, N.Y.: Eastman Kodak, 1981.

Rempel, John I. *Building With Wood and Other Aspects of*

Nineteenth Century Building in Ontario. Toronto: University of Toronto Press, 1976.

Rennsselaer County Surrogate Court Library. *Will File Box 192*. Troy, N.Y.: 7 Aug. 1879-1 April 1883.

Reuss, Martin. Telephone interview. 10 Oct. 1988.

Reynolds, Helen Wilkinson. *Dutch Houses in the Hudson Valley Before 1776*. New York: Dover Publications, 1965.

Reynolds, Hezekiah. *Directions for House and Ship Painting*. Worcester, Mass.: American Antiquarian Society, 1978.

Riedel, James. Telephone interview. 25 July 1987.

Rifkind, Carole. "How To Read an Old House." *Historic Preservations*, Jan./Feb. 1988. 44-47.

"Right-handedness." *Funk & Wagnalls New Encyclopedia*. 1979 ed.

Robertson, Deane and Peggy. Letter to author. 20 June 1988.

Rochester Museum and Science Center. "Seneca Falls Walking Tour of Architectural Styles." 26 Sept and 3 Oct. 1976.

Rochester Public Library. "House Research in the Local History Division." ROchester, N.Y., n.d.

Sanford, Wayne. Telephone interview. 21 July 1987.

Saylor, Henry H. *Dictionary of Architecture*. New York: John Wiley and Sons, 1952.

Schell, Ernest H. "Tracing the History of an Old House." *Early American Life*, Oct. 1981, 32, 95-96, 104.

Schick, Timothy F. and Rosemary O'Hara. "Tax Dollars Fund Firehouse Perks." *Sunday Times-Union*, 12 July 1987, Sec. A, p. 8, cols. 2-4.

Schick, Timothy F. and Rosemary O'Hara. "Volunteer Companies Lack Public Oversight." *Sunday Times-Union*, 12 July 1987, Sec. A, p. 1,8. cols 1-2.

Schwarz, Joel. "Historic Housework." *American Way*, Oct. 1984, 46-47, 49.

Seale, William. "How I Research a Historic Interior." *Historic Preservation*, May/June 1988, 14, 18-20, 85.

Semerow, Robert W. *Questions and Answers on Real Estate*. Englewood Cliffs, N.J.: Prentice-Hall, 1964.

"Set in Stone." *Kansas!* No. 4 (1986) 34-35.

Shafer, Charles. "How Much Is It Worth?" *Preservation News*, Oct. 1988, 7.

Shauers, Margaret. "Native Know How." *Kansas!* No. 1 (1987) 24-25.

Shephard, Albert to James Shephard. Original Deed. Hillsdale, N.Y.: 5 May, 1837.

Shephard, Judy. "Household Clues Help Owners Be At Home With House's History." *Sunday Times-Union*, 15 Dec. 1985, Sec. G, p. 1, cols. 1-2.

Sherrer, Joan. Telephone interview. 16 March 1989.

Simon, Leslie. Telephone interviews. 27 July 1987 and 25 Oct. 1988.

"Sir Christopher Wren." *Funk & Wagnalls New Encyclopedia*. 1979 ed.

Smith, Bill. Telephone interview. 2 June 1988.

Smith, Mary Lou. Telephone interview. 2 June 1988.

Sobon, Jack and Roger Schroeder. *Timber Frame Construction. All About Post and Beam Buildings*. Pownal, Vt.: Storey Communications, 1984.

Solomon, Charles. *Mathematics*. New York: Grosset & Dunlap Publishers, 1971.

Stanley, Linda and Ellen Manning. *Inside/Outside. Finding a Sense of Place*. Albany, N.Y.: Albany County Hall of Records Publication, 1986.

Stein, Martin, Telephone interviews. 17 May 1988 and 16 March 1989.

Stewart, Elizabeth H. "How To Do Historical Research On a Building." Rochester, N.Y.: The Landmark Society of Western New York, n.d.

Stoddard, Brooke C. "Picking the Right Paint Color." *Historic Preservation*, Sept./Oct. 1987, 16, 18-19.

Stryker-Rodda, Harriet. *Understanding Colonial Handwriting*. Baltimore: Genealogical Publishing 1986.

"Surveying." *Funk & Wagnalls New Encyclopedia*. 1979 ed.

Sweeney, Thomas W. "The Adobe Art of Anita Rodriguez." *Preservation News*, March 1988, 15, 17.

"Taconic Mountains." *Funk & Wagnalls New Encyclopedia*. 1979 ed.

Tarbell, Ida M. *In the Footsteps of the Lincolns*. New York: Harper & Brothers, 1924.

Temple, Martha W. "The Partridge Brook Inn: History and Hospitality." *Early American Life*, 18, No. 5, (1987), 46-47.

Thayer, Anita, Telephone interviews. 1988.

Thomas, Earle. *Greener Pastures: The Lovalist Experience of Benjamin Ingraham*. Belleville, Ontario: Mika Publishing, 1983.

Thomas, Graham Stuart, *Shrub Roses of Today*. New York: St. Martin's Press, 1962, 54-55.

"Thompson, Bejamin, Count Rumford." *Funk & Wagnalls New Encyclopedia*. 1979 ed.

Thompson, Katherince Wilcox. *Penfield's Past 1810-1960*. Penfield, N.Y.: Christopher Press, 1976.

Thompson, Katherine Wilcox. Telephone interviews. Sept. 1987.

Tichler, William. Telephone interview. 8 March 1988.

"Tracing Your Home's History." *Remodeling Ideas*, Fall 1987, 14-15.

Traupman, John C. *The New College Latin and English Dictionary*. New York: Bantam Books, 1966.

Trento, Salvatore Michael. *The Search For Lost America; The Mysteries of the Stone Ruins*. Chicago: Contemporary Books, 1978.

Trigonometry." *Funk & Wagnalls New Encyclopedia*. 1979 ed.

United States Copyright Office. Library of Congress. *Form TX*. Washington, D.C.: U.S. Government Printing Office, 1988.

United States Department of Agriculture. *Trees, The Yearbook of Agriculture, 1949*. Washington, D.C.: U.S. Government Printing Office, 1949.

Upton, Dell, ed. *American's Architectural Roots; Ethnic Groups That Built America*. Washington, D.C.: National Trust for Historic Preservation, 1987.

U.S. and Special Census Catalog, An Invaluable Aid To Genealogical Research. Salt Lake City: Ancestry, 1985.

Van Allen, Gary. Personal and telephone interviews. 15 July 1987 and 19 Oct. 1988.

Van Ravensway, Charles. "America's Age of Wood." *The Proceedings of the American Antiquarian Society for April 1970*. Worcester, Mass.: American Antiquarian Society, 1970, 49-66.

Van Rensselaer, Stephen to Simeon Holmes. Original Deed. Rensselaerville, N.Y. 6 May 1793.

Vider, Elisa. "Getting To Know Your House." *Historic Preservation*, March/April 1982, 22-24.

Voorhis, Harry Stephen. *History of Columbia Lodge No. 98-F. & A.M. of Chatham, New York*. Chatham, N.Y.: Columbia Lodge, 1932, 11.

"Wall Coverings We Have Known." *Yankee Homes*, 4, No. 1 (1988), 24-25.

"Wallpaper." *Funk & Wagnalls New Encyclopedia*. 1979 ed.

Wambach, Louis, Jr. Telephone interview. 2 Sept. 1987.

Warner, Sam B., Jr. "Writing Local History: The Use of Social Statistics." *History News*, 25, No. 10 (1970).

Watson, John. Telephone interview. 25 Aug. 1987.

"Weights and Measures." *Funk & Wagnalls New Encyclopedia*. 1979 ed.

Wells, Camille, ed. *Perspectives in Vernacular Architecture*. Annapolis: Vernacular Architecture Forum, 1982.

Wells, Camille, ed. *Perspectives in Vernacular Architecture, II*. Columbia, Mo.: University of Missouri Press, 1986.

Whiffen, Marcus. *American Architecture Since 1780. A Guide to the Styles*. Cambridge, Mass.: The MIT Press, 1985.

Whiffen, Marcus and Frederick Koeper. *American Architecture 1607-1976*. Cambridge, Mass.: The MIT Press, 1981.

White, C. Albert. *History of the Rectangular Survey System*. Washington, D.C.: U.S. Government Printing Office, 1982.

White, Earl E. *150 Years in Ogden, 100 Years in Spencerport*. Albion, N.Y.: Eddig Printing Co., 1967.

Wiley, Barbara. Telephone interview. 19 April 1988.

The World Almanac and Book of Facts 1986. New York: Newspaper Enterprise Association, 1985.

Zelinsky, Wilbur, et al. "United States of America." *The New Encyclopaedia Britannica*. 1982 ed.

Zim, Herbert S. and Alexander C. Martin. *Trees*. New York: Western Publishing, 1956.

Zohn, Harry. Telephone interview. 15 March 1989.

Zwinger, Susan. "Adobes of God." *Americana*, 15, No. 5 (1987), 65-69.

Index